The Awakening
of the Soviet Union

GEOFFREY HOSKING

The Awakening of the Soviet Union

Enlarged Edition

Harvard University Press
Cambridge, Massachusetts
1991

In memory of Kostya Bogatyrev
who did not live to see it

Copyright © 1990, 1991 by Geoffrey Hosking
All rights reserved
Printed in the United States of America
10 9 8 7 6 5 4 3 2 1

Library of Congress Cataloging-in-Publication Data
Hosking, Geoffrey A.
The awakening of the Soviet Union / Geoffrey Hosking.—Enl. ed.
p. cm.
Includes bibliographical references and index.
ISBN 0-674-05551-9
1. Soviet Union—Politics and government—1985–   2. Soviet Union—
—Intellectual life—1970–   3. Soviet Union—Social life and
customs—1970–   4. Perestroïka.   5. Glasnost.   I. Title.
DK288.H67   1991
947.085—dc20

91-15070
CIP

Contents

Preface to the enlarged edition   vii
Preface to the first edition   viii

1   A great power in crisis   1
2   Communities and ideals in Russian society   21
3   The return of the repressed   41
4   A civil society in embryo   55
5   The flawed melting pot   82
6   Religion and the atheist state   117
7   The paradox of Gorbachev's reforms   137
8   From 'informals' to political parties   170
9   Towards the dissolution of the Soviet Union   186
   Conclusion   211

Notes   220
Index   240

Preface to the enlarged edition

When the publishers suggested bringing out a paperback edition of this book, I had to think quickly. It did not seem right, on such a fast-changing subject, to publish a text which by its appearance would be nearly two years out of date. On the other hand, a thorough revision looked like a daunting task.

So indeed it proved. Yet in fact the eighteen months which have elapsed since I completed the first edition have provided ample further evidence for both my major theses, on the vigour of the Soviet Union's independent political movements, and on the baleful nature of the totalitarian heritage. While, therefore, I have had to write two completely new chapters, and substantially rewrite and update some of the others, I have not had to rethink radically my main argument.

I have continued to receive valuable help from many of the colleagues mentioned below. I am especially grateful to Alexander Suetnov and Martin Dewhirst for their generous help with documentation, and to Peter Duncan for finding time during a very busy period to comment on my new chapters. Responsibility for errors and over-hasty judgements remains, as before, my own.

School of Slavonic & East European Studies
University of London

December 1990

Preface to the first edition

Most studies of the exciting changes taking place in the Soviet Union focus on Gorbachev and the reform programme he has launched. That is understandable, but it nevertheless gives a misleadingly one-sided view of the situation. The present book grew out of my desire to see things from the viewpoint of the society he is trying to transform. Reform in the Soviet Union can only be initiated from above, but the vital motor lies below, among the peoples and social groups whose autonomous activity Gorbachev has encouraged.

The kernel of my ideas was contained in an inaugural lecture delivered at the University of London in February 1987. My purpose then was to counter the misleading tendency, common among western scientists, to assume that the Soviet Union was just a variety of authoritarian regime now at last evolving into something better. At the same time, I wanted to contest the opposite image, offered us by some émigrés, of a new socio-biological species, *Homo sovieticus*, said to have been irreversibly bred by debilitating Soviet conditions, and congenitally incapable of generating any independent civic or cultural life. I was convinced, from my own experience, that the Soviet Union was a totalitarian society, but that nevertheless a kind of political emancipation was possible within it, indeed was waiting to come about. I believed that, if the then embryonic policies of glasnost and perestroika developed into real democratisation, then the

Soviet peoples would prove readier to make more fruitful use of it than we in the west usually gave them credit for. The events of the last two years have borne out that assertion more emphatically than I could have conceived at the time. So it seemed worth attempting to give a fuller historical explanation for the unexpected vigour with which social movements unfolded, once they got the chance. The BBC's invitation to me to deliver the Reith Lectures in the autumn of 1988 provided the perfect opportunity. I have extensively rewritten the lectures and brought them up to date, in order to produce this book.

While putting these chapters together, I have been sorely aware of the precarious posture which the contemporary historian adopts. Much of the evidence in favour of my views has been accumulating in the last few months. That is reassuring, but poses problems of perspective. Even as I round off my writing, the turbulent proceedings of the Congress of People's Deputies fill Soviet television screens and raise the possibility that we may be moving on to a qualitatively new stage in the emergence of civil society. At such close quarters it is difficult to tell. So I am painfully conscious that my judgements may prove fallible.

I am grateful to the staff of the Library of the School of Slavonic & East European Studies who have provided for most of my needs in the way of documentation, supplemented by the library of the London School of Economics, and by the archives of Radio Liberty in Munich, and of the Forschungsstelle Osteuropa at Bremen University. My efforts to follow the tracks of so many heavenly bodies simultaneously would have been in vain without the help of numerous colleagues. The SSEES Soviet Press Study Group has furnished me with abundant information and opinion every Wednesday lunchtime. Shirin Akiner, Jane Ellis, Peter Frank and Bob Service have read earlier drafts and offered valuable advice and suggestions. Nora Beloff and Alex Shtromas took a lot of time and trouble to give me their views on the Reith Lectures. Some colleagues rallied round with invaluable cuttings and references, or by allowing me to see their own work in progress: Tamara Dragadze, Martin Dewhirst, Peter Duncan, Stephen Jones, Walter Laqueur and Peter Rowland. Murray Pollinger, my literary agent, steered me through the difficult transition between broadcasting and publication. Helen Fraser, Lisa Glass and Patricia Williams were encouraging and perceptive editors. I am most grateful to those numerous people in Moscow, Kiev and Tbilisi who took time off in the spring of 1988 to explain to me what was happening in their country: their personal insights form an essential part of what follows. But my greatest professional debt is to David Morton, who as BBC editor guided me through the Reith Lectures: with his perspicacity, sympathy and profound knowledge of the Soviet Union, he saved me from many errors, and sometimes spotted what I was thinking before I did.

My wife, Anne, and my daughters, Katya and Janet, have borne with an unpredictable and semi-absentee husband/father while this book was being prepared, and have nevertheless offered their love and support when it was needed. To them I owe most of all.

This book is dedicated to the memory of a friend who was murdered in Moscow ten years to the day before the Chernobyl' explosion. Paradoxically, since that terrible anniversary I have felt what he stood for come alive as never before in his own homeland: may it not be brutally cut short as his life was.

June 1989

A great power in crisis

In the last few years one of the most intriguing sections of any Soviet newspaper has been the readers' letters column. Take the following cry of indignation, published recently in *Pravda*: 'I cannot be silent! Look at what is going on around us. In Leningrad – the cradle of the revolution – well-fed, insolent thugs parade on the streets with swastika armbands . . . At an Estonian song contest a half-naked singer cavorts about with a cross round his neck, and this on television! In Armenia there are strikes – people skiving without any reason. Where is the law? Why is it silent? And why are those responsible for law enforcement inactive?'[1]

The writer signs himself 'Member of the Communist Party since 1945, Sverdlovsk' – the rough Soviet equivalent of 'Disgusted, Tunbridge Wells'. Life has been very unkind to such staunch party members recently. They have seen their own leadership sponsor changes which affront their most cherished beliefs. State ownership of the means of production is undermined with impunity, as they see it, by speculators and private marketeers. Rock music and western clothing are corrupting the youth. The party itself no longer seems to know where it's going: why, it's even permitted a self-styled opposition to come into existence. And, worst of all, the old stalwarts' hero, Stalin, is pilloried in the press as a mass murderer. As a Second World War invalid wrote from Kiev: 'Still as unfledged youths, we went into battle with the cry, "For the motherland, for Stalin! Hurrah!" Those were the last words that many of us ever spoke. And now you want us to blot that period out of our memories, to admit that we gave our lives or became cripples in a struggle for injustice?!"[2]

While his Tunbridge Wells counterpart works himself up over trivia, Disgusted Sverdlovsk has a real point. However blinkered his own approach to it, what he is witnessing is a real and fundamental crisis. He may blame Mr Gorbachev for it, but actually it is rooted in the very nature of the Soviet system, and Gorbachev has done no more than bring it to the surface in order to tackle it. Even so, the risks involved in his programme of radical reform are so serious that one is bound to ask: why did he attempt it at all? Why not just muddle on as Brezhnev did for eighteen years?

In a sense that was a real option, but muddling on would have had consequences which might not be acceptable to the leaders of a great power. Largely as a result of the ambitious military and foreign policy of the Brezhnev period, the Soviet Union suffers from what the historian Paul Kennedy recently called 'imperial overstretch', that is, strategic commitments so diverse and military power so overgrown that they drain the resources of the economy on which they depend.[3] The danger was intensified by the American Strategic Defence Initiative, which challenged the Soviet Union to develop a new generation of weapons involving lasers, supercomputers and sensitive long-range guidance systems. These are precisely the technological areas where it lags farthest behind. A nation which can outproduce the world in steel, cement and coal is, in effect, panting along one industrial revolution behind its major rivals, its preponderance in conventional arms liable to be nullified by the deployment of new weapons it cannot hope to match. If, then, the Soviet Union is to remain a great power even in the one sphere where it has hitherto excelled, the military one, it must create an economy which possesses the capacity to generate and assimilate independent technological innovation. This is the heart of the matter as all the Soviet leaders see it, whatever their shades of difference over perestroika, and that is why they are not prepared to just muddle on.

The economic deficiencies were merely part of a deeper crisis which permeates the whole society. It had already been diagnosed in 1970 by three distinguished Soviet scholars then in official disfavour: the nuclear physicist Andrei Sakharov, the historian Roy Medvedev and the mathematician Valentin Turchin. Writing to Brezhnev, they warned that the economy had entered a stage of 'dislocation and stagnation', the roots of which lay in the structure of society itself, in the 'anti-democratic norms of public life' established in the Stalin era and never properly disavowed. Without democratisation and the guarantee of civil liberties, they warned, any purely economic reforms would fall on stony ground. They proposed political reforms remarkably similar to those which Gorbachev is adopting today: greater openness, or glasnost, in public life; a press and information law; increasing the powers of the soviets as organs of self-administration; and restoring genuine elections, with multiple candidacies, in both party and soviets.[4]

There is plenty of evidence that Soviet society was ripe for such reform at the time when Sakharov and his colleagues proposed it, and it was even more so when Gorbachev came to power. The Soviet Union is far from being the backward, largely peasant country it was even a generation or so ago, when de-Stalinisation was first begun. In 1960 half the Soviet population lived in the countryside: today the proportion is not more than a third, and only a quarter at most can be called peasants.[5] When one thinks of the weight of the peasant problem in Russian history, that is a momentous change. The Soviet Union is now a highly urbanised society – though one in which the peasant heritage is still strong: as recently as the late seventies half the townsfolk had been born in the villages.[6]

No less important: during the same period the Soviet Union has become a highly educated society. If in 1939 only just over 10 per cent of the population aged ten and over had secondary education (often incomplete), that figure had reached 36 per cent by 1959 and 70 per cent by 1986. And whereas in 1939 only just over half of those doing non-manual labour had any secondary education, by 1959 that proportion was 90 per cent and today is virtually 100 per cent. Over the last thirty years there has been a fourfold growth in the proportion of people with higher education, from just over two per cent in 1959 to nearly nine per cent now. An important aspect of this educational revolution is that women have partaken of it as much as men: in 1986, among the working population, the proportion of women with secondary education was virtually identical with that of men, at 88 per cent.[7] Occupationally speaking, the fastest-growing sectors of the population have been the administrative and professional strata which absorb those college graduates. They have expanded seven-fold since 1940, and the growth shows no signs of easing.[8]

This educational development is of great importance, for education in the Soviet Union is a more crucial social mechanism than it is in the west. In a society where birth and property play a minor role, educational attainment is the principal agency for the transmission from one generation to another of privilege, status and power. Admittedly, nowadays it functions in a para-doxical fashion. Whereas at one time, higher or even secondary education was sufficiently rare to guarantee high social status of itself, this has long ceased to be the case. Higher education is a necessary prerequisite for the social climber, but it is no longer sufficient. It is also much harder to achieve: the chances of getting into university are today only half what they were twenty years ago.[9] So young people have much more difficulty in attaining something which simultaneously offers fewer rewards. There has been a growth of what, in purely functional terms, one can call 'over-education', the PhD on the building site. This mismatch has engendered considerable frustration; on the other hand, it has also brought the ferment of education into relatively humble forms of employment. We may expect nowadays to see receptivity to ideas at *all* levels of urban society in the USSR.

Overall, then, even since the last round of serious reforms was attempted under Khrushchev, the Soviet social structure has become markedly more urban and professional. Now, on the face of it, a population which in education, lifestyle and occupation has become so much more like the west should be ready for an open, democratic style of politics. And indeed, there has been evidence for more than two decades that society and politics were out of phase with one another, that society was starting to outgrow the crude and rigid integument of the party-controlled political system. An unofficial or 'black' economy has been mushrooming to meet the needs which the cumbersome planned state economy left unsatisfied. Similarly, extruded by the narrow confines of the Communist political monopoly, a new kind of semi-underground politics was taking shape, which we in the west referred to as 'dissent'. And the dreary output of official culture was increasingly being challenged by the primitive technology but lively appeal of *samizdat* – self-publishing.

In this sense, we might hypothesise that Gorbachev is doing no more than belatedly bringing the political system up to date with a more developed society. Or, as one American observer has put it, that he is not so much impelling change as 'uncorking' it.[10]

But it is not as simple as that. There is no straightforward transition from social to political change. A sophisticated society is a necessary condition for sophisticated politics, but it is by no means a sufficient one.

So what stands in the way? The obstacle, as I see it, is the political system handed down from Stalin, which has proved remarkably tenacious and resistant to change. All this would be obvious enough, were it not that Sovietologists have displayed so much uncertainty about how to describe that system. Thirty years ago nearly all observers of the Soviet scene would have agreed in calling it 'totalitarian': they'd have pointed to the monopoly mass party, with its grip on all political and social institutions; the single dominant leader; the single permissible ideology; the totally controlled culture and mass media; the completely planned, centrally directed economy; and the ubiquitous and terroristic security police.[11]

Ever since Khrushchev eased the terror in the late fifties, though, there have been warnings that we were misunderstanding the country, that the term 'totalitarian' was a misnomer, a relic of Stalinism and the cold war, an obstacle to understanding a society which was becoming more open, diverse and internally differentiated. What designation might be more appropriate was widely, though inconclusively, debated: 'modernising', some thought, or 'corporatist' or 'state socialist' – even 'pluralist'.[12] There is some sense in all of these epithets, except the last, 'pluralist', which is precisely what the Soviet Union is not. But none of them has ever replaced the term 'totalitarian' as an instrument for enabling us to see the Soviet system as a whole. None of them defines the essence of the system as opposed to characterising certain of its aspects. The danger of partial labels is that they can mislead us into seeing in Soviet society superficial analogies with western institutions, precisely because we lose sight of the overall context. Terms like 'socialisation', 'public opinion' and 'interest groups' tend to degenerate into being used as if they meant roughly the same as in the United States or West Germany.

It is true that the 'totalitarian' concept has weaknesses, at any rate in the form in which it has been employed up to now. It first took hold among a generation of American scholars emerging after the Second World War, somewhat guilty about past isolationism, ready to transfer morally absolutist feelings about Nazi Germany to the new enemy, as the Soviet Union then appeared to be, and sensitive to the experience of Central European refugees who had suffered terribly at the hands of both regimes.[13] As a result the concept has tended to imply an implacably hostile approach to the Soviet Union, and it still bears the nasty aftertaste of the McCarthyite witch-hunts. It has, moreover, usually been applied in a top-heavy and static manner. That is, it has over-emphasised political control mechanisms, giving the impression that society was mere malleable putty in the hands of the ruling party. And it has proved ill equipped to explain, still less predict, change: those who use it have on the whole assumed that, once in place, the totalitarian polity is permanent, not susceptible to the processes of internal evolution which affect most political systems. Richard Pipes, for instance, has asserted that it is 'by definition incapable of evolution from within and impervious to change from without'.[14]

As it stands, this statement is plainly wrong, but its partial blindness harbours an important element of insight. Totalitarian systems *are* quite unusually rigid, as Gorbachev is discovering to his cost. But nowadays we have enough information about the lower levels of Soviet society; and we can look back on a time-span sufficient for gradual change to be obvious. Nor are we unduly influenced by cold-war sentiment any more. So there is no reason why we should perpetuate the obvious deficiencies of the model, which have led so many scholars to reject it altogether.

For a totalitarian society is neither demonic, nor unchanging, nor totally manipulated from above. Actually, it is 'human, all too human'. If we can rehumanise our understanding of it, see it in its historical context, and reawaken our sense of how the various social strata, nationalities and religions operate and inter-act under it, then I believe the totalitarian model is capable of affording us a more complete view of Soviet society than any alternative yet propounded. Indeed, it provides the most satisfac-tory explanation of the processes which have generated the country's current crisis, as well as making it clear why thorough-going reform (or as Gorbachev prefers to call it, 'restructuring': *perestroika*) is so extraordinarily difficult to bring off. 'Stag-nation' is a logical result (though not the only possible result) of Lenin's revolution of 1917. His determination to pursue his utop-ian vision alone, even in the face of opposition from the other socialist parties, to risk civil war rather than enter coalitions and agreements which would require him to compromise any of his programme, led naturally to a political monopoly which, given the technical accomplishments of the twentieth century, assumed unprecedented proportions.

So I make no apologies for resurrecting the notion of 'totalitarianism'. I believe that it enables us to understand both why radical reform has become so urgently necessary, and also why it is proving so difficult to carry out. Remove the term 'totalitarian', and it is not obvious how the Soviet Union differs from say, Spain under Franco or Chile under Pinochet. But these differences are crucial.

Until Gorbachev's perestroika began to take hold, the Soviet Union was a society marked by three decisive features. Its political life was entirely monopolised by one body, the Communist Party, which dominated organisationally all governmental and public institutions, and governed appointments to all responsible jobs through the *nomenklatura* system. The party's ideology was the only permitted intellectual system, and it was projected to the population using all the resources of the media, culture and the educational system. Its economy was wholly directed from the centre (with the sole exception of the peasant garden plots), and everybody was directly or indirectly an employee of the state.

Of course this system functioned in a different way under Brezhnev than it had under Stalin. Institutionally, perhaps the most significant change was that the security police had been brought under party control and could no longer apply indiscriminate terror against the party itself under the direction of a single dictator. Correspondingly the arbitrary power of the leader diminished and became diffused among an oligarchy at the apex of the party-state apparatus. Underneath, too, radical social change was taking place in a way which pointed towards eventual political reform, but was not enough in itself to shake the tough framework of the system.

The first and perhaps most important feature of the totalitarian polity is that it produced a nation traumatised by its own past. It is difficult for us to grasp the sheer scale of the human suffering involved, but we know that, according to recent Soviet estimates, the mass collectivisation of agriculture in the thirties subjected ten to fifteen million peasants to forcible expropriation and deportation.[15] We know that a substantial proportion died, many of them in the ensuing famine. Moreover, from about the mid-thirties to the mid-fifties, millions of Soviet citizens were in slave labour camps, where the death rate may have been 10 per cent a year. Some historians believe the victims of Stalin's brutality may well have outnumbered the twenty million usually cited by Soviet sources as the figure for those killed in the Second World War.[16]

And this is not to mention the tens of millions uprooted from their homes by less abnormal social processes, like industrialisation and military service. When Boris Pasternak wrote his *Essay in Autobiography*, he broke off before this period with the words: 'To continue would be immeasurably difficult . . . One would have to write in such a way as to make the hair stand on end and the heart falter.'[17]

I myself have found over the years that, as I get to know Soviet citizens of the middle and older generations, I discover that all of them have been scarred in one way or another by that terrible epoch. One will remember being deported in a cattle truck to Siberia; another that, when he was six, his father simply disappeared and was never heard of again; another recalls standing with her mother in long queues outside prisons, waiting to deliver food parcels and hoping for a scrap of information about her father. Those who were in labour camps and came out alive are usually very reluctant to talk about the experience, perhaps agreeing with Varlam Shalamov, survivor of Kolyma, that 'the camps were a negative school of life in every respect . . . There was much there that no man should know or see, or, if he has seen it, it is better he should die.'[18]

Shalamov, fortunately, did not follow his own precept: he chronicled his labour camp experience in a series of gritty, icily factual stories.[19] But most Soviet people have preferred not to dwell too much on the grim past. Now when a nation cannot face its own past, it will have difficulty with its future too. We have seen something of this in German society since the war, but the effect is far deeper in the Soviet Union, for there the regime responsible for the trauma is still in place, and till very recently it had only feebly and indecisively denounced its own crimes. A whole nation has been unable properly to mourn its murdered and tormented. This theme of the belated and halting recovery of memory is one to which I shall return, for it helps to explain the travail in which Soviety society is rebuilding its civic consciousness.

Another crucial feature which distinguishes the totalitarian regime from the merely authoritarian is that it has created its own society. Whereas Franco and Pinochet (and arguably even Hitler) inherited social structures from the past and sought by and large to preserve them, the Communist Party began its rule by destroying an old society and creating a new one in its own image. The new ruling class was delineated by the *nomenklatura* system, set up in the early twenties, through which party committees began to keep regularly updated files on all individuals whom they regarded as potentially suitable for nomination to public office. Since a party recommendation is crucial to any appointment, in this way the party Central Committee directly or indirectly controls the patronage of all responsible posts in Soviet society, including those which are in principle elective. All other social classes – and, for that matter, nationalities – fall into place in a hierarchical pyramid whose framework the party has constructed. It is true that with time these raw social classes have gradually acquired their own way of life, their traditions and customs, but the party is integrally woven into these as the guiding and directing institution.

That basic fact governs the next major distinct characteristic of the totalitarian system: its unique pervasiveness. The Communist Party not only leads and guides society, it penetrates it. It has its cells in every factory, farm, office, school, and block of flats. It unceasingly supervises, indoctrinates, exhorts, and mobilises –

not always successfully, it is true, but its presence is invariably evident. Through the *nomenklatura* network, it has a grip on patronage in every social hierarchy. It watches over the economy and sorts out the muddles and bottlenecks which inevitably arise when the planning system gets tangled in its own tentacles. It socialises the people through the education system. It speaks to the people through the mass media. It preaches to the people through its propagandists and agitators. It both claims and exercises an exclusive right to all these forms of authority, a prerogative bestowed upon it by history, of which its guardians profess a superior understanding.

Since this right to rule rests on ideology, it follows that totalitarianism is a system which attributes paramount importance to ideas. The ideas may be debased, but they are everywhere. Every student, whatever his subject of study, has to pass examinations in Political Economy, Dialectical Materialism, Scientific Atheism, and the like. The acquaintances of my student days at Moscow University used to say they were bored silly by these subjects: they would knit or write letters during the lectures, and then desperately mug up the material out of a textbook the night before the exam. One might think that studies pursued in this way could hardly have a profound effect, but in fact I feel that the impact of all this ideological cramming is not altogether superficial. Rote-learning has a way of clinging to odd corners of the mind, and turning up unexpectedly, maybe years later. In any case, the effect is constantly being reinforced by the ever present slogans on street banners, wall-posters, in the newspapers, and on radio and television. As the émigré novelist Alexander Zinoviev puts it, Soviet citizens are 'in constant contact with the powerful magnetic field of ideological influence . . . They absorb from it a certain electrical charge . . . There is physically no way they can escape from it'.[20] This, of course, is especially true for the literate, for those who live in towns, and those who perform administrative or intellectual work, that is, the fastest-growing sector of the population.

This all-pervading ideological 'static' does not necessarily make everyone a Marxist-Leninist zombie. Far from it. But it does inculcate in the average Soviet citizen the habit of systematic, monological thinking on social, political and philosophical issues, an inclination which remains with him even if he disavows the official ideology. The instinct for seeing problems as a whole, and taking up vehement, unambiguous stances on them, has permeated the gradual revival of civic consciousness in the Soviet Union, as we shall see.

Another paradoxical fruit of the ascendancy of ideology is that it confers high social status on people whose profession is ideas. In the west such people often have to seek niches in jobs where ideas are a by-product. In the Soviet Union, by contrast, the purveyors of ideas are more independent of day-to-day utilitarian pressures: they can work in the party's huge ideological apparatus of instructors, propagandists and agitators. They can go to ground in one of the many research institutes maintained by the party, the government or the Academy of Sciences, none of which ever sees anything so demanding as a student wishing to be taught. They can join one of the creative unions, such as the Union of Writers, which exists to free authors from the need to support themselves by mercenary drudgery (ironically, many of them in consequence produce their own species of dreary hack-work, but then that itself is a tribute to the respect accorded even to derivative ideas).

In short, there exists in Soviet society a certain confidence that ideas, especially all-embracing, systematic ideas, are worthy of respect as such and require no extrinsic justification. Given the normal human propensity to discern charm in forbidden fruit, this confidence bestows on alternative, non-Marxist intellectual, cultural and philosophical systems a considerable creative, or should one say subversive, potential.

Last among the key distinctive features of the totalitarian society is the unusual depth of the divide it opens up in the individual between the public and the private persona. To some extent we are all familiar with this divide. No one in any society behaves towards his employer exactly as he would with a close friend. But nowhere is the split so radical as under totalitarian rule. Most people, whatever their private views, cultivate in public a façade of conformity and anonymity: they do what is expected of them. 'A meeting', in the apt definition coined by the satirical novelist Vladimir Voinovich, 'is an occasion when people gather together, some to say what they do not think, and others not to say what they really do.'[21]

This institutionally induced doublethink engenders what appears on the surface to be an almost limitless flexibility of outlook. People's opinions change, or seem to, with the same abruptness as the party line. How many unexpected 'liberals' did the advent of glasnost not suddenly reveal! Editors and critics who had not stinted in their paeans to what later became known as 'the era of stagnation' were transformed overnight into convinced exponents of perestroika. Which of the two they really believe remains an enigma. We should not take too seriously, then, what passes in the Soviet media for 'public opinion'.

As against the impressive but brittle unanimity of public life, Soviet citizens cultivate their private pursuits and attachments with an intensity seldom seen in more relaxed societies. Behind the carefully contrived façade of anonymity and conformity, they discreetly 'do their own thing' in the company of like-minded individuals. That 'thing' can vary from rock music to abstract art to the discussion of Hegelian philosophy to Yogic meditation. What such groups have in common is that they are dealing in cultural artefacts and ideas. Many of them have turned, naturally enough, to their own semi-suppressed national traditions, whether Russian or non-Russian. As an occasional privileged interloper in such gatherings over the last quarter of a century, I can testify to their remarkable warmth, humanity and spiritual intensity. This is the milieu in which the political anecdote flourishes – that backhanded tribute of oppressed intellectuals to the rulers who subjugate them. It is also a milieu in which the exchange and exploration of ideas proceeds with utter spontaneity and at the same time concentration. In my experience, the art of conversation is pursued in Moscow at a higher level than anywhere else in the world.

Until recently, one could have stated confidently that this intellectual ferment produced little discernible social result. It remained perforce essentially private. It is true that the movement called 'dissent' grew out of it. 'Dissidents' were people of this kind, forced to 'go public' because the state had invaded their private domain, charging them and their colleagues with 'anti-Soviet propaganda' for circulating among themselves thoughts not admitted to the official canon. Nearly all westerners misinterpreted dissent, in a classic example of the failure to see the whole Soviet context. They took it for a political movement aiming to bring about political change, and accordingly judged it a failure. Actually it was the mere dislocated tip of an iceberg, whose depths harboured a powerful reaffirmation of personal identity and community – a spiritual not a political movement. Judged in its own terms it was not a failure but a remarkable success, and ultimately it has brought forth political fruits as well, in the diverse and beneficial flowering of glasnost, which is otherwise impossible to explain.

Elements of pluralism do emerge, then, at least potentially, under the totalitarian carapace. But they are very different from the competing interest groups with which we are familiar in western societies. They are formed on the basis not of material interests, but of culture and ideas, in keeping with the society to which they belong. They do not compete in an open forum for media attention or for influence on the electoral process. On the contrary, until recently they have deliberately shunned all publicity, seeking it, if at all, only when the state violates their fragile boundaries. The Soviet Union has been a deeply segmented society, in which a multitude of diverse associations existed but did not interact with one another. Nowadays they are beginning to, generating the 'turmoil' which is normal politics, but which so disconcerts Mr Gorbachev's colleagues.

All of which brings me back to Disgusted Sverdlovsk. The crisis he is witnessing is the crisis of Soviet totalitarianism. The system is undermining itself through its own inherent contradictions, putting at risk the great power status which that system once achieved.

From the leadership's viewpoint, the totalitarian pathology is most evident and damaging in the economy. The decision to set up centrally administered planning under Stalin was fateful, for it delivered the economy into the hands of a ruling class of a historically unprecedented kind. Founded by Lenin and brought to perfection by Stalin, this ruling class has both its anchor and its forum in the party Central Committee. Its origins go back to the years during and after the civil war, when the Bolsheviks were tightening their at first precarious grip on a country in deep turmoil. Lenin's 'professional revolutionaries' were becoming professional administrators (or, if they proved unsuited to this new role, were being replaced by Stalin's nominees), responsible for a huge country in extreme disorder and poverty. Their methods of rule were not the traditional ones. They infiltrated the structures of power as well as dominating them from above. The party rules published in December 1919 laid down that wherever there were three or more party members in any organisation, it was their duty to form a party cell 'whose task it is to increase party influence in every direction, carry out party policies in non-party milieux, and effect party supervision over the work of all organisations and institutions'.[22]

One of the ways in which the party cell carried out this instruction was by keeping lists of employees in all organisations, and especially of people suitable, from the party's point of view, for promotion. The 'great and the good', as it were. These lists were passed up the party ladder and, under Stalin as General Secretary from 1922, they were extended, systematised and kept up to date.

Not for nothing did Stalin's comrades dub him 'Comrade Card Index.'

Those who have lived through revolution and civil war tended to assume that, as Mao Zedong later put it, 'power grows out of the barrel of a gun'. It took them a long time to realise that, on the contrary, in a one-party system where the state soon became the sole employer, power was henceforth to proceed from the filing cabinet. Stalin's personnel lists became the instrument of the *nomenklatura* system, under which every single appointment to any responsible job, in whatever walk of life, was decided only after approval by a party committee at the appropriate level. The committee would make its nomination only on the basis of reports filed and kept up to date by the potential appointee's previous employers, by his trade union committee, by his party organisation, and by the security police. Thus was constituted an all-embracing network of information and patronage without equal in any previous society.[23]

It was buttressed by a panoply of honours and privileges. Since responsible office-holders could not be expected to tolerate the wretched conditions in which most Soviet citizens lived, they were granted access to more spacious housing, superior medical care and special stores with cheap, good quality food. As it developed, the ladder of privilege became minutely graded according to the ranking of one's post in the *nomenklatura* hierarchy: those at the very top would receive the best apartments, doctors and groceries, and in addition might qualify for a country dacha, a chauffeur-driven car and a holiday abroad.

The *nomenklatura* hierarchy is, then, not just of power and patronage, but also of material interests. Money and inheritance, as they operate in most societies, are replaced by privilege and political clientelism. The result is an unprecedentedly monolithic and dominant ruling class.

Of course, some things have changed since Stalin's death, but not in such a way as to endanger the grip which the *nomenklatura* office-holders have on society. On the contrary, Stalin may have created them, but they can exist very well without him. Better in fact than under him. While he was alive, they flourished as a class, but individually they had to tremble for their positions and indeed their lives. Since his death the party Central Committee (which we may think of as the *nomenklatura* 'inner circle') has brought his murderous security police firmly under control. Under Brezhnev's slogan of 'stability of cadres' the *nomenklatura* appointees have been able to regard their posts as virtually lifetime incumbencies. Benefitting from corruption, personal acquaintances and their own subordinate patronage, they have consolidated their position by dispensing favours downwards to selected recipients, while using the police, the procuracy and the law courts to stifle their opponents. If you like, 'stability of cadres' was the 'little Stalins' charter.'

The planned economy is the principal arena in which these office-holders have deployed their power, and from it they derive their generous emoluments. It is both their *raison d'être* and their feeding trough. The Soviet economy is in effect a huge institutionalised sellers' market, run for the benefit of those who operate it, not of those who have to use its products. It flourishes on grandiose projects – which increase the scope of patronage – but cannot respond to the highly differentiated demands of today's consumers. It actually penalises both innovation and high quality work, the driving forces which are needed to ensure for the Soviet Union an economic base appropriate to a twenty-first-century great power.

The resulting milieu of low pay and permanent under-production is the familiar home of the great majority of Soviet citizens – those, that is, who do not have access to privileges assigned from above. Prices of housing, transport and basic foodstuffs are relatively low, and the authorities prefer to keep it that way. When Khrushchev raised meat prices in the early sixties there was rioting in the streets, and the leaders are regularly reminded by developments in neighbouring Poland how defiant workers can become when asked to pay more for their food. To fulfil this side of their tacit social contract with the workforce, the Soviet state pays out the equivalent of some fifty billion dollars a year in subsidies.[24]

Of course, cheap commodities in short supply have to be rationed somehow, and in the Soviet Union they are rationed by the queue. Most Soviet citizens expect to spend part of the day standing in line along with hundreds of their surly, frustrated fellow-citizens. They tend, indeed, to regard the right to do this during working hours as another aspect of that tacit 'social contract': 'They pretend to pay us, and we pretend to work.' In order to keep the queuing down to a minimum, though, most of them also devise at least some private arrangements, through bribery, or personal acquaintance, or mutual favours, to obtain the supplies or services of which they have most regular need. Thus a shop assistant may keep back a good cut of meat in return for a tip, or a garage mechanic may perform motor repairs for imported clothing. The permutations are endless, but they nearly always involve time, tools or goods diverted from the official economy. The 'second economy' is essential to a tolerable life, but it is also parasitic on the official one and therefore dependent upon it. Its devices are precarious, and both seller and customer have an interest in their remaining undisturbed.

This situation gives most Soviet citizens a certain stake in the status quo. They cannot afford to have their private arrangements disrupted unless successful reform of the entire economy follows, so that goods and services hitherto obtainable only clandestinely become regularly available at affordable prices. Much of the unease provoked by Gorbachev's measures derives from the fear that in his drive against corruption he will upset existing contrivances without putting stable patterns of supply in their place.

It is not, then, only the *nomenklatura* élite who have an interest in the prevailing system. To some extent most people have become dependent on it, or have at least sought out a tolerable niche within it which is vulnerable to the winds of perestroika.

Yet the system inspires only a limited and conditional loyalty.

For in other ways it engenders evils which people are well aware of and find extremely irksome, even oppressive. The general squalor and neglect, the confined intellectual life, the cultural censorship, the religious restrictions, the obstacles to foreign travel, the bureaucratic obstructionism, the degradation of the environment: all these deficiencies are perceived by most Soviet citizens as products of the system and as serious impediments to what they nostalgically like to call 'normal life'. And that includes a lot of members of the élite. To eliminate these evils, or even some of them, most people would be prepared, in my experience, to support an out-and-out reformer, if only they could be sure that their present precarious sufficiency would not be destroyed without anything more lasting and satisfactory being substituted. For that reason, the natural reaction to a reforming leader is initial caution, even inert resistance. But this could give way to enthusiastic support if he is seen to be succeeding. In most people's eyes, however, Gorbachev has not yet made the vital breakthrough. That is one major source of his difficulties.

Another is that his reform programme entailed a crucial paradox. A serious loosening of the economy, let alone of politics and intellectual life, dislocated the mainspring of the power which the Communist Party's full time officials, the *apparatchiks*, had arrogated to themselves. They were well aware of the fact. To be fair to them, some party secretaries also recognised the seriousness of the present crisis, and the need for drastic remedies, at least to judge by their speeches at the 19th Party Conference in the summer of 1988. But the bulk of the medium and lower level *apparatchiks*, who were perhaps less well informed and certainly had narrower perspectives, were resentful at any prospect of losing their grip on power and privilege. And they could still claim the mandate of history in support of their prejudices.

So do the reformers stand a chance, or are their efforts doomed to failure? To a considerable extent, the answer depends not on them, but on the response of Soviet society. We in the west tend to write Russians off as passive, even slavish, and to assume that, because they have no native tradition of democracy, they are incapable of ever creating a more open and pluralist policy.

There is, of course, something in this: Russians do not have a heritage of democracy as we understand that term. All the same, I do not believe they are condemned to eternal civic passivity. On the contrary, I believe that they have derived, from their past, traditions of political participation and mutual solidarity under pressure which are proving to be decisive elements in the new situation, and which are creating the makings of a civil society.

2

Communities and ideals in Russian society

Visiting the Soviet Union today, one is tempted at times to believe that Russia's past has disappeared entirely. Standing in a modern Soviet street, I sometimes feel as if I were in a society afflicted by communal amnesia, disoriented like an alcoholic who wakes to discover he can't remember what happened the day before. The town may be old, but it now bears a brand new name, that of some Soviet hero, and the gigantic architectural monoliths in which most Soviet citizens live have obliterated all traces of previous settlement, of ancient fields and pathways. It does not seem possible in the Soviet *tabula rasa* that any form of social institution or even memory can have survived revolutions, wars, purges and forced industrialisation to offer a foothold for a more pluralist mode of politics today.

At the start of my career I studied the State Duma, the short-lived parliament of tsarist Russia's last years. The Duma had serious powers, it contained a variety of political parties, and it debated the issues of the day in an unconstrained and well informed manner. At its birth the British House of Commons sent it a telegram welcoming it to the international family of parliaments. Perhaps there, I thought, one might find a thread from the past, the first rudiments of a democratic tradition. But I soon discovered that today's Soviet intellectuals, even those with a concern for freedom, are not reading the ideas of Milyukov or

Guchkov, who were the two leading liberal members of that assembly.

While I was in Moscow, I did, though, discover something else, something which pointed to at least some kind of inherited sense of community. Take the following scene, which I believe will be familiar to most people who have spent some time in the Soviet Union. You have been invited to a friend's home one evening. You want to take a little present, so you trudge round the shops looking for something – a box of chocolates, flowers, even just some decent sausage meat. But the shelves are empty and the salesgirls sullenly unhelpful. Tired and discouraged, you struggle on to a crowded bus where all the other passengers have oversized elbows and feet. Getting off again, you tramp through the freezing air, and make your way into the filthy, evil-smelling vestibule of a block of flats.

Then you ring at the doorbell . . . and a magic transformation takes place. Your friends welcome you. Whether or not you have managed to bring a contribution, you are seated in front of a feast which may be modest but must have taken hours of ingenuity to assemble. The vodka – or in the Gorbachev era, the tea – begins to circulate. You plunge into discussion of literature, philosophy, science, politics – everything under the sun. You feel for a while – and is it an illusion? – that you are part of a warm human community talking about the things which really matter in life.

This is, I believe, the archetypal Russian experience, and it goes far back into history. A freezing climate, squalid externals, a harsh and inadequate official system contrast with a warm interior, a humane and cultured personal life. If we are to understand Russians at all, we have to take this dichotomy into account. It is both geographically and historically determined. In order to hold their vast, frozen territories together, and on the basis of them to claim the status of an international great power, Russian governments over the centuries have had to extract the maximum resources from a scattered and poverty-stricken population. From the time of Peter the Great in the early eighteenth century, and arguably earlier as well, Russian governments have endeavoured to create institutions which would make it possible to raise and maintain a huge army, to create industry backed by modern science and technology, and generally to mobilise the population for the tasks incumbent upon a great power. The remarkable thing is that they have succeeded to a considerable extent, but usually in ways that have something of the *trompe l'œil* about them, and that leave Russians themselves feeling surprisingly vulnerable.

Institutions in Russia never function quite as intended by the government that set them up. There are a number of good reasons for this: immense distances, harsh climate, economic and cultural backwardness (compared with the western models on which Russian institutions are usually designed), and the inadequate provision of resources by the government itself. Indeed, institutions take on a life of their own, determined by the needs of the human beings who actually man them. These needs do not necessarily coincide with the purposes of the government, and may indeed run directly counter to them. Hence the feeling the historian has, when reading the papers of Russian statesmen, that they are wearily doing their best, with their impeccable juridical phraseology, to grasp a reality which constantly eludes them. At the grass roots, people improvise a façade for the occasional appearance of the dreaded 'government inspector', but otherwise do their own thing in their own way, treating officials as just another unpredictable element in a forbidding environment.

This cardinal characteristic of Russian society has always been difficult for historians or social scientists to grasp. For we are largely dependent on documents, and documents come on the whole from governments, not from the grass roots, where indeed people may actually be anxious to *conceal* the reality of what they are doing. So we write history from above, and marvel that Russians have been able to survive at all the asperities of their climate and their political system, not to mention repeated foreign invasions.

But they *have* survived, battered, bruised and intimidated

though they may be. Indeed, in some respects, they have flourished, as one realises if one looks at the best of their culture, science and learning, which are on the highest international level. I believe, in fact, that the Russian people have demonstrated an extraordinary capacity to improvise humane and functioning grass roots institutions in extremely adverse circumstances. If I accepted the Hegelian notion that each nation has something distinctive to contribute to the Universal Spirit, then I would say this is what the Russians have to offer, and we have all been enriched by it. Not, as we shall see, that the political consequences of this community spirit are always happy.

The archetypal grass roots institution in Russian society was the peasant community, the *mir*, whose principal aim was simple survival in extremely adverse conditions. It achieved this by the minimisation of risk and by collective attenuation of extremes of fortune, whether good or bad. Inside it the belief prevailed that the isolated individual was weak and vulnerable, and also prone to error and sin. For that reason emphasis was placed on conformity and collective discipline: individual aberrations were regarded as dangerous, and even individual enrichment was viewed with suspicion.[1]

The *mir* was consolidated during the seventeenth and eighteenth centuries, along with the strengthening of the absolutist state. It was a dual institution, both official and unofficial in nature. Official, in that the government utilised it for tax-collecting, recruitment and local administration; unofficial, in that the peasants themselves used it as their forum for collective decision-making, for mutual aid, and for the maintenance of ethical norms.[2] The gathering of heads of households, the *skhod*, would fix the dates of common agricultural work, provide for the upkeep of roads, bridges and wells, and for the hiring of shepherds and night watchmen. It would decide which members should be permitted to seek work outside the village and on what conditions. It held the ultimate ownership of the land, and could redistribute holdings, assigning more to families who had new mouths to feed, and reducing the holdings of those whose members had recently died or left the village. The *skhod* would sometimes even intervene to try to settle family disputes, or to examine moral questions, for example the accusation that a village girl had lost her honour.

One imagines that such a community must have been almost stifling in the degree of its concern for the behaviour of every one of its members. The records suggest that its outlook was often arbitrary, intolerant and highly deferential to the opinions of its older or wealthier male members, one of whom, the *starosta*, or elder, had authority vested in him which was limited only by the community's moral concepts. In such a community to be young, or a woman, or weighed down by some possibly unjust accusation from the past must have been very trying. On the other hand, at times of real need or difficulty, the community could and would help out. The notion of *pomochi*, or mutual aid, was fundamental. When a household suddenly lost its breadwinner, or was struck by illness, or its home was burnt down, then the *skhod* would decree that their neighbours, or perhaps even the whole village, should turn out to help them with the heaviest or most urgent work. The beneficiaries of this help would provide hospitality – perhaps including vodka – for their rescuers if they could, but if they were destitute, then it was accepted that help should be provided anyway free of charge.[3]

When Russian peasants found themselves working outside the village – which happened quite frequently, because the soil was infertile and the income to be derived from it insecure – then they tended to reproduce the familiar communal structure, in amended forms appropriate to the new environment. Hence the widespread institution of the *artel'*, or workmen's co-operative. As the nineteenth-century populist Stepniak commented in his classic work on the Russian peasantry, 'All the hundreds of thousands of peasants who move from the village in search of work either start by forming *arteli*, or join some *artel'* when they reach their destination.'[4] Thus building workers, masons, carpenters, fishermen, barge-haulers, stevedores would band together, sometimes just for one major job of work, sometimes for long periods. Each member would contribute what he could, in the form of money, equipment, skill or just brute strength. They would elect one of their number as *starosta*, and he would have responsibility for finding work, concluding a contract, receiving and distributing pay and profits. Sometimes the *artel'* arrangement covered board and lodging as well, in which case one member would act as *ekonom*, bursar, if you like, and another as cook.

Even where no common work was involved, the existence of an *artel'* could do much to simplify the arrival in a city of a peasant looking for lodging and work. When in the 1890s Semyon Kanatchikov was brought as a teenager into Moscow by his father to seek employment, his path was smoothed in this way. 'We rented an apartment communally, as an *artel'* of about fifteen men. Some were bachelors, others had wives who lived in the village and ran their households ... Our food and the woman who prepared it were also paid for communally. The food was purchased on credit at a shop; our individual shares were assessed twice monthly.'[5]

Of course, we must be quite clear what kind of institutions the *mir* and the *artel'* were. They displayed no democracy or civil freedom in the western sense. They encouraged no concept of citizenship, individual ownership or individual rights. The predominant force in them was not the rule of law, but that of custom and authority. Nevertheless, as human communities operating in a grim and oppressive environment, they had much to commend them. They certainly afforded security and a means of getting things done. Moreover, even in this relatively primitive form, they have not entirely disappeared. As every foreign student at a Soviet university knows, he and his co-nationals will be expected to form a cohesive group and elect a *starosta* who will conduct all their dealings with the authorities. Any other method of getting things done will be met not just with disapproval, but with incomprehension.

If, then, we want to understand the Russian revolution and the Soviet state, it is very important to bear in mind that they sprang from this capacity of the Russian people for improvising grass roots institutions in circumstances of difficulty or emergency. In my view, the dogged radicalism of Russian workers and peasants in 1917 derived not from Marxism, but from the unusually late survival into the industrial world of popular institutions of primitive solidarity, accustomed to steering round governments, offering their officials passive resistance or profiting by their inadequacies.

Take, for example, the institution of the soviet, which gives the Union of Soviet Socialist Republics its present name. It first arose in the textile city of Ivanovo-Voznesensk, when a general strike was called there in May 1905. Delegates from the various mills gathered on the banks of the River Talka: they were the men whom the workers had chosen to represent them on the so-called Shidlovskii Commission, set up by the government to examine possible industrial legislation. Now, consulting on the river bank, in a position where they were challenging both employers and government, these delegates decided to put their representative functions to a completely new use, that is, to represent their fellows in negotiations with both employers and government, and in the meanwhile to improvise minimal services for a city in which the normal administrative bodies were paralysed.[6]

So a completely new institution was born, the Soviet of Workers' Deputies, embryo of the present-day Soviet state. It acted at one and the same time as strike committee and temporary local government assembly. It was elected by the workers of the various mills, any of whom had the right to attend its debates. Delegates could be recalled at any time, if their electors disapproved of what they were doing, and replaced by others. Outside the market square of Athens it was perhaps the closest approach to direct democracy that can be conceived.

The idea caught on fast. During the next few months similar

soviets sprang up all over Russia, the most famous of which, the St Petersburg Soviet, paralysed the capital city in October, and pressured the tsar into promising civil freedoms and the establishment of a national legislative assembly. And when the tsarist regime fell in March 1917, the first thought of workers all over Russia was to rush to form soviets of the kind they had briefly experienced in 1905.

If one believes the commonly accepted picture of Russian workers as politically unformed, then this rapid spread of effective political institutions is difficult to explain. Some of course would attribute it to the skill and vigour of the revolutionary parties, and there is unquestionably something in this. Both the Social Democrats and the Socialist Revolutionaries offered cogent explanations of the workers' discontents, and an inspiring mandate for action. But most accounts, even from the revolutionaries themselves, agree that the socialist politicians were taken aback by the swiftness with which the workers improvised their own organisations. Lenin, in particular, initially viewed the soviets with grave misgivings, though he later changed his mind in view of their obvious effectiveness.

No, I believe the relative success of the soviets in 1905 and 1917 was chiefly due to the long experience of both peasants and workers in creating and running their own grass roots institutions, an experience long ago lost in more advanced countries where the environment was less harsh, the economy more productive and the government more effective.

In the villages of 1917 the peasants displayed a similar capacity for collective action. With the breakdown of law and order – or at least of the law and order imposed by church, police and landowner – they saw their chance to assert their own conception of how affairs should be run. The natural place for them to meet, discuss the situation, and take decisions was the *skhod*, the communal assembly. And there they would often come to the conclusion that an opportune time had come for them to rectify age-old injustices, by invading the landowners' land and taking his timber, pasturing village cattle on his fields, harvesting his crops, or even driving him out and burning down his manor house so that he could not easily return. Having reached such a resolution, they would implement it as a body, sharing the responsibility and the risks. They would sound the *nabat*, or alarm bell, gather with their carts, and troop together up to the manor house, to demand from the bailiff the keys to the barns and store-sheds, and then, provided there was no resistance, they would escort the squire and his family courteously off the premises.

The village commune had in other words its own conception of law and order, which it endeavoured to put into practice. Maverick fellow villagers who tried to grab more than their fair share, or who looted the squire's liquor supply for their own consumption, were treated as criminals by the community.[7]

In short, then, in the freedom, but also dangers, of 1917, peasants and workers reacted by improvising their own institutions, such as would enable them to take advantage of opportunities offered, and to defend themselves against threats. They drew in the revolutionary parties to help and advise them, where possible. But they did not always accept their advice, and where such help was not forthcoming, went ahead anyway.

The Bolsheviks came to power in October not least because they were the party best attuned to the mood in these popular institutions. They sponsored the popular demands for bread, land, workers' control in the factories, and an end to the war. Most of the workers, soldiers and peasants who supported the Bolshevik seizure of power in October thought they were fighting for 'All Power to the Soviets', as Lenin's slogan put it.[8]

In reality, of course, things turned out differently. The soviets and their equivalents held effective power only for a few months at most under the Bolshevik government. Then the pressures of economic collapse, and civil war and the ingrained authoritarianism of Lenin brought a steady tightening of central control over all popular institutions. Instead of being elected, their officials came to be appointed from above. Rival political parties were gradually squeezed out, and then even alternative platforms within the Bolshevik party were banned, rendering genuine political debate more and more difficult. The Bolsheviks proved far more competent than the tsarist government at asserting effective control over the grass roots. They were better organised, more ruthless, had a far more developed sense of propaganda and mobilisation. Besides, many younger peasants and workers from poorer families – the very ones who had found the old village commune stifling – were thoroughly committed to the new regime, and were prepared to act as its devoted agents through thick and thin. They formed the indispensable basis of social support for the new one-party state and the totalitarian system which it erected.[9]

Having sponsored and led this revolution of workers' and peasants' communities, the Communist Party later also destroyed them, partly in the civil war, partly a decade later in the whirlwind collectivisation of agriculture. The soviets of town and country became mere instruments of one-party domination.

It is my impression, though, that even after these popular communities were destroyed, something of their *spirit* survived in distorted form in the dwelling patterns of the city, in the so-called 'communal apartments', where for decades families lived squeezed next to one another owing to the desperate housing shortage. There, in shared poverty, they had perforce to devise a consensus about the common use of kitchen and bathroom, and they kept an even closer eye on one another than was possible in the village. Even today, when the communal apartment is no longer universal, the basic unit of Soviet urban life, the large block of flats grouped round a courtyard, still has something rural about it. The men sit at table and play cards or dominoes, the women gather and exchange gossip, the children amuse themselves in the sandpits. Such scenes can be found in Moscow as much as in smaller towns, and are very different from the texture of urban life in most of Europe.

Nor is it just a matter of dwelling patterns. The underlying habit of mutual aid, combined with mutual supervision, has survived and indeed spread to other strata of the population as former peasant children have left the village and moved up the social scale. The very speed of the urbanisation process, reinforced by the absence of pluralist political institutions in the towns, may actually have artificially preserved elements of rural culture inside the urban environment. In this way the totalitarian polity may have accidentally perpetuated an archaic communal outlook that would otherwise have faded more rapidly.[10]

I believe, in fact, that attitudes derived from the village have permeated the middle and lower levels of the Soviet political and economic systems, and still make themselves felt today. They should help us to understand how the totalitarian system works in practice. Since absolute control from the top is impossible, even the totalitarian state has to transmit its commands through intermediate institutions, and these tend gradually to evolve their own forms of internal solidarity. In his classical study of Soviet politics, written in the 1950s, the American political scientist Merle Fainsod hypothesised that totalitarianism tends to engender its own antibodies, even within the apparatus of power itself. 'Faced with demands from the party leadership which are difficult if not impossible to fulfil, and confronted with the constant possibility of a crossfire of criticisms from many directions, party as well as government functionaries are tempted to seek a degree of independence from control by organising mutual protection associations in which they agree informally to refrain from mutual criticism and to cover up for each other's mistakes and deficiencies.'[11]

In this way transmission belts can also become islands of resistance, indeed a whole network of resistance which eventually clogs up the system. This is entirely in keeping with the ambivalent Russian spirit of community: the peasant *mir* served both as the lowest rung in the ladder of authoritarian control, and yet also as a means by which ordinary people could cushion themselves against the excessive demands of the state. I suspect the same applies to Fainsod's 'mutual protection associations' and indeed to many grass roots Soviet institutions. In his study of industrial managers, Joseph Berliner calls them 'family circles', which well catches the analogy with rural congeries.[12]

So far westerners have not had the experience and Soviet scholars have not had the theoretical insight to write systematically about institutions at the lowest level. As a result, we know very little about the way village soviets, collective farm meetings, house committees and so on operate. The only observer who has attempted an extensive survey of the grass roots is Alexander Zinoviev, the philosopher who emigrated in 1977 at the age of 54, and has expatiated on his experience in a series of monographs in semi-fictional, semi-scientific form. He sees Soviet society as a network of tightly knit primary cells, centred at the workplace, which he calls 'communes'. In his presentation they sound like degenerate extended peasant households, held together by a web of material dependence, servility towards superiors, and mutual support adulterated by mutual jealousy and supervision.

These are the basic features of what Zinoviev calls 'communality', which he holds to be a universal human trait, restrained in most societies, but given free rein by Communism. Their inescapable result, as he sees it, is 'a tendency to make everyone mediocre. Be like everyone else: that principle is the very cornerstone of a society in which communal laws are paramount.'[13] Of course, one must remember that Zinoviev's vantage point is that of a highly talented intellectual who had been trying to publish unorthodox works. He naturally, therefore, emphasises the levelling effects of the primary cells. But there is no doubt in any case that Russian communities have always tended to crush or extrude their eccentrics, even (or especially) those who were talented, since divergences from the collective norms always seemed hazardous to a community on the edge of survival. As Zinoviev sees it:

'A person who can live in society independently of a primary collective is a threat to the very foundations of society. He is like a soldier who doesn't march in step with the rest of the platoon, but wanders about at random independently of the rest. He annoys the rest.'[14]

These 'communes' are the most important units of Soviet society, and their attitudes shape all the others, including families, circles of friends, even official institutions. This is because they dispense to each individual the basic ingredient of material and social life, including simple sociability, many of which are otherwise difficult to secure at all in Soviet society.

'At the level of the primary collective people not only work, they spend their time in the company of people they know well. They swap news, amuse themselves, do all kinds of things to preserve and improve their position, have contact with people on whom their well-being depends, go to innumerable meetings, get sent on leave to rest-homes, are assigned accommodation and sometimes supplementary food-products.'[15]

These are the daily confines of Soviet society, and in Zinoviev's opinion they render control from above superfluous. (For that reason, he rejects the term 'totalitarian', but we are not obliged to follow him: in any case, he clearly considers the hierarchical context within which the 'communes' operate to be crucial.) On their own they suffice to explain the homogeneity and conformism of *Homo sovieticus*. The security police is no more than the concentrated quintessence of society's outlook, usually superfluous since the communes will spontaneously eject their own mavericks and dissenters.

Zinoviev is perhaps unaware of the cultural limitations of his view. The kind of 'communality' he describes is not necessarily characteristic of humanity everywhere. But it may well be characteristic of many peasant societies, and its prevalence in Russia may be explained by the fact that the pre-modern peasant community survived there till more recently, and in harsher circumstances, than in most European countries.

I believe that, for all its limitations, Zinoviev's loquacious analysis opens up significant insights. He offers us what Philip Hanson has aptly called 'totalitarianism from below'.[16] If we want to understand how change can come about from below in such a society, then this is the unit from which we must start. However, as I said in the first chapter, the bearers of change in totalitarian society are intellectuals, so we must consider how these 'communes' function among them.

The Communist Party, which first supported, then took over and finally emasculated the popular assemblies, grew from the ranks of the radical intelligentsia, whose ideas and whose forms of community life are therefore of fundamental importance in understanding the influences which have shaped Soviet society.

The intelligentsia were the bastard children of Peter the Great, who in the early eighteenth century set out to make primitive Muscovy into a great European power. He succeeded, despite the enormity of the task, by using the power of the monarchy to transform all Russia's social institutions. In particular, he made the landed nobility into state servitors of army and bureaucracy, and he moulded the Church into an instrument for education, social welfare and the supervision of the common people. In the process, he laid the foundation for a tradition of public service which was one of the most attractive and abiding features of Imperial Russian society. But he also gravely weakened both the nobility and the clergy, depriving them of the autonomy which enabled them, in most European societies, to make their own distinctive input into the political process.

This enthralment was particularly damaging to the clergy, especially the parish clergy, who in the course of the eighteenth and nineteenth centuries became a subordinate estate, in effect almost an inferior caste, bereft of the financial provision, institutional independence or social standing which an established church normally enjoys.[17] Even the anti-clerical French republic of the late nineteenth century did not treat its clergy so shabbily. Yet the tsar still claimed to rule by divine right: this was expressly stated in the Fundamental Laws. The legitimacy of the Russian state, and therefore its symbolism, were religious, but its aims and methods were secular. It humiliated the very institution on whose sanction it rested its authority.

This fundamental incongruity created fertile soil for a revolutionary movement. Russia's revolutionaries came mainly from the two estates – nobility and clergy – which also provided its state servants. A study of the biographies of revolutionaries of the 1860s and '70s shows that they went through their formative experiences at educational establishments – universities, colleges and seminaries – designed to train them for public service. There, however, many of them came to the conclusion that the existing state and church were too corrupt and degraded to fulfil their proper function. Some students thereupon switched their allegiance to the revolutionary movement in the hope that it could do what state and church could not: genuinely serve the people.[18]

What had the revolutionary movement to offer them? Its basic unit was the *kruzhok*, the small circle of devotees who would meet, discuss, carry on impassioned arguments on philosophy or politics late into the night. Hermetic and secretive because of the oppressive political atmosphere of tsarist Russia, these circles were warm and supportive internally, yet also (with equal and opposite animus) chronically suspicious of outsiders, especially of neighbouring circles with rival programmes.

When they originated in the 1840s, the *kruzhki* derived their ideas from German idealist philosophy, which they embraced with a fervour no doubt intensified by the abject condition of the Russian Orthodox Church. It is almost as if there were a church-shaped vacuum in nineteenth-century Russian society. In effect the radicals channelled their religious aspirations into a philosophy of secular utopianism, promising social revolution as the means of man's final deliverance from evil.

Official censorship ensured that no such ideal could be openly put forward. The nearest radical thinkers could come to the public avowal of their aspirations was in literature – or, to be more accurate, through the literary journals, which were actually by no means purely literary, but combined prose, poetry and drama with social, philosophical and scientific treatises and with informed comment on the issues of the day. Literature absorbed some of the religious impulses which the Church was unable to channel: as a recent student of Tolstoy had commented, 'much of the finest fiction of the period was in essence theology in narrative form'.[19] And Vissarion Belinskii, one of the founders of the radical movement, went so far as to claim that 'all our moral interests, our whole spiritual life, have been focused exclusively on literature, and it will probably long remain so: literature is the living fount from which all human feelings and concepts flow into society'.[20]

If with literature the intelligentsia entered a marriage of convenience which developed into a passion, it was also extremely attracted by the prospects of science, especially after Russia's defeat in the Crimean War discredited the autocracy and opened the way for the tsarist version of perestroika in the great reforms of Alexander II, which did much to renew the Petrine vision of the state as the engineer of social progress. Radicals were drawn by both the natural and social sciences: the first for its promise of industrial development and increased mastery over nature, the second for the assurance it purported to offer of progress towards a more humane society. 'Without science,' the early Russian socialist Alexander Herzen once said, 'there is no salvation for modern man.'[21]

Their earnest zeal was not unlike that of the English Utilitarians: they wanted to jettison tradition and superstition in favour of hard-headed, realistic work to better the people on scientific principles. With no parliament to implement reform, however, most of them believed this goal could only be achieved by overthrowing the autocracy. Hence the need for revolution.

The man who best united in his person all these aspirations was Nikolai Chernyshevskii. He was the son of a clergyman, a seminarist who abandoned the priestly calling because he lost his faith both in God and in the Church. Like Marx, he regarded political economy as an extension of the natural sciences, a source of certain knowledge and soundly attested principles for ensuring social progress. Himself an editor of *Sovremennik (The Contemporary)*, the leading radical journal of its day, he also published a novel, *Chto Delat'? (What is to be Done?)*, which captured the imagination of two generations of radical youth. In it he shows how young women, emancipated from the oppressive patriarchal rule of their fathers, pool their resources, work together and share their income in a seamstresses' co-operative, or *artel'*. This co-operative Chernyshevskii presents as a model primary cell, a prefiguration of the human future society whose advent is being prepared by the austere young intellectuals, in fact revolutionaries, whom he calls euphemistically 'the new people'.

It is here that the foundations were laid for the secular utopian project of the Communists. Lenin greatly valued *Chto Delat'?*. 'This novel provides inspiration for a lifetime,' he once remarked.[22] He called his doctrine 'scientific socialism' and insisted that 'Marxism is all-powerful because it is *true*'. And Bukharin and Preobrazhenskii, authors of the first popular guide to Soviet Communism, roundly asserted that Communism, being scientific, had finally replaced religion: 'Scientific Communism . . . is guided by the data of the natural sciences, which are in irreconcilable conflict with all religious imaginings.'[23]

The regime which Lenin founded generated a singularly frustrating milieu for the intelligentsia. In one sense, they were the creators of the system, the custodians of its ideals, and many of them tried to live up to that calling. Yet at the same time, they were collectivised and oppressed, just like the peasants, their own ideals turned against them and used for their enserfment. Some of them – often the compliant and untalented – were co-opted by the regime in order to organise and supervise the rest. Under Stalin, they were required to peddle a crude, paranoid and reductionist view of the world, in which the utopian vision of the Old Bolsheviks was converted into a propaganda instrument to justify the regime's authority.

One of the most important and damaging aspects of this manipulated utopianism was its relentless drive into the future, given administrative form in the series of Five Year Plans begun in 1928. The science of economics played very little part in the elaboration of these Plans: they were not based on a projection of present productive trends into the future, nor did they attempt to balance one sector with another (industry, say, with housing or food supply). Rather, the first Five Year Plan (in particular) represented what the economist Naum Jasny has called 'Bacchanalian planning': setting apparently impossible targets in certain key heavy industrial sectors, and letting everything else line up behind.[24] 'There are no fortresses which Bolsheviks cannot storm,' Stalin exhorted.

This obsession with heavy industry and with the future was achieved at the cost of crushing everything which conflicted with it: the peasant community, serious intellectual life, the natural environment, even in a sense history itself. The advance into the future acquired a sacral character, measured out in five years spans. Both past and present were important only for what they contributed to the Great Future.

The state monopoly of information and mass communications, backed by a vigilant security police, made any serious intellectual or cultural life impossible. The conflict of diverse viewpoints and the assimilation of uncomfortable facts, both prerequisites for the formation of public opinion and the conduct of serious politics, were altogether precluded. While some intellectuals were fanatically devoted to the cause, others merely professed opinions, no longer quite knowing what they really thought, and succumbed to apathy and cynicism, or to the ambivalence which George Orwell so aptly termed 'doublethink'.

The Stalinist degradation of intellectual life wrought terrible destruction in the intelligentsia's own sanctuaries of science and literature. In science the nadir was reached with Lysenkoism, a pseudo-biology based on the theory, unproven by experiment, that man himself can intervene and direct the process of genetic change – a notion fully consonant with Stalin's slogan about fortresses and Bolsheviks.[25]

In literature, the authoritatively imposed doctrine of 'socialist realism' made obligatory a banal and sugary mode of writing, while the Writers' Union made the text a kind of collective product, on which writer, editor, censor, reviewer, party cell and literary critic all left their mark.[26]

Yet in the long run, science and literature were to prove to be channels by which intellectual emancipation re-entered Soviet society. In a way, it was natural that this should be so. Science and literature cannot serve even the purposes for which the regime requires them while they are confined in the totalitarian strait-jacket. A science which is not up to international standards, which is not meticulously verified by experiment and not open to new information and argument, cannot nourish a productive economy nor (even more important) sustain strong armed forces. In literature, which is by nature semantically rich and often ambiguous, the authoritative imposition of the banal and monological text becomes self-defeating. It no longer fulfils even its intended pedagogical function because it undermines normal communication between writer and reader. Readers no longer look for information in what the text states, but rather in what it implies or even omits. They become insensitive to the deadeningly omnipresent norm, reacting only to the fleeting aberration.[27]

In one respect the Stalin period brought a disguised blessing to the intelligentsia. In the nineteenth century they had tended to idealise the *narod*, the common people, aspiring to serve or emancipate them, while not really *knowing* them. In Soviet society, and particularly under Stalin, they could not avoid close acquaintance with the *narod*, being forced into unsought intimacy with them in schools, the army, building sites and labour camps.

I have dwelt at length on the traditions of the peasantry and the intelligentsia because they underlie such habits of community as have survived at all into the modern Soviet Union. These traditions played a decisive role in making the Russian revolution and in shaping Soviet society. Even under Stalin, though distorted and abused, they did not die out altogether. When one seeks to understand the present Soviet crisis, one must take them into account once again, for a new society can only be constructed out of the materials which are to hand. Furthermore, the reconquest of memory has to begin there too.

3

The return of the repressed

In Stalin's time, any real sense of community among the intelligentsia was rendered virtually impossible by the massive mistrust which the ubiquitous security police informers aroused. Since people could not be sure who might be reporting on them, they tended to keep social contacts down to a minimum. Ordinary human solidarity was confined either to specially trusted close friends or to Fainsod's 'mutual protection associations': informal coteries of officials helping each other out by covering up each other's mistakes and shortcomings. Stalin, of course, tried to break such islands of passive resistance to his rule: that was one of the aims of his purges. But no regime, no matter how tyrannical, can succeed in eliminating all such improvisations.

However, after Stalin's death, with the mitigation of terror, something more like normal social life gradually resumed. Among the intelligentsia, rapidly growing at this time with the expansion of higher education, it usually took the form of evening gatherings of colleagues or friends round a table loaded with black bread, sausage meat, cucumber, whatever happened to be available in the sparsely stocked grocery shops. They would discuss everything under the sun – literature, philosophy, science, religion – but especially the latest political events and all the frustrations of everyday life. These penurious salons had little to offer gastronomically, but they were, in the words of a participant, 'sumptuous, endless feasts of the spirit. In these circles theories were propounded and disputed, old authorities were felled and new ones erected.'[1]

This was classical soil for the matchless Soviet anecdotes, in which the oppressed cocked a snook at their oppressors and mocked the infuriating anomalies of Soviet life. Let just one, which I heard many times, illustrate the boundless paranoia of the authorities and the helplessness of the victims under Stalin. Three men are sitting in a prison cell and talking about their past. 'Why were you arrested?' 'Because I was late for work, so they accused me of sabotage. And you?' 'Oh, I arrived early for work, so they accused me of being a spy.' They both turn to the third cell-mate: 'And what happened to you?' 'I arrived for work punctually, but in their eyes my zeal was just a cloak to conceal my hostility to Communism.'

This was the time of Khrushchev's so-called 'secret speech' – actually not very secret though not published till 1989. People sought each other out and tried to understand what had happened to them all in the whirlwind years of war, purges and officially sponsored falsehood. Their exchanges of thought and experience were soon seasoned by the accounts of those returning piecemeal from labour camps, able to tell of a nether circle of the Stalinist inferno which everyone had dimly guessed at, but which few had survived to bear witness to. Among those homespun chroniclers of the underworld were even a few singers, bards with guitars, who refashioned popular ditties through the medium of the labour camp song, and thus resurrected long-submerged folk wisdom in modern guise: a Soviet version of the blues, if you like.[2]

It was also the time when more and more Soviet citizens were acquiring short-wave radio sets and listening to foreign broadcasts. More was becoming known about the present and recent past, enough to stimulate animated gossip without fully satisfying anyone's curiosity. The business of exchanging information thus assumed a crucial importance. The assimilation and mutual discussion of uncomfortable truths – a prerequisite for the formation of public opinion anywhere – was resumed for the first time since the twenties. This was the essence of the apparently aimless conversations which Russians call *tryop*. The ignorance and 'opinionlessness' of isolation was being overcome. As the human rights activist Lyudmila Alekseeva puts it: 'These conversations helped one to grope towards an understanding of the nature of Soviet society, how one should live in it, what one could accept and what reject.'[3]

In this setting *samizdat* developed almost spontaneously. Indeed, one could regard it as a natural extension of conversation, born of the desire to fix little-known information, put new ideas into circulation (even if very limited), remember and disseminate unpublished literature, whether of the past or of the present. The technology was primitive: one person would type four or five copies, each more faded than the last, and pass them on to friends, who, if they felt strongly enough about the material, would repeat the process. Whole journals and even novels were circulated in this way. So inadequate was the supply that one might be offered a 300-page novel for just one night to read: then one would invite the friends one trusted and sit up, passing pages from one to another. An ideal milieu for the formation of tightly knit circles – *kruzhki* – with their own ardently held views. Again, the setting was very reminiscent of that which had given birth to the nineteenth-century radicals, though the terrible lessons of the Stalin years were to lead their successors to very different political conclusions.

Such gatherings existed not only in Moscow and Leningrad, but also in a few Russian provincial towns, in Ukraine, in the cities of the Baltic and the Transcaucasus, where they helped to generate a much sharper awareness of national culture, history and tradition. The first cells of a potential civic society were germinating, but because of the totalitarian soil in which they were embedded, they were still isolated and helpless, often ignorant even of each other's existence.

The post-Khrushchev leadership took the decision to criminalise these activities – or at least their outgrowth, the dissemination of *samizdat* – without, however, restoring indiscriminate mass terror. This decision converted the more determined and self-aware of the participants in these gatherings into what became known as 'dissidents'. The turning point was a cultural one: the arrest in 1965 of two writers, Andrei Sinyavskii and Yulii Daniel', for allowing their *samizdat* not only to circulate among friends, but to be published in the west under pseudonyms. The event soon became widely known, thanks to western radio stations. Professional people, and writers in particular, were afraid that it might herald a return to Stalinist methods of secret trials, savage sentences and the victimisation of friends and relatives. They wanted to try to ensure that the proceedings would be public and that the court would at least observe the laws under which it claimed to operate.

This was an important new development. The idea that the Soviet authorities should observe their own laws was a novel one, and it struck them at a vulnerable point. Anxious to prevent for good and all the resumption of illegalities on a Stalinist scale, Khrushchev had launched a programme of 'socialist legality', which his successors endorsed. So to be publicly seen to be over-riding the law in Stalinist style was something they wished to avoid. But this enabled individuals for the first time to behave as if the Soviet constitution were a serious document, as if they were citizens of a free country. Such behaviour, as the human rights activist Vladimir Bukovskii later commented, 'presupposed a small core of freedom in each individual'.[4]

The authorities' relative restraint and the protestors' boldness made possible the first political demonstration in the Soviet Union since the twenties. It took place on 5 December 1965 at the Pushkin monument in Moscow, with banners demanding 'Glasnost for the trial of Sinyavskii and Daniel'!' and 'Respect the Soviet constitution!' There was scarcely time to read them, though, before the banners were torn down and the demonstrators were bundled off to police vans.

At the trial itself the new human rights activists were not admitted, and they had to stamp their feet in the freezing cold outside the court room, where, however, they timidly made their first acquaintance with western correspondents, a significant expansion of their channels of communication.[5] Despite the difficulties, Alexander Ginsburg, who had already been imprisoned under Khrushchev for issuing a *samizdat* journal, succeeded in making a transcript of the trial, revealing its judicial irregularities, and compiling the letters and press comment it provoked at home and abroad. In this way he breached the regime's monopoly of information, filling in what George Orwell would have called a 'memory hole' (but what in current Soviet parlance is referred to as a 'blank spot') before it was created. He distributed his so-called White Book among friends, sent copies to the Soviet leaders, and made sure that some reached the west, where it was published for re-smuggling into the Soviet Union.

Altogether, then, the Sinyavskii–Daniel' trial brought concerned individuals together, gave them the watchwords of 'publicity' and 'legality', and opened up the possibility of continued communication with each other, with the outside world, and even indirectly with Soviet society itself. Sympathy for the accused became a moral basis for the formation of *kruzhki*. As one witness has commented, 'it was the ethical gauge by which young intellectuals chose one another's association. To denounce the trial privately was to give oneself an identity badge that like-minded people could recognise.'[6]

Therewith the pattern was set for the gradual emergence of an alternative public opinion, a crucially important process for understanding what is taking place now. Its centre of gravity was initially human rights, but this concept expanded in due course to embrace issues of nationality, religion, culture, the environment – issues which people gradually articulated more clearly to themselves and to each other as they acquired ever more diverse information, exchanged opinions, and gained a sense of mutual solidarity.

Adopting such viewpoints meant, of course, in the long run that the human rights movement could not remain unified. In view of the size and diversity of the Soviet Union, this was inevitable. But in the short term immediate needs united the various participants. The focus of the movement throughout was the *samizdat* journal austerely called *The Chronicle of Current Events*, which first appeared in 1968. It bore on its masthead Article 19 of the UN Declaration on Human Rights: 'Everyone has the right to freedom of opinion and expression; this right includes freedom to hold opinions without interference and to seek, receive and impart information and ideas through any medium regardless of frontiers.' Otherwise eschewing any explicit editorial policy, this crudely produced typewritten bulletin collated and presented without comment examples of the Soviet authorities violating their own laws in their dealings with citizens. Natalya Gorbanevskaya, the first editor, would turn out seven copies on her typewriter, one for herself, one for a western correspondent, and five for friends, who were expected to retype their copies in similar fashion and pass them on. The journal's distribution channels functioned in the reverse direction as channels of information. To judge by the growing number of locations which furnished information for its pages, its circulation became more widespread over the years. According to one estimate, it may have attained as many as 10,000 copies by the early eighties, with perhaps ten readers for each copy.[7]

Lyudmila Alekseeva, one of its editors, has testified that working for the *Chronicle* 'meant to pledge oneself to be faithful to the truth, to cleanse oneself of the filth of doublethink which has pervaded every aspect of Soviet life . . . This created among people who scarcely knew one another, but who were connected with the *Chronicle*, very strong spiritual ties of the kind that probably existed among the early Christians.'[8]

With this loose co-ordinating centre in place, the movement was able in the seventies to diversify into specialised groups, some dealing with national rights, others with women's rights, invalids' rights, the rights of religious believers and of those confined in mental hospitals. Many of these produced their own specialist journals on the general pattern of the *Chronicle*. The Soviet government's signing of a European Security Agreement at Helsinki in 1975, with clauses on human rights and the free contact of peoples, provided an international validation for their concerns, and imparted renewed impetus to their work. A number of Helsinki Monitoring Groups appeared in various Soviet republics.

The Soviet authorities were embarrassed by the movement, and had difficulty in dealing with it effectively. The KGB was like a huge regular army faced with guerrillas, unable to place consistent informers in the network, and too centralised and clumsy to trace the informal, decentralised and unauthoritarian pattern of its contacts. Besides, to try to break it by mass arrests would have risked returning to Stalinist terror. They reacted therefore with apparently piecemeal and haphazard sanctions: arrests here, expulsions from the party there, job dismissals elsewhere, in some cases psychiatric confinement or enforced exile from the Soviet Union.

This pressure did not succeed in breaking the dissenting movement, indeed if anything the reverse is true, but it did begin to change its nature during the late seventies and early eighties. Participants began to go underground, seeking anonymity as a natural response to the increasing inevitability of sanctions against them. The movement's social composition began to change as ordinary workers and employees began to become involved. And it moved away from a primary concern with human rights towards an involvement in socio-economic, environmental and practical problems.

In 1977 the Donbass coal-mining engineer Vladimir Klebanov established the first independent trade union. It began, in traditional dissenting style, by protesting openly about violations of the legal rights of employees: it was formed by workers whose pursuit of justice against their employers had brought them to the waiting-room of the Presidium of the Supreme Soviet in

Moscow. Most of its members were detained on various pretexts soon after the foundation of the Union, and Klebanov himself was confined in a mental hospital.[9]

In the light of that experience, the second attempt to set up a free trade union took a different source. The Free Inter-Professional Association of Workers (known as SMOT) soon ceased to publish the names of its members, and confined itself to offering legal advice and to publishing surveys of socio-economic problems – for example, on food supply difficulties, price rises and rationing.[10] SMOT has survived to the present day, and thus provides a link between the dissenting movement and the rise of the 'informal associations'.

The human rights movement drew its strength from the cultural and scientific intelligentsia. Of its initial activists, the signatories of protest letters in the late sixties, more than half were scholars, many of them natural scientists, and a quarter were writers.[11] The public tribune of the movement was Andrei Sakharov, whose nuclear weapons work had alerted him to the unscrupulous and irresponsible way in which the Soviet leaders were exploiting the formidable technological power at their disposal. He had become convinced that only resolute defence of human rights could render governments accountable to their peoples, and thus restrain them from mortally dangerous abuses of power. The sight of his bald head outside a courtroom was a source of comfort to a good many dissenters.

Few scientists had Sakharov's saintly single-mindedness, but as a social stratum they were unusually well placed to identify abuses of power, and they enjoyed the prestige, the confidence of being indispensable, which enabled them to voice their concern. In the late sixties, scientific institutes became for a time centres of human rights protest activity. The authorities would react, sometimes with job dismissals and expulsions from the party, but more often with milder penalties, such as official rebuke, which at least left those affected still holding their jobs and able to pursue further research. There is some evidence that quiet resistance by academic councils and even by party organisations within the Academy itself dissuaded the authorities from taking harsher reprisals.[12]

Most striking is the fact that the Academy of Sciences, though it did not treat Sakharov well, never expelled him from membership, even at the time of his deepest official disgrace. This was not necessarily a sign of civic courage: more likely it was a defence of privilege. But still, the life tenure of academicians is a rallying cry which, however unheroic, in practice limits the power of the party and establishes a tiny bridgehead for political pluralism.

Of course, the great majority of scientists were not involved directly in human rights agitation and did not become open dissenters. But once Stalin's mass terror had ended, many of them shut themselves away in their institutes to devote themselves, along with a few like-minded colleagues, to what they considered promising fields of research, regardless of ideological implications. Whole branches of science, neglected or suppressed under Stalin – cybernetics, genetics, the social sciences – were revived and discreetly cultivated. In some of these new fields, even or perhaps especially ones which accorded ill with Marxist ideology, Soviet science established itself as a world leader, as in literary theory and semiotics, thanks to the seminar of Professor Yurii Lotman at Tartu University in Estonia.[13]

Another more practical example was the work of the Institute of Economics and Industrial Organisation at the Academy of Sciences in Novosibirsk. After Avel' Aganbegyan was appointed its director in 1967, it became the leading centre for research into what might be called the 'socialist market economy', as distinct from the centrally administered model which Stalin had introduced and Brezhnev was restoring. Every month the institute produced a journal which gained a world-wide reputation for its penetrating analyses of Soviet economic weaknesses and its propounding of alternatives. In 1983 the institute sent a long report to the post-Brezhnev leaders, written by Tatyana Zaslavskaya, Aganbegyan's colleague, devastatingly critical of the state of the economy, and recommending radical decentralisation. In many ways this report laid the foundation stone for the current economic reforms. Non-conformist work, long discreetly pursued, thus fed into the mainstream of perestroika.[14]

If scientists were able to get away comparatively lightly with such free-thinking enquiry, it was because the work they were doing was important to the political leaders, and also because scientists quite simply enjoyed a high standing which pre-dated the origins of the Communist Party. Much the same kind of prestige attaches to writers, which explains why the institutions of literature, and especially, the 'thick journals', became the other major centres of what might be called 'establishment non-conformity'.

The Soviet 'thick journal' has a certain Victorian quality to it. It would look far more familiar to subscribers of the *Quarterly Review* than to today's periodical readers in Britain. It is a kind of monthly intellectual hamper of goodies which lands on the doormat. Predominantly but by no means purely literary, it combines prose, poetry and drama with criticism, reviews and comment on the great issues of the day. Social, philosophical and scientific problems are grist to its mill. If controversial, they are often tackled in the form of literary criticism, which is a convenient and acceptable camouflage.

This has made the 'thick journal' the ideal forum for discussing the more serious problems of Soviet society. Until very recently such discussions had to be couched in an oblique and allusory style, to circumvent the censorship, and this has made them difficult for outsiders to follow. In a sense, though, their enigmatic quality was part of the mystique which journals found it expedient to cultivate, involving readers in an intellectual cryptogram accessible to a quite numerous but still limited circle of initiates and fellow believers. So each journal evolved not only its own political attitude, but also its own distinctive clientele, its relationship with whom created a kind of social magnetic field.

The most celebrated example of the type was *Novyi mir (New World)*, especially in the sixties under the editorship of Alexander

Tvardovskii. Tvardovskii was the son of a peasant expropriated during the collectivisation of agriculture and deported to Siberia, so that he experienced personally the harsh realities of the Stalin era. This did not prevent him being a loyal Communist, and a very popular war poet, whose literary hero, the peasant lad Vasilii Tyorkin, a kind of Tommy Atkins of the Red Army, was to be found in the knapsack of many a Soviet soldier. Tvardovskii's party loyalty was, however, of a distinctive variety. He interpreted party-mindedness in literature to mean telling the truth about what the ordinary people had undergone in the upheavals of Soviet history, not concealing the suffering Stalin had inflicted on them. Such frankness was officially tolerated as long as Khrushchev's de-Stalinisation was in progress, but Tvardovskii persisted with it, even deepened it, after Khrushchev's fall in 1964.

I was a Moscow University student myself at that time, and I recall with what eagerness the monthly arrival of the pale blue volume was awaited. One had to be a personal subscriber: there was no chance of buying a spare copy at a bookstall. On the evidence of readers' letters, Vladimir Lakshin, Tvardovskii's deputy, had asserted that *Novyi mir* 'became part of people's lives' and 'inspired a faith in the indestructibility of the truth'. I too remember the earnest enthusiasm of its loyal readers. In a world where everyone knew the public media were full of distortions and evasions, Tvardovskii's skill and courage in fighting for authors in whom he believed kept open a unique channel of unclogged communication. '*Noyvi mir* was read in the corridors of power, in remote villages, and in the most distant provinces, and its readership spanned labourers on construction sites, librarians, village schoolteachers, agronomists, passionate lovers of truth and lonely seekers after faith.'[15]

Perhaps his greatest contribution to Soviet culture was to make possible a serious re-examination of the Stalin period. Alexander Solzhenitsyn's story *A Day in the Life of Ivan Denisovich*, which Tvardovskii personally steered through formidable political obstacles, recounted candidly the routine of a Stalinist labour camp in all its squalor and inhumanity. The publication in 1962 of this sober but cogent *aperçu* released a flood of popular memory. Thousands of ordinary Soviet citizens wrote heartfelt letters to Solzhenitsyn, thanking him in glowing terms for daring to disclose what they had lived through but had never ventured to talk of openly. Many of them appended their own detailed accounts, providing for Solzhenitsyn the first of the materials he later wove into his much more comprehensive survey, *The Gulag Archipelago*.

Overnight Solzhenitsyn became, as it were, honorary archivist for a nation which had lacked its own memory. This was the 'return of the repressed', not in the individual psyche, but in the cultural community. And as Freud has taught us, the repressed always returns with tremendous emotional force. Such was certainly the reaction of Solzhenitsyn's readers to *Ivan Denisovich*:

'I could not sit still. I kept leaping up, walking about and imagining all those scenes as taking place in the camp I myself was in.'

'Now I read and weep, but when I was imprisoned in Ukhta, for ten years I shed not a tear.'

'After reading it, the only thing left to do is to knock a nail into the wall, tie a knot and hang oneself.'

'Although I wept when I read it, I felt myself a citizen with full rights among other people.'[16]

Tvardovskii and *Novyi mir* performed another signal service for the folk memory, and that was the cultivation of a school of rural authors, peasants by origin, who had risen with the precipitate upward social mobility of the Soviet era to receive their training at the Gor'kii Institute of Literature and to become writers. Their personal experience bridged a profound chasm in Soviet society, between the urban and the rural. For millions of Soviet citizens alive today, the decisive life event was the migration from village to town, usually at an early age, initially to do military service or to acquire an education, after completing which they would not return home, but would move heaven and earth to find a job in town and somewhere to live – often enduring years, even a lifetime, in crowded and sub-standard accommodation in order to realise their ambition. In a sense, their feat of individual dedication to the urban ideal replicated the total historical experience of Soviet society, with its worship of industry, technology, education and culture. Both in the macrocosm and the microcosm, this dedication was achieved at the cost not only of turning one's back on rural life, but also of denigrating it, devaluing it as something from which to escape at all costs. How many Soviet citizens have, in this way, denied their own childhood?

The village writers thus tapped a deep and long blocked up stream of feeling. Their leisurely evocations of the work and customs of the peasant community stimulated a strong reaction among readers who had once known that way of life, or had heard their parents talk about it. Again, this was a kind of 'return of the repressed', for the values of the village community had been repressed for at least a generation, partly because the official ideology imposed such amnesia, but partly also because individuals making their way in the modern world preferred to turn their backs resolutely on what they were abandoning.

The intensity of the reception given to 'village prose' also owed a good deal to the perception that the urban world had not brought with it the unclouded contentment of the utopian vision. Far from it: by the mid-sixties, when the Soviet Union was at last becoming a predominantly urban society, towns seemed to entail ugliness, pollution, stress, loneliness, alcoholism, delinquency and unstable family life. Such at least was a widespread impression. Many Soviet writers of the last generation have been actuated by motives similar to those of our own Victorian novelists: by fear of a new kind of contagious moral and spiritual disorder, spread by the teeming industrial towns. They strove to combat this disease by reasserting values inherited from an earlier, ostensibly more stable and humane era. Among these values was traditional religious belief: a vague, non-denominational but unmistakable Christianity. At a stroke the Promethean Soviet drive towards the future had been inverted, had become the worship of a lost Golden Age!

Altogether, the Brezhnev years may have been an era of stagnation, but they were also one of convalescence. A society which had been atomised and traumatised under Stalin was slowly and painfully reconstituting its memory and reknitting the fabric of social solidarity. It turned out that the Soviet people were not afflicted by total amnesia. A dim sense of loss of community was reawakening, together with an intellectual inheritance which had not completely succumbed to the totalitarian rewriting of history. So a certain basis did exist for the revival of autonomous social institutions and eventually of genuine politics. The preoccupation with human rights was the first sign of recovery, but it gradually broadened to embrace underlying issues of nationality, religion, culture and the natural environment. The articulation of these concerns will form the subject matter of the next three chapters.

4

A civil society in embryo

In 1987 a great turning point was reached in Soviet history. The government passed a decree banning tree felling around Lake Baikal and requiring the Baikal Pulp and Paper Combine to phase out the production of cellulose.[1] Hardly the stuff of historic turning points, you might think. It doesn't sound all that sensational, I must admit. But if you consider the implications for a moment, it actually contradicts the relentless drive towards economic growth which Soviet Communists have always regarded as a paramount priority. Lenin after all was fond of saying that 'Communism equals Soviet power plus electrification of the whole country'. And that meant accepting everything which electrification and the accompanying forms of modernisation entailed.

Nor is Baikal the only example of this kind. As I shall explain below, the great project to divert the north-flowing rivers southward to irrigate the semi-arid areas of Central Asia and the Volga basin has been halted, if not finally cancelled. And the nuclear power programme, crucial to the Soviet Union's energy needs, has faltered since the explosion in the Chernobyl' power station. In fact, some of the most cherished ambitions of the Soviet regime are being seriously challenged. How did this come about?

In the formative years of the Soviet system, and especially during the thirties and forties, the primacy of economic growth was so undisputed that no heed whatever was paid to environmental damage resulting from industrial development. The predominant attitude to nature was that it was there to be conquered! Nor in any case were the cumulative effects of pollution readily apparent at first. Blast furnaces, power stations and chemical plants were built at frenzied speed and left to belch their fumes into the air and discharge their effluents into the rivers. Lenin's 'electrification of the whole country' was pursued at headlong pace. Films were made and poems were composed about Dnepro-ges, the hydroelectric project on the lower River Dnieper which was one of the great showpieces of the first Five Year Plan, but no one at the time deemed it worth mentioning that thousands of acres of agricultural land and forest had been destroyed to make way for it. Equivalent degradation could result from poorly executed irrigation and drainage schemes. In Central Asia the intensive irrigation of cotton plantations has gradually deprived Lake Aral of its normal water inflow, so that much of the lake has become brackish marsh or even desert. And the marshy Pole-sye area of Belorussia has been so ineptly drained that in places sand dunes have formed and even dust storms have developed. As a local wit commented, aping the propaganda machine: 'In the next Five Year Plan let us transform all the marshes of Belo-russia into deserts!'[2]

In the early sixties, though, a few writers and scientists began to sound a warning note. One reason for this was mounting disillusionment inside the party with Khrushchev's headstrong character, his refusal to heed the advice of scientists about the damaging side effects of his grandiose projects. Take, for example, his much trumpeted programme for sowing vast areas of western Siberia with grain – the so-called virgin lands – which caused massive soil erosion because elementary precautions were not taken. But this was not just Khrushchev's personal foible. In his own idiosyncratic way he was only reflecting a general character-istic of the system: the fascination with size and speed, the drive to construct everything as big as possible and as fast as possible. This drive was institutionalised, it was inherent in the political structure: any ministry which was made responsible for a major project would automatically receive increased funding and additional personnel. Ministerial empire-building had its own logic, regardless of the effects any particular scheme might have on the rest of the economy or on the environment, and regardless even of whether it had any prospect of ultimately paying for itself. This is a classic example of the complete absence of checks and balances within the totalitarian system: although laws existed to protect nature, any powerful minister who could persuade the party's ruling bodies of the desirability of his pet project would receive an unconditional green light for its implementation.

The object of the first ever environmental campaign in the Soviet Union was the very same Lake Baikal which the government finally agreed in 1987 to protect. The purity of Baikal's water was threatened by careless timber felling and by the effluent from two planned cellulose factories designed to produce especially tough cord for the tyres of heavy bombers. Interestingly enough, it was conservative and Russian nationalist writers who first raised the alarm: the Siberian V. Chivilikhin[3] and Mikhail Sholokhov, who made an impassioned appeal at the 23rd Party Congress in 1966: 'Our descendants will not forgive us if we do not preserve this glorious lake, this sacred Baikal.' A number of the Soviet Union's best known scientists, such as Academicians Berg, Zel'dovich and Kapitsa, issued statements in support of them. A scientists' committee was set up to defend the lake, and Andrei Sakharov went personally to make representations to Brezhnev.[4]

This has been a quarter-century-long battle royal: on the one side are ranged the strategic imperatives of the military-industrial complex, with its grip on the party apparatus, on the other the status of Baikal as the world's largest reservoir of fresh water, home to unique forms of aquatic life, and backed by well-informed writers and scientists. By the time the censorship was tightened again during the late sixties, Baikal had already become a *cause célèbre* and could not just be stuffed back into the bottle. It was the first occasion in Soviet history on which it was recognised, at least by some participants in the controversy, that national pride and maximum industrial production might be in conflict with one another.

The result has been a prolonged and somewhat muffled war of attrition between the industrial ministries and the ecological campaigners. Today the campaigners are headed by the Siberian novelist Valentin Rasputin, who complains that, as a result, he has very little time left for his creative writing. It has been a long story of official decisions to reduce pollution of Baikal being stealthily circumnavigated by industrial ministries eager to maximise their output and minimise their expenditure, and until recently able to count on uninquisitive public media.[5] In 1987 the campaigners achieved a success in the form of the government decree which I described as a turning point. But even this is not total victory. Rasputin himself reports that the new combination of supervision from above, *and from below by the public*, is at last producing results, but he also warns that the battle to ensure beneficial decisions are actually implemented is far from over. 'Baikal is like a battlefield where a ceasefire has just been declared. Some are observing it, but others have got used to sniping and find it inconvenient to change their way of life.'[6]

Over the years environmentalists have been able to establish a foothold partly because their concerns reflect genuine economic dilemmas of the kind that pitch one ministry against another and therefore divide the party leadership. The American political scientist Thane Gustafson has pointed out that what appear to be pressure groups in the Soviet Union cannot actually become effective unless the party leadership is genuinely uncertain or divided about which of two alternative policies to adopt. As he rightly remarks, 'this is not pressure group politics, but the politics of waiting for the open window'.[7]

Apart from Baikal, one or two other 'open windows' have appeared during the last twenty years or so, and a semi-tolerated public debate has been taking place. During the sixties, for instance, it became possible to cast doubt on the advisability of constructing huge hydroelectric power stations. The institution responsible for them, Gidroproekt, had originally been part of the immense NKVD economic network, which included Stalin's labour camps, and it inherited from those days an imperious and secretive manner.[8] Criticism of Gidroproekt became possible mainly because other equally powerful agencies found their own interests impaired by its activities. The Ministry of Fisheries discovered that its catches were declining in the lower reaches of rivers dammed upstream. The timber industry lost valuable sources of raw material. And the higher priority which Khrushchev assigned to agriculture alerted everyone to the loss of fertile arable land.

It still needed a scholar of insight and pertinacity to crystallise this opposition. This was Academician Vendrov, of the Institute of Water Problems, who made it his business to assemble information and direct it to influential quarters, as well as training graduate students to support and continue his work. According to Gustafson, who interviewed some of them: 'In the early seventies Vendrov's students were filled with a crusading spirit. They saw themselves as the front line defence of the environment, and had detailed knowledge of the work done by similar groups in the west.' Being a member of an advisory panel attached to the State Planning Committee (Gosplan) Vendrov was able to press his points home at the highest level, and to contribute, perhaps decisively, to a moderation of the all-powerful hydroelectric urge.[9]

One environmental battle which has especially fired the public imagination was fought over the proposed diversion of Russia's northern rivers. It has been one of Russia's great geographic misfortunes that most of its major rivers flow unproductively into the Arctic Ocean, while large areas of the Volga basin and Central Asia are semi-arid or worse. Even in tsarist times one of two engineers had put forward schemes for diverting some of these rivers so that part of their flow went southwards; and a Communist regime which prided itself on its ability to 'transform nature' was not likely to remain permanently resigned to the cussedness of geography.

The only problem from the government's point of view was the breathtaking cost of the hydraulic works required. However, the 25th Party Congress in 1976 felt affluent enough to order full-scale scientific studies of the possibility of diverting water from the rivers Ob', Irtysh, and perhaps Enisei, through a 2000-kilometre-long canal to flow into the Aral and Caspian Seas, with feeders to provide irrigation for the cotton-growing areas of Central Asia and for the industrial towns of Western Siberia. An auxiliary project was also envisaged, to divert northern European Russian rivers towards the Volga basin.[10]

Among the project's principal protagonists were the Central Asian Communist Party organisations, eager to receive cheap supplies of water to sustain a wasteful and corrupt local economy resting on the over-planting of cotton. But most influential of all was Minvodkhoz, the Ministry of Water Resources and Melioration. This ministry is one of the prime Soviet leviathans. Responsible for all hydraulic, irrigation and drainage work throughout the country, it employs by its own account one and a half million people, including building workers, which I estimate at something approaching one per cent of the entire Soviet population of working age. When I spoke to some of its leading officials in May 1988, they were unbowed by recent setbacks and confident that the country would one day recognise again the need for river diversions and come running back to them for help. They were polite but unmistakably scornful about the temporary fashion for taking notice of ignorant amateurs expressing opinions on such complex matters. No doubt that would pass, they implied. Meanwhile, they were stockpiling the feasibility reports of no less than 150 research institutes on various aspects of the project, against the day when they would be needed. Even casting an eye over these mounds of paper, I could sense the sheer scope of the patronage that lies stored up in a project like this, capable of employing and paying hundreds of thousands of people for many years.

Initially the opponents of Minvodkhoz took longer to make their views felt. Economists have always tended to oppose the project, reckoning there must be cheaper ways of preserving water, and over the years they have signalled their reservations in specialist journals. But once again, it was natural scientists and writers who were eventually more successful in making opposition effective. The writer Vasilii Belov – ecological spokesman for northern Russia as Rasputin is for Siberia – was especially worried about the monasteries and churches of his homeland, most of which lie along river banks and hence are vulnerable to any rise in the water level. Unable to publish his views in the Soviet press, he eventually resorted in the summer of 1982 to an émigré newspaper in Paris.[11] Under Gorbachev such subterfuges became unnecessary, and the Writers' Union congress of summer 1986 turned into a concerted forum for public opposition to river diversions.'Glasnost is all very well,' complained Rasputin, 'but what use is it if nothing changes as a result?'[12]

Scientists were also stirring themselves to take advantage of the new political conjecture. They were worried about the effects of flooding on the soil, and about the dangers to the world climate of curtailing the flow of so much relatively warm water into the Arctic Ocean. The Academy of Sciences held interdisciplinary seminars in 1985, which aroused such interest and concern that a voluntary commission was set up under Academician Yanshin to study the whole project and present an alternative report on it. This commission brought together specialists from a variety of fields: soil science, geography, biology, ethnography, law and so on. One of its members, to whom I talked, emphasised that it was a voluntary enterprise, set up from below out of shared concern, without official instructions of any kind. He also told me that Minvodkhoz and the Central Asian party organisations had tried to have it banned, but in vain.[13]

The commission's report argued that, quite apart from the cost, the environmental consequences of the project were incalculable and potentially very damaging, and the commission recommended abandoning the whole thing. Together with the appeal from the Writers' Union, this report seemed to catch the Politburo at a moment of critical indecision of the kind hypothesised by Gustafson. At any rate in August 1986 it ordered the suspension of all construction work, pending further study. It was not quite a conclusive victory for the ecologists, but it was nevertheless a remarkable success. Sergei Zalygin, chief editor of *Novyi mir*, and himself a hydraulic engineer by training, hailed the decision as the first ever major triumph of 'public opinion' over Gosplan and the industrial ministries.[14] It was certainly an indication of a sea change in the official attitude to the environment, and also in the capacity of writers and scientists to articulate views – or at least doubts and fears – hitherto widely held by people powerless to change anything.

It may be no accident that this decision followed quite closely on the explosion at Chernobyl', which demonstrated as no previous incident had the dangers inherent in allowing the economic leviathan to get out of control.

The explosion's full significance was dramatised two years later by one of the foremost architects of the Soviet nuclear power programme, Valerii Legasov, first deputy chairman of the Kurchatov Atomic Energy Institute. On the second anniversary of the explosion Legasov committed suicide, and in a *Pravda* article which was part suicide note, part testament, he called the disaster 'the apotheosis of the whole misguided way of running the economy which we had been pursuing for decades'.[15] By this he meant not only the secrecy – nuclear authorities everywhere are inclined to be secretive – but also the grandiose ambitions backed up by haste, wilfulness and slovenly workmanship.

The Soviet nuclear power programme was speeded up in the late seventies because of difficulties over other sources of energy. It promised to be clean, cheap and efficient, and it looked attractively 'modern', the sort of thing a self-respecting superpower could not afford to be without. In practice, however, it was often carried out, as most Soviet construction schemes are, with shoddy materials and to hurried schedules. Legasov was once horrified to find a welder failing to finish off the seams on a water cooling pipe properly, simply because he had so many seams to get through to complete his daily output target. The staff installed to run the stations were sometimes inadequately trained because the speeded-up building programme had left no time. Once the novelty of nuclear power had worn off, moreover, they got used to sloppy procedures and habits. As one station director once remarked to Legasov: 'What are you worried about? A nuclear reactor is only a samovar. It's much simpler than a thermal plant . . . Nothing will ever happen.'

This spirit seems to have underlain the fateful experiment which took place on the night of 25/26 April 1986. It was conducted in order to discover whether energy output could be continued even when the station was receiving very low levels of electric current from its own turbines, for example during a repair or a temporary power failure. We do not know why it was judged necessary to test this, but of course maximum output in all circumstances has always been a motto of the Soviet economy, and Gorbachev had only recently made it clear at the 27th Party Congress that he was looking for *uskorenie* or 'acceleration'. (Is it merely my imagination, or has he used the word a lot less since Chernobyl'?) At any rate, since it was important to complete the test before the plant's imminent annual shutdown for repairs, the normal safety precautions (which might have accidentally aborted the experiment halfway through) were overridden. The result was that when a sudden increase in power unexpectedly took place, there was no way to prevent it surging into a full-scale nuclear explosion.[16]

Thereupon heroism mingled with duplicity and furtiveness in characteristic Soviet fashion. While firemen and technicians struggled self-sacrificingly (literally: some of them died) to bring the blaze under control, local officials tried to minimise what had happened and to localise information. Some of them even made hasty arrangements to evacuate their own families while leaving the public at large in the dark about the hazards. This obfuscation must have delayed Moscow's response to the crisis. Legasov first heard of 'some kind of accident at Chernobyl'' several hours before he was flown off to the site as a member of an emergency commission, and even by the time he arrived he was quite unprepared for the scale of the disaster which lay before him.

The local population was needlessly exposed to presumably high levels of radiation (precise readings have never been disclosed) for up to a week after the explosion. The rest of the world heard about the disaster before those most closely affected, who had to pick up what they could from (sometimes exaggeratedly alarmist) western radio reports. Evacuation was begun belatedly, and some anxious parents besieged railway stations to try to get their children out of the danger zone.[17]

Faced with evidence that its customary minimal information policy was discrediting the Soviet Union abroad and sowing panic at home, the Soviet regime abruptly changed the policy, and started to put some beef into glasnost, which had hitherto existed on paper rather than in reality. It began to publish regularly updated information on radiation levels, monitored food supplies and advised on health precautions. It invited a commission of the International Atomic Energy Authority to come and inspect the disaster site.

Nevertheless, much uncertainty persisted and still persists. The public have remained worried that facts vital to their health were being withheld from them. This anxiety was intensified by the trial of officials from the power station in July 1987: foreign correspondents were excluded from most of the trial, and the impression was deliberately fostered that a few negligent officials were *entirely* responsible for the disaster. Questions of design, location, poor materials and bad workmanship in the construction of the station were neglected.[18] I myself recall a meeting held in the Ukrainian Writers' Union building in Kiev two years after the disaster, at which members of the public fired questions at officials about radioactive dust, the topsoil, the state of the rivers, and the safety of the 'sarcophagus' in which the stricken reactor had been encased. They evidently felt a good deal of scepticism and anxiety about the reassurances they were given.

With the lapse of time, in fact, public disquiet has not abated, but on the contrary been reinforced, both by official evasions and by further incidents at nuclear plants. In 1988 it seemed to reach a critical level. The publication of Legasov's testament undoubtedly contributed to this upsurge, as did Academician Sakharov's stated view that all future nuclear power stations should be built underground.[19]

An extreme view has been expressed by Ales' Adamovich, one of the leading writers of Belorussia, the republic which, because of the direction of the wind, suffered most from the early fallout of the explosion. According to him, the real scale of the disaster was still being concealed from the public by the unholy alliance of three bureaucratic leviathans: Minenergo (the Energy Ministry, with powers similar to Minvodkhoz), solicitous of its nuclear power programme; Agroprom (the agricultural and food processing authority), straining to keep up its output figures; and Minzdrav (the Ministry of Health), eager to present a reassuring picture of a healthy population. 'All their efforts are bent towards concealment, not disclosure of the sources of danger. As they see it, atomic energy must be saved at all costs. Why, they've even invented the expressive word "radiophobia" to describe anyone who doesn't blindly put his faith in the specialists.'[20]

Adamovich's dig at the 'specialists' highlights a remarkable aspect of the recent public agitation over environmental matters: the loss of faith in 'specialists' and the assertion of the right of 'non-specialists' to express concern on matters which affect their lives. As Adamovich himself declared, 'I cannot afford not to take up matters which are "none of my business". I don't have the right not to. What specialists do, the results of their decisions, affect us all too closely.'[21] This is a novel sentiment in a society which has traditionally accorded almost unlimited respect to the 'men from the ministry' and taken a deferential view of science and learning. The strain of violating this deep-seated taboo may help to explain the somewhat hysterical tone of Adamovich's outburst.

Belatedly, then, concern over the consequences of Chernobyl' has built up into a broad questioning of the whole Soviet nuclear energy programme. The progress of the campaign is confusing to follow, since announcements that construction of a certain power station is being stopped are sometimes followed by further news that it is continuing. Perhaps there is an element of dissembling on the part of Minenergo, which after all has to find alternative employment for its workers or lay them off, which is almost unheard of. Departmental pride will not permit a ministry to admit to a shrinking work schedule.

Most of the protests over nuclear power have been in non-Russian republics, where environmental fears mingle with ethnic resentment in a way I shall return to in the next chapter. At the Kiev meeting which I alluded to earlier, many of those present seemed suspicious that the persistence with nuclear generation at Chernobyl' was in some way an attack on the Ukrainian nation. In Lithuania, after a fire in the Ignalina nuclear power station in September 1988, the Initiative Group in Support of Perestroika (embryo of Sajudis) organised a huge petition campaign calling for the station's closure and improvised a human chain of several thousand people round it. At about the same time, the Riga consultative meeting of non-Russian national democratic movements singled out the nuclear issue as one of especial concern: participants called the Soviet atomic energy programme 'a greater threat to European states than Soviet military might'.[22]

The upshot of all this public agitation was that by September 1988 an expert western observer felt able to remark that 'these protests have effectively made redundant the Soviet Union's ambitious programme for nuclear reactor construction to the year 2000'.[23] If so, this is an achievement even more remarkable than the prevention of the river diversion project. Of course it signifies no more than an uneasy stalemate, and Minenergo is probably reacting like Minvodkhoz, shelving the projects in the hope (or confidence?) of being able to resume them when more favourable weather returns. Besides, the stalling of nuclear power faces the Soviet Union with a potentially very serious energy shortage. Nevertheless, it seems clear that public organisations, inspired by writers and scientists, have proved themselves able to block, at least temporarily, vital components of the economic plan.

The growing public concern over the environment illustrates the way in which a potential constituency did exist for agitation over political problems, even when Soviet society, apart from a few human rights activists, seemed in a state of deep apathy. An analogous concern, widely felt but little expressed, was over the seemingly endless escalation of the international arms race, with its heedless consumption of resources and its threat to life on the planet. Now, an official Soviet Committee for the Protection of Peace did (and does) exist with the ostensible purpose of voicing this public concern, but few took its claims seriously, since, unlike western peace movements, it spoke in favour of a government which, by the late seventies, was the principal instigator of the arms race.

No unofficial peace movement arose on the western model until 1982, at a time when the long-established human rights movement was fading away or going underground. Then a circle of Moscow intellectuals set up a 'Group for Establishing Trust between the USSR and the USA'. Its first activity, a press conference held with western journalists, was very much in the spirit of the human rights movement: declarations of conscience using the western media to bypass the deaf-and-dumb Soviet information channels. Before long, however, the Trust Group began to experiment with other means of reaching the Soviet public. It would hold seminars in private apartments on subjects such as the Soviet nuclear arsenal, the theory of non-violent action, or the conversion of the arms industry to peaceful purposes. It established contacts with visitors from western peace movements and used their materials to stage an exhibition on the consequences of the Hiroshima bomb and of children's paintings on peace. It was embarrassing for the security police to be seen removing exhibits so patently in accord with the ostensible policies of the Soviet government.

In the summer of 1984 the Trust Group transferred some of their action on to the streets of Moscow. On the Arbat, members collected signatures for a petition urging the Soviet and American leaders (Chernenko and Reagan, then in a relationship of glacial hostility) to hold a summit meeting as soon as possible. Passers-by proved less timid than was feared and, though surprised by an initiative which had no official approval, 300 gave their signatures in the two hours which passed before the police woke up to the fact that the action was unauthorised and rounded up the petitioners. In similar fashion in 1986 the Group handed out leaflets in Gor'kii Park, providing facts about the Chernobyl' nuclear explosion, and passing on recommendations about precautions to be taken. It was carrying out a public service which the government had neglected, on a subject which caused most people deep and legitimate worries.

Participants in these and other public demonstrations were rewarded with brief spells in prison, and one or two of them with severer penalties, such as psychiatric detention and compulsory military service. But the resilience of the Trust Group showed that there were some prospects for a movement taking up causes which the Soviet government itself affected to support and using to the full the limited scope available for making contact with western colleagues and a wider Soviet public. The Group was feeling its way towards overcoming one of the major problems of the human rights movement – its relative isolation from the broad mass of the Soviet peoples.[24]

Another success of the Trust Group was its relative attractiveness to young people, anxious to do something practical about the serious problems affecting their society. Young people in the

Soviet Union today are in a paradoxical and, in some ways, dispiriting situation. On the one hand their lives are materially more comfortable than those of their elders, and they have not been obliged to endure war, revolution or social upheaval. They are more educated and sophisticated, with a wider range of interests. On the other hand they are moving into a society which can offer them no obvious role. Whereas in earlier generations people gained interesting and responsible jobs on the basis of meagre educational attainment, the impressive qualifications held by some of today's young people are often not matched by the work they do. In fact their way is blocked by the *nomenklatura* appointments monopoly which installed their elders with life tenure. As Dr I. Il'insky, Director of Research at the Komsomol High School, has pointed out, demographic ageing has led to a reduction of the hiring of young people for administrative work, science and the arts. This both weakens their involvement in society and also limits their access to consumer goods, which often depends on professional position. Their civic maturation is slowed, and their sense of alienation intensified.[25]

Older people sometimes display a striking lack of understanding of their younger compatriots. Last year I talked to two writers in their fifties, men of real culture and human insight, who nevertheless assured me that today's young people, not having lived through serious deprivation and difficulty, were spiritually empty, and their literary attempts therefore insipid and lightweight. The Writers' Union, incidentally, is a classic instance of an official organisation unresponsive to youth: of its recent recruits only 20 per cent have been under 35 *at the age of entering*.[26]

The party's youth organisation, the Komsomol, is supposed to induct the young into this greying milieu, and so has naturally found itself in a classic 'piggy-in-the-middle' situation. Intended to reflect the aspirations of young people, it also has to convey to them an authoritative world view elaborated in quite different conditions and carrying little conviction today. Membership is not compulsory, but is more or less expected of young people with any ambitions in life. At least it was till very recently, but in 1988 Viktor Mironenko, its first secretary, revealed that membership had dropped by 10 per cent over the last three years, and that a quarter fewer 14- and 15-year-olds were joining it.[27]

The reasons for the decline are not far to seek. More than 50 per cent of the Komsomol's own members consider it bureaucratic and unresponsive to ideas from below.[28] Since about the mid-seventies, and in some cases even earlier, more and more young people have been taking things into their own hands, setting up their own voluntary associations and clubs to pursue all kinds of interests and aims, from basketball to yoga, rock music to international peace, breakdancing to environmental protection.[29]

Now Soviet law certainly permitted voluntary associations, but it also demanded that they register and attach themselves to a sponsor institution (RSFSR law of 10 July 1932). More enlightened or flexible Komsomol organisations came halfway to meet them, offering premises, advice and facilities. But not all voluntary associations found sympathetic sponsors, and some of them did not bother to register at all, meeting instead in members' flats or hiring premises wherever they could, in schools, palaces of culture, municipal buildings and so on.

Informal groups have been multiplying with remarkable speed. Early in 1988 it was reckoned that some 30,000 of them existed in the Soviet Union: a year later the estimate was 60,000. As many as 50 to 70 per cent of young people are estimated to belong to one or more, though the number of active participants may be much lower.[30] The range of their concerns is very broad, but perhaps half are in the field of culture or sport. About a tenth are estimated to be addressing political and social problems, while quite a large number of others are active in defending the natural environment or historical and cultural monuments.[31]

The great change since 1986 is that some groups of this kind have been encouraged by the official policy of glasnost to project their activities and ideas to a wider audience. The natural means by which they can achieve this broader publicity is by raising matters which arouse the concern of an educated and increasingly suspicious public: culture, the environment, history, ethnic and religious identity. The lively public response to them has in turn provoked a further increase in their numbers and in the vigour of their activity.

In Leningrad, for example, there has been for more than a decade a lively alternative culture, tacitly tolerated by the authorities. Its focus was the so-called Klub 81, which was allowed to hold poetry readings and even bring out an uncensored literary journal, provided its members circulated it strictly among themselves and did not seek western publication.[32] But the alternative groups sought a broader public only when early in 1987 the City Soviet announced that it was planning to demolish the Hotel Angleterre – distinguished, apart from its architecture, by the fact that the much-loved poet Esenin committed suicide there in 1925. Klub 81, together with other historical and ecological groups, collected signatures in the street for a petition to save the building. Partly by deception and partly by brute force, the city council cleared the demonstrators and moved their demolition workers in. The protestors then stationed an information kiosk on the square in front of St Isaac's Cathedral to hand out leaflets and answer questions. By this time nothing could save the hotel, but the activists drew from their failure the lesson – already long ago learnt by the human rights movement – that they must regard state and party as potential adversaries, and so must work together better in future and be more assiduous in seeking publicity.

Accordingly, they set up an umbrella organisation, the Cultural Democratic Movement, or Epicentre. Using the primitive technology of *samizdat*, Epicentre began to issue its own monthly journal, *Mercury*, carrying the watchword 'Claws and teeth for public opinion!' This contains open letters on cultural and environmental problems, as well as announcements of public discussions, lectures and meetings. Its editor, P. S. Filippov, set the tone in the first number: 'The activation of public opinion, its mobilisation as an effective instrument of perestroika – this is the main road which leads to socialist democracy.'[33] The spirit is very much that of Edmund Burke: 'When bad men combine, the good must associate; else they will fall, one by one, unpitied victims in a contemptible struggle.'

In Moscow, though there was no comparably dramatic event, the picture was similar: disparate groups of young concerned people doing their own thing and gradually being drawn together by the need for information, mutual aid and solidarity. The idea of a co-ordinating body first sprang from the apparently unprom-ising soil of the 'red corner' (communal meeting room) of a block of flats on the Arbat. In early 1986 a youth discussion group which regularly met there conceived the idea of an enabling group to help people with practical proposals for social work. They helped to launch a theatre studio, a computer club, and a building detachment to construct a home for the deaf and dumb. The official resistance they encountered to these projects raised broader political issues in their minds, and Gorbachev's calls for support from below emboldened them to establish a Club for Social Initiatives. Similar clubs arose at about the same time in Leningrad, Riga, Vil'nyus, Kaunas, Vinnitsa, Chelyabinsk and Novorossiisk.[34] They received the encouragement of the econom-ist Tatyana Zaslavskaya (author of the famous Novosibirsk eco-nomic report of 1983) and of the Soviet Sociological Association, which, through its own Committee for Social Initiatives, was doing its best to regain some influence on social change, lost long ago under Brezhnev.[35]

According to its own charter, the Club for Social Initiatives aimed 'to involve broad strata of the population in the process of self-government'. The activities it sponsored were extremely diverse: helping the old and ill; preserving old buildings; sponsor-ing games for the disabled; holding seminars for workers on the recent 'self-administration' law; offering advice to people whose legal rights had been infringed; agitating for a monument to Stalin's victims; sponsoring discussion meetings on draft laws published in the Soviet press. Altogether, it was in danger of becoming Amnesty International, Greenpeace, Age Concern and the Citizens' Advice Bureau rolled into one. Accordingly, it sensibly divided up, spawning sub-groups to specialise in particular problems: one called 'Social Self-administration'; another, 'Civil Dignity', to advise and aid people who feel that their legal rights have been infringed; and the 'Philanthropic Society' to provide practical help for the old, ill or handicapped by shopping for them, cleaning their flats, or just talking with them.[36]

Sometimes political and social aims like these were married to a religious or philosophical orientation, like the Cosmos Club in Moscow, which combined the restoration of old buildings and international peace work with contemplative jogging in the Yoga spirit and shared meals which they began with a joint meditation, imagining the mutual love that bound them to each other, to the city, the nation and the whole world.[37]

Some informal groups emerged under the wing of official institutions, like the Perestroika Club, which originated in the Central Economic-Mathematical Institute in Moscow. It grew out of discussions on the new enterprise law held there in the spring of 1987, which brought together economists, sociologists, jurists, political scientists and others. The discussions were wide-ranging and spontaneous, and soon outgrew their original theme, raising issues which concerned the whole of Soviet society and attracting in the process a wider non-academic public. Some participants decided to move beyond discussion and set up action groups, each taking responsibility for a particular set of problems: one for legal rights, another for political questions, another for historical and cultural issues. One group, later called *Memorial*, set itself the task of arousing public concern for the building of a memorial to Stalin's victims – an aim eventually crowned with success at the 19th Party Conference.

But as the Perestroika Club grew politically more active, a symptomatic schism took place within its membership. This was between those who wanted it to act as a ginger group *within* the establishment, and those who felt it would be better to dissociate the club from existing authority structures and agitate from outside. In a nutshell, we have here the dilemma which confronts all informal activists in present-day Soviet conditions, a dilemma which in turn reflects the ambiguity of the current political scene, where a totalitarian party is proposing reforms which would end the totalitarian system. At any rate, the club split into Democratic Perestroika – more technocratic, strict about membership admissions, and in favour of working within the system; and Perestroika-88 – more libertarian, more open about membership, and less prepared to compromise with existing institutions.[38]

This kind of fracture may not be too damaging, since both sides seem to maintain good personal relationships – in contrast with the bitter splits of the nineteenth-century radicals. In the uncertain and ambiguous current situation, both modes of activism are probably fruitful in their own way. One view of the requisite strategy was put to me forcefully by Aleksandr Podrabinek, editor of the unofficial journal *Ekspress-Khronika*. If a cart is stuck in a bog, he said, then the best way to haul it out is not to wade into the mud, but to stand back from it, on firm ground, so as to have a reliable foothold. His own foothold is Orthodox Christianity, which he learned from Dostoevskii, and a belief in freedom and the rule of law as the basic preconditions for the existence of society. As he sees it, those who profess 'socialism' as the fundamental principle, or who hope to work through existing power structures, are merely slithering about in the mud and are likely to share the fate of the cart they are trying to extricate.

Ekspress-Khronika as a journal consciously moulds itself on the *Chronicle of Current Events*. In the late seventies Podrabinek edited an information bulletin on psychiatric abuse and wrote a book on the subject, *Punitive Medicine*, which was published in the west. For this he was charged with slandering the Soviet state and sentenced to five years' exile. Compared with the *Chronicle*, *Ekspress-Khronika* is much shorter and also much more frequent;

otherwise its aim is exactly the same, dispassionately to record and publicise violations of human rights in the Soviet Union. Its editors meet every Saturday morning in a flat on the outskirts of Moscow, in the afternoon the typists get to work, usually going on far into the night, and on Sunday morning the journal is distributed on the Gogol Boulevard in the centre of the city. People come to pick up copies, pay what they can afford for them, and usually stay to ask questions. The police stand around in the background and watch, but usually do not interfere.[39]

An unofficial publication of this kind puts an immense strain on those involved. There are constant telephone calls to be answered, often from people distraught over what has happened to them, and their reports whenever possible must be checked. Typists and paper must be found, also couriers to distribute the final product – in spring 1988 *Ekspress-Khronika* was going to 53 towns, in 11 of which it was further typed and distributed. And all this must be done by people who have jobs of their own, and often families to look after in overcrowded apartments where books and paper seem to overflow from every shelf and table, and with technology which is utterly inadequate to the task.

The authorities' attitude to these unofficial journals was, as one would expect, ambivalent. They did not forcibly close them down, but on the other hand they declined to legalise them by official registration. Podrabinek, for example, was brushed off by the Moscow City Council with the comment: 'Your views on the freedom of the press are not consistent with Marxist-Leninist philosophy'. And Sergei Grigor'yants, editor of the unofficial journal *Glasnost*, was told by an official of the State Committee on Publishing that there was no need for new publications, since there already existed thousands of newspapers and periodicals, and besides there was a shortage of paper.[40]

At a meeting in October 1987 the editors of some thirty unofficial journals agreed that legal status was their most pressing need. As Podrabinek said: 'If we enjoyed the status of a co-operative, we could open a bank account, buy paper, rent premises, conclude a contract with a printing firm, have our own copying equipment.' They also requested 'open access to reprographic technology', which they called a prerequisite for genuine freedom of the press.[41]

Many informal political activists believed, unlike Podrabinek, that their place was in the mud alongside the cart, that unless someone puts his shoulder to the wheel, it will remain mired for ever. Those associations which were prepared to try to work with reforming elements in the party-state apparatus first came together in August 1987 at a conference in Moscow convened by the Club for Social Initiatives. Nearly 600 individuals from some 48 different groups participated. Most of them were of a 'broad left' persuasion, seeing Marx through the prism of Gramsci, Marcuse, the Yugoslav revisionists and the protagonists of the 1968 Prague Spring. They repudiated the Soviet version of 'real socialism', but did not disavow the idea of socialism altogether: they hoped to evolve a new version, responding to Gorbachev's calls for 'initiative from below' to develop links with ordinary people in their workplaces and homes and to prod the bureaucracy into more fruitful activity. They put particular emphasis on 'workplace democracy', on encouraging and helping workers to take advantage of their new rights under the 1987 enterprise law to participate in and monitor management decisions. At the same time, they rejected the methods of the human rights movement of the sixties and seventies as élitist, too remote from the interests of the masses. They also regarded with suspicion the market-oriented reform projects of economists like Aganbegyan, which they felt were likely to generate greater inequality, social injustice and probably unrest.

With so many groups represented, it is not surprising that many diverse views emerged at the congress. Not all groups could accept the majority consensus outlined above, and in the end two federations of informal political associations were formed, one of which (FSOK, the Federation of Socialist Clubs) required that its members acknowledge 'socialism' as their aim, while the other (KOI, or the Circle for Social Initiative) made no such insistence.[42]

The latter federation seems to have faded away, but the former continued and extended its activities in an ambivalent relationship with the authorities. In January 1988 FSOK arranged a joint conference with the Komsomol, to see whether common ground could be discovered for permanent co-operation. However, when it became apparent that the Komsomol intended to swamp the conference with its members and to take over the agenda, FSOK withdrew and broke off contacts for a time, provoking a bitter attack in the Komsomol newspapers.[43]

The more democratic electoral system announced by the special 19th Party Conference in July 1988 offered an opportunity for an alternative mode of coalition-building. During the summer FSOK joined with many other associations in trying to put together Popular Fronts in Support of Perestroika, with the aim of mobilising public backing for Gorbachev, especially among young people, against the conservative rump of the apparatus. This support, in the eyes of the movement's initiators, should not be uncritical: in fact, the Popular Fronts could be seen as performing many of the functions carried out in parliamentary systems by the official opposition.

Some of the more enterprising members of the Soviet legal establishment were evolving similar ideas. Professor Boris Kurashvili, of the Institute of the State and Law, for example, had formulated the theory that in a one-party system the competence and probity of the apparatus tends to degenerate unless someone is providing what he called 'social opposition'. Writing in a youth newspaper in April, Kurashvili proposed that Popular Fronts should monitor the work of government and party, criticise their legislative drafts, formulate alternatives, and keep data banks for the public to draw on for the purposes of informed discussion.[44]

Welding the disparate political clubs together into an organisation generating mass appeal proved extremely difficult. The clubs had all forged their own identities and loyalties, which it was painful to adapt to the needs of larger associations. As Boris Kagarlitsky, who was in the thick of it, has testified: 'The lack of political experience, even among the leaders of the movement, a shortage of information, a pathological fear of even the most democratic forms of centralised leadership (which led at times to a complete incapacity for collective action), the clash of personal ambitions – all these combined to obstruct the development of the Popular Front from the very outset'.[45]

There were serious ideological divergences, too. While some clubs, like Democratic Perestroika and Socialist Initiative, wanted the movement to proclaim itself 'socialist', others, like Civil Dignity and Perestroika-88, believed that the whole concept of 'socialism' had been utterly discredited by the Soviet experience, and that it was essential to build a broader alliance to include all those committed to democracy and the defence of civil rights. Even Kommuna, the anarchist group, though socialist in orientation, took the latter stance, because of its belief in avoiding centralism of all kinds.[46]

Those who most fervently rejected 'socialism' and any cooperation with the Soviet authorities, even in support of perestroika, formed their own movement, the Democratic Union, which proclaimed itself an 'opposition party' (the first since 1921), rejected the entire heritage of the October revolution and called for a return to the principles of February 1917. It refused to join the Popular Fronts, dismissing them as stooges 'pinning their hopes on the authorities and on international public opinion' instead of conducting a truly political struggle by appealing to the people.[47]

In contrast, those who joined the Popular Fronts felt it was necessary to cooperate with reforming elements in the party-state apparatus *as well* as to appeal to the people. The rift between 'liberals' and 'socialists' proved very difficult to heal. Although the 'liberals' eventually accepted the words 'democratic socialism' in the first programme of the Moscow Popular Front, the tensions aroused by the dispute kept coming back to the surface.[48]

The actual circumstances in which such Popular Fronts were

founded often brought them into direct conflict with authorities who were inflexible or reluctant to tolerate criticism. An example of this kind was seen in Yaroslavl, where a Popular Front was formed at a public meeting on the bank of the Volga on 8 June 1988. It had been learned that the long-standing first secretary of the district party committee, one F. Loshchenkov, had been chosen as a delegate to the 19th Party Conference without any consultation with the rank-and-file party members. He was unpopular because he had encouraged the construction of a new chemical works in the town. The improvised meeting demanded Loshchenkov's recall and new elections, a demand to which the district party committee eventually acceded. Encouraged by their success, the initiative committee went on to organise weekly meetings in the football stadium, each of which would end by passing resolutions for action on local matters. In this way a Popular Front came into being, grudgingly tolerated by the authorities. When, however, the new Front wanted to publish its own programme – including open elections for leading public posts, and the abolition of privilege stores for *apparatchiks* – the local party newspaper refused to publish it. The editor told outraged leaders of the Front: 'I answer to the party. If they tell me to publish this, I will. But they haven't, so I won't.'[49]

The election campaign for the 19th Party Conference stimulated some lively provincial political activity of this kind. In Omsk an 'action group' comprising engineers, lecturers, students and Komsomol officials organised a rally in the Dynamo stadium one Sunday in May to discuss perestroika and to protest about 'the undemocratic nomination of candidates to the conference'.[50]

In the Urals industrial city of Sverdlovsk, popular opposition was aroused even earlier by the dismissal from the Politburo of their popular former first secretary, Boris El'tsin. An initiative group called Meeting-87 was set up at a public gathering. It brings out a lively journal, *Herald of the Urals (Ural'skii vestnik)*, and has organised public meetings on subjects like 'The Democratisation of Soviet Society'. Ecological and Russian national groups have also been set up in the town.[51]

The elections of March 1989 to the Congress of People's Deputies demonstrated that, even in their current amorphous and loosely organised state, the informal political associations could have a considerable impact on public opinion. The procedure for the nomination of candidates was complex: official electoral commissions had to validate candidacies at each stage, and this offered plenty of opportunities for the apparatus to interfere. Sergei Stankevich, Popular Front candidate in Moscow, likened the process to the Minotaur's labyrinth.[52] Here the role of the Popular Fronts and equivalent movements was to act as Theseus: to choose good candidates, thread them through the formal obstacles and then campaign for them in public.

In Leningrad a number of political clubs got together and formed an alliance called 'Elections-89' to coordinate an electoral challenge to Yurii Solovyov, first secretary of the regional party committee, and alternative member of the CPSU Politburo. It proved impossible to nominate an opposing candidate. Undaunted, Elections-89 printed leaflets and paraded the streets with slogans such as 'Long live unsanctioned restructuring!' and 'No to elections without choice!' They won a sensational victory: Solovyov, though unopposed, failed to be elected because he did not muster even 50 per cent of the electorate.[53]

In Moscow oppositional efforts focused on the person of Boris El'tsin. His status as popular hero persecuted by the apparatus made him a natural magnet, especially after the CPSU Central Committee decided on 16 March to investigate him for breaches of party discipline. Without the support of the informal groups, though, he would probably neither have fought his way back on to the political stage, nor been able to develop a coherent programme of his own. Popular Front support brought him the advice of intelligent and able people, some of whom had spent years reflecting on the country's problems in the twilight world of the private discussion groups. It also gave him an organisation capable of bringing thousands of people out on to the streets – as many as 35,000 at the final pre-election rally in the Luzhniki Stadium.[54]

The result was sensational: El'tsin won 90 per cent of the vote against the party's official nominee. Results elsewhere were patchy, probably reflecting the local strength or weakness of the 'informals', but nomenklatura candidates were also defeated in Vladivostok, Khabarovsk, Kemerovo, Chita, Tyumen', Volgograd, Perm', Ivanovo and Kirov, in the Belorussian towns of Minsk, Gomel' and Mogilev, and the Ukrainian towns of Kiev, L'vov, Chernigov, Voroshilovgrad and Zakarpat'e. There is little evidence at the moment to suggest how many of these defeats resulted from the agitation of informal groups, but in Zhitomir, for example, a woman journalist, Alla Yaroshinskaya, won a remarkable victory after denouncing the privileges accorded to *apparatchiks*.[55]

A unique situation pertained in the Baltic republics, for there the Popular Fronts were no mere haphazard coalitions, but well organised mass movements (see next chapter). Candidates enjoying their backing won more than two-thirds of the seats; and the fate of the official candidate in those seats they did not contest was usually determined by whether or not they certified him as acceptable.[56]

Most observers were astonished at the results of the Congress elections. Of course, everyone knew that the public was bitterly resentful at the decades of misrule by the apparatus, the shortages of food, consumer goods and housing. But few expected the voters to register their discontent in such a concerted manner. The scale of the reformers' local victories – and also their very patchy distribution – suggests that the agitation of local informal associations, their posters, leaflets, public meetings and demonstrations, probably played a vital role in encouraging the voters, at least in certain regions, to articulate their feelings at the polling booths.

5

The flawed melting pot

The national question in the Soviet Union provides a striking illustration of Tocqueville's celebrated dictum that 'the most dangerous moment for a bad government its when it seeks to mend its ways'. When Gorbachev came to power, it seemed not especially pressing. Though many non-Russian intellectuals resented in private – and occasionally in public – the domination of their culture from Moscow, their concerns appeared to outsiders esoteric, and it was not self-evident that their resentment was shared in any consistent fashion by workers and peasants. As for the local *apparatchiks*, though mostly indigenous, they owed their power, directly or indirectly, to the centre, and dispensed their loyalty accordingly. Despite sporadic outbursts of popular ethnic animosity, there did not seem to be a basis for asserting nationhood in opposition to Moscow. Above all, there were no autonomous associations to undertake the task.[1]

Yet a mere five years later, the picture is quite different. The resentful intellectuals have proved capable of mobilising the mass of their fellow countrymen and of asserting the sovereignty of their nations. How can this be so? What has happened, I think, is that the factors which gave birth to informal associations in Russia have made themselves felt, with redoubled intensity, in the non-Russian areas. There issues of history, culture and the environment are even more salient, as symbols of national distinctiveness, and for the same reason writers and scholars enjoy a uniquely respected status. The whole dynamic of glasnost and democratisation has propelled ethnic factors to the centre of the Soviet political stage. That which totalitarianism repressed has surged powerfully to the fore, uniting people of disparate social backgrounds and career paths. An explosive realignment of loyalties and political structures has resulted.

The Soviet multi-national state is the last of the great European empires and since the others have all fallen apart in the present century, it was in some ways to be expected that the Soviet one too should come under pressure from national liberation movements. However, things are not as simple as that. The Soviet Union is a decidedly unusual imperial entity. It resembles the Habsburg or Ottoman Empires, contiguous agglomerations of territory held together by military and administrative power. More than either of those, though, it is numerically and politically dominated by one nation, the Russians. But – and here the paradoxes start – that domination has not enabled the Russians to flourish economically, even by comparison with many of their ostensible 'colonies': compare, for example, the poverty of a village in central Russia with the relative prosperity of its counterpart in Estonia or Georgia. Nor indeed have the languages and cultures of the principal non-Russian peoples withered: in fact, in some ways they have developed and strengthened as a result of membership of the Soviet Union.

The truth is that this is not, in fact, in the normal sense a *Russian* empire. It is a Communist one, the first empire in history to be ruled over by a political party. From that fact flow the anomalies and contradictions of this unprecedented multinational union.

The anomalies result from the unintended as well as the intended effects of the Bolshevik revolution. To take the intended effects first. Lenin held that classes, not nations, were the most fundamental social formations. Ultimately, he believed, nations would wither away along with states, and the proletariat would create an international community of peoples. In the short and medium term, however, he recognised that the national sentiment of Imperial Russia's subject peoples was a very useful ally in the struggle against the tsarist regime, and later in the civil war against the Whites. So before and during the revolution itself the Bolsheviks launched the slogan of 'national self-determination', supporting the emancipation of the subject peoples from Russia. In the immediate sense, the slogan was a great success: most of the non-Russians did ally themselves with the Reds and did gain some kind of independence, at least temporarily.

Once the Bolsheviks themselves were the masters, however, they inevitably took a much dimmer view of separatism, not only because they were the party in power, but also because theoretically they regarded 'national self-determination' as subordinate to the ultimate goal of 'proletarian internationalism'. During 1918–21 the Reds gradually and where necessary forcibly resumed control of most of the old Imperial Russian territories. Only Finland and Poland remained permanently independent, though it was 1939/40 before the Soviet Union could regain the Baltic region, eastern Moldavia and western areas of Belorussia and Ukraine.

So by 1922, when the Soviet Union as a political entity was finally formed, the way should theoretically have been open to introduce 'proletarian internationalism'. In practice, however, especially in the absence of socialist revolutions elsewhere, the Soviet state was not in a position to offer the non-Russians any kind of internationalism, proletarian or otherwise. The most it could extend to them was membership in a multi-national amalgam dominated demographically, linguistically and administratively by Russians. And this in turn was difficult to distinguish from actual Russification, the very evil against which the non-Russians had so recently fought, with explicit Bolshevik support.

This was the kind of 'proletarian internationalism' which Stalin favoured, but Lenin was well aware of the dangers. In the last years of his life he repeatedly warned of crude Russian chauvinism making its reappearance in the leather-jacketed breast of the

Soviet commissar. He did not, though, have any political solution to the problem: indeed, the political structure he had instituted aggravated it. The Soviet Union was nominally designated a federal state, with considerable autonomy – and even the right of secession – granted to its constituent national republics. But in reality its administrative structure was highly centralised, with not only diplomatic and military power, but also economic power firmly located in Moscow. The Russian Republic (RSFSR), nominally just one of seven (later fifteen) republics, actually contained 90 per cent of the Soviet Union's territory and 72 per cent of its population. So it could scarcely help becoming the dominant member of the Union. Added to this was the fact that the Communist Party did not even *pretend* to federalism. Lenin always intended that power should reside unambiguously with the all-Union Central Committee in Moscow: the national communist parties of the constituent republics were, and have remained till very recently, no more than subordinate provincial units.

All the same, alongside this redoubtable concentration of political and economic power, a genuinely decentralised and pluralist approach to culture and education did prevail for a time. There were cogent reasons for this. Lenin had always believed that the political revolution needed to be complemented by a cultural one. He felt especially strongly about this when he surveyed the abject state of the country after the civil war. The Communists might be in power, but, as he saw it, they were not really running the country because they and most of the population lacked 'culture', that is, basic work habits and elementary notions of punctuality, probity and even literacy. Lenin hoped to overcome this lacuna by a crash programme of cultural propaganda, starting with the inculcation of basic literacy.

It made little sense to conduct such a programme in a language which people did not understand. So, like the medieval Catholic Church facing rural paganism, the party had to make use of local languages and show some consideration for inherited popular traditions. The twenties and early thirties saw the introduction of universal primary schooling in the various native languages, as well as the publication of books, journals and newspapers in the vernacular. In some cases this meant the revival of ancient cultures threatened with eclipse by the growing dominance of Russian under the tsars; in others it meant the transformation of what had been largely rural or tribal dialects into full-scale urban and literary languages with their own emergent high culture.

It is important to remember that not all ethnic communities survive into the modern world and become full nations. For every potential nation which makes it to nationhood there are a far greater number which fall by the wayside. Many dialects and folklores gradually fade away, or at least remain behind in the rural ghetto, when their bearers come to the city and are swamped by the broader, more sophisticated culture dominant there.[2] This was a fate which might, for example, reasonably have been expected to overtake the Ukrainian and Belorussian peoples in the early twentieth century. But Soviet nationality policy unintentionally ensured that this did not happen. If most Ukrainians coming into the towns during the Five Year Plans had been illiterate, then they would probably have acquired the habit of using Russian as an everyday language and would in effect have assimilated to Russian culture. Soviet education policy, however, ensured that they were mostly literate, and in Ukrainian. As a result, the towns became *more* Ukrainian during the industrialisation. Whereas in 1926 65 per cent of Ukrainian town-dwellers named Ukrainian as their native language, in 1959, the next time the question was asked in a census, the proportion had grown to 77 per cent. In Belorussia the effect was even more marked, with a rise from 38 to 64 per cent.[3]

This movement of an ethnically aware rural population into the cities helped to lay the social base for the intensely nationally conscious intelligentsia of today. The effect was deepened by the elaborate administrative divisions of the Soviet Union, which gave even quite small ethnic groups their own miniature version of statehood in the form of an Autonomous Republic or an Autonomous Region. It was party policy that all such subdivisions should have their own indigenous cadres, that is to say, local nationals promoted through the *nomenklatura* ladder to hold high office in their territory. These people were closely supervised by representatives of Moscow in the party and the KGB, but they none the less symbolically embodied the attributes of nationhood and were usually able to act as powerbrokers on behalf of their ethnic colleagues.

Stalin, it is true, tried to re-establish a centralised Soviet hegemony with marked Russian nationalist overtones. Alarmed by the growing influence of these indigenous cadres, he purged them, accusing them of 'bourgeois nationalism'. He insisted on a Russian imperialist version of history being taught in schools, and was in the habit of referring to Russians as 'elder brothers' in the Soviet family. Worse than that, he tried to destroy some nations completely, by uprooting them and deporting them to distant and unfamiliar territories; or if they were too large, then he deported or murdered their élites, as he did in the Baltic, Belorussia and Ukraine in 1939–40. Yet never did he end the practice of conducting primary education in local languages, so that the nourishing of national feeling from below continued unbroken throughout his rule, irritated and intensified by his repressions and by the crude mixture of Marxism and Russian chauvinism which he imposed as cultural pap. Moreover, when in 1932 he introduced pass books, which all Soviet citizens had to carry, he included in them the category 'nationality'. A citizen's ethnic background thus became a permanent administrative fact, which would affect his fate every time he applied for education, a job or a residence permit. So whatever the official rhetoric about the ultimate merging of nationalities, their separate existence was authoritatively registered, with far-reaching consequences for everyday life.

All in all, the contradictions of Soviet policy have set the agenda for the conspicuous national revival which is going on today. Like other civic movements in the Soviet Union, this revival bears all the emotional force of the 'return of the repressed', the fervour of the sudden rediscovery of community amidst the rubble of the totalitarian heritage. The key role in this process has been played by writers and scholars, who are in a better position than most of their countrymen both to identify potential dangers and to articulate alarm at them. Whereas in the sixties and seventies such dissent did not often spread beyond limited circles, because the authorities used an array of sanctions to keep it within bounds, in the last three or four years various issues, different in each nation, have sparked off contact between these circles and a broader public which feels that its grievances are best encapsulated in ethnic demands.

The specific aspirations of each nation differ according to history and circumstance. For some the paramount concerns are territorial. It is easy to understand why: a nation without a homeland is deprived of the most elementary condition of community life. Already in the sixties, the Crimean Tartars, deported from their native soil by Stalin and forbidden to return by his successors, were able to mobilise most of their co-nationals for a mass campaign of demonstrations and petitions. The Jews are in an analogous condition: without a proper homeland in the Soviet Union, they saw an alternative one established in Israel in 1948. Feeling discriminated against in jobs, housing and education, they encapsulated their national aspirations in the demand for the right to *emigrate*, a desire little understood by other Soviet nations and easily dismissed as mere lack of patriotism.

The territorial issue which has most recently attracted the headlines is the Armenian demand to have the Autonomous Region of Nagornyi Karabakh incorporated into their republic. This is one of those emotionally overburdened problems whose implications are very difficult for outsiders to appreciate. The Armenians are an ancient people, one of the oldest Christian nations in the world, with much more than a mere millennium to celebrate. But for them territory and statehood have always been a sensitive issue, since for many centuries their population was uprooted and scattered between different empires. This has made them vulnerable to inter-communal violence, of which the Ottoman massacres of 1915 were only the worst example.

Nagornyi Karabakh is the easternmost area of Armenian settlement, a mainly pastoral and viticultural region. From a monastery within it the seventeenth-century Armenian Patriarch is said to have first written to the Russian tsar requesting protection against the infidel tyranny.[4] That is why the decision of 1921 to include Karabakh in the Azerbaijani Republic, with its Turkic population, has always deeply offended Armenians. The region was at that time more than 90 per cent Armenian in population, and the subjection to an alien race reminded them forcibly of the orphaned and vulnerable condition in which their people had so long lived.

Nor is it merely a matter of a historically based insult. In the one-party state, administrative subordination affects all aspects of life. Jobs, housing and economic development all depend ultimately on the Azerbaijani republican authorities in Baku, who tend to give preference to their own co-nationals over Armenians. Moreover, after four years of primary schooling, all parents must choose for their children whether to continue their education in Russian or in Azerbaijani, the language of the republic: Armenian is not an option.[5]

Armenians' loyalty to the Soviet state – which after all has remained their protector against hostile Muslim neighbours – long inhibited them from serious agitation to put the anomaly right. But they made discreet representations about Karabakh, and even organised a street rally in 1974.[6]

Gorbachev's proclamation of glasnost encouraged the Armenians to raise the issue more publicly. In autumn 1987 they sent a petition with 75,000 signatures to the party Central Committee calling for the historical injustice of Karabakh to be rectified. They never received a proper reply. This tacit slighting of their claim coincided with agitation over another grievance which has figured frequently in recent ethnic protest, that of environmental damage. The air in the Armenian capital city of Erevan is so

polluted by chemical factories that intellectuals sent an open letter
to Gorbachev, talking of 'biological genocide' and citing a huge
recent increase in cancer, cardiac and respiratory disease, and in
birth defects.[7] The merging of these two streams of protest
imparted the decisive mass appeal to the Armenian national
movement. On 25 February 1988 a crowd estimated at between
500,000 and a million demonstrated in the streets of Erevan
with banners proclaiming 'Karabakh is part of Armenia!' and
'Karabakh is a test case for perestroika!'[8]

The bursting of the genie from the bottle discredited the Armenian Communist Party, which had for decades acquiesced in both
the territorial and the environmental affronts. The protests of
1988 were co-ordinated by a so-called Karabakh Committee,
which according to the Soviet press was formed by writers,
journalists and scholars, as well as officials acting in a private
capacity.[9] It placed its branches in factories, offices and educational establishments – just like the Communist Party, and,
practically speaking, in rivalry to it. It was in effect an unusually
successful Popular Front facing a demoralised local Communist
Party. The Armenian Supreme Soviet actually came down on its
side against the party by voting for the incorporation of Nagornyi
Karabakh.

Symptomatically, it was two writers, Sil'va Kaputikyan and
Zorii Balayan, who were mandated to go to Moscow in March
1988 to lay before Gorbachev the concerns of the Armenian
people. They returned to report that Gorbachev had promised
them 'a new beginning' in Karabakh. He did not, however,
honour this pledge in the sense in which they had understood
it, by awarding Nagornyi Karabakh to the Armenian Republic.
Presumably he feared a backlash among the Soviet Union's fifty
million Muslims, and was reluctant to open the way to irredentist
demands in other disputed border areas. The feeling of being
let down naturally intensified Armenian bitterness. Apart from
writers, the Armenian Church also began to play a more active
role, with its head, Catholicos Vazgen, supporting the Armenian

claim, but urging the people to behave responsibly and peacefully in pressing it.

In the end, after months of fruitlessly trying to ban the Karabakh Committee, Gorbachev took advantage of the earthquake of December 1988 to weaken it by arresting the eleven members of its Central Committee. Shortly after, he introduced direct rule from Moscow in Karabakh, supplemented by a virtual military occupation of the Armenian Republic.

The Azerbaijanis, not surprisingly, also regard the Karabakh issue as a test case for the ability of the Soviet Union to satisfy their national aspirations. They share with all Soviet peoples the sense that their economy and culture are not under their control, but are being alienated from them for someone else's benefit. The oil wealth of Baku is running out, having mostly been siphoned off to fuel the Soviet economy as a whole: the Azerbaijanis, as they see it, are left only with the pollution.[10] Their past culture has been placed at two removes from them by not one but *two* alphabet reforms. For them the Armenians are rich neighbours who have enjoyed an undue share of the Soviet Union's aggregate wealth: many of the better-off or more privileged citizens of Baku and Sumgait are Armenians. Doubtless such frustrations lie behind the appalling massacre in Sumgait, where a hundred or so Armenians were murdered in what seemed to many like a systematic fashion by their Azerbaijani neighbours.

In Georgia the Communist Party managed to retain more effective power for longer than in Armenia, but did not use it wisely, and has in the end suffered the same collapse of reputation as in the neighbouring republic. Like the Armenians, the Georgians are an ancient Christian people who have lived under constant external threat from expansive Muslim empires. In most other respects, though, their national experience has been very different from that of their neighbours. They had a great medieval kingdom, that of David the Builder and Queen Tamara, in which other small peoples were subject to their rule. Over the centuries that kingdom fragmented into petty principalities, and was only reunited under the Russian crown in the nineteenth century.[11]

Georgian national sentiment thus manifests itself in deep mistrust of outsiders, together with a fierce and anxious desire to hold together the nation's fissiparous territories and peoples. In that sense Georgia is a kind of microcosm of the Soviet Union as a whole.

This proud, militant patriotism is exemplified by Merab Kostava and Zviad Gamsakhurdia, in whose company I spent a number of memorable hours in April 1988. Gamsakhurdia's father, Konstantin, was a writer whose epic novel *David the Builder* chronicles the rise of the medieval kingdom. Zviad showed me his father's statue (significantly unnamed, for the Communist Party distrusts national heroes): he sits with stiff dignity, holding a curved sword at his knee. Sitting in a room austerely furnished but lined with books and prints, Zviad and Merab expounded to me in luxuriant detail the glories of their nation's history, and recounted their struggle, as leaders of the Il'ya Chavchavadze Society (called after an early twentieth-century writer now thought to have been murdered by the Bolsheviks in 1908), in defending Georgia against Russian encroachment. Their enthusiasm was infectious, but also mixed with passionate hatred of all their opponents, especially their rivals within the Georgian national movement. (I later learnt that their leadership of the Chavchavadze Society was disputed.)

This meeting equipped me well to understand the intractability of the Georgian question. The intransigent militancy of Georgian national feeling has made compromises extremely difficult to achieve. The Il'ya Chavchavadze Society was set up in October 1987 to defend the Georgian language, culture and environment against gradual erosion by Russian immigration, Russian cultural hegemony and industrial projects imposed by Gosplan (like the Caucasian Mountain Railway which threatens a peaceful mountain valley carrying the bulk of Tbilisi's drinking water). It subsequently split into moderates and irreconcilables, the latter led by Gamsakhurdia. The irreconcilables formed the nucleus of the National Democratic Party, established in August 1988 as an explicitly opposition party calling for the revival of an independent Christian Georgian state. 'The Georgian people', proclaimed the National Democrats, 'made its choice on 26 May 1918, when it voted for democracy and pluralism in the conditions of a free Georgia. 26 May was destroyed by Bolshevik bayonets, but the idea of freedom and democracy remain undefeated in the Georgian people . . . The revival of Georgian independence would set right a great historical injustice. It is worth living, fighting and dying for that.'[12]

The National Democratic Party is by no means the only mouthpiece of Georgian national feeling, but it has probably attracted the strongest public support, especially among young people. It has raised impressive numbers of people to support its meetings, strikes and demonstrations, over matters like human rights violations, the destruction of historical monuments, and the continual pollution caused by the Batum oil refinery. They brought out 100,000 people on the streets of Tbilisi on 12 November 1988 to protest against the proposed changes in the Soviet Constitution which would rescind the theoretical right of constituent republics to secede from the Union.[13] The National Democrats have reacted strongly to perceived threats against Georgians from the other peoples living in the republic. They are especially sensitive to demands from the Abkhazians, a half-Christian, half-Muslim people who form about 15 per cent of the population in the extreme north-west of Georgia, to break away and amalgamate their Autonomous Republic with the RSFSR.

Such demands were the immediate precipitant in April 1989 of the most serious act of violence committed by the Soviet authorities on their own people for a quarter of a century. Demonstrations in Tbilisi which began in protest against the Abkhaz demands turned into all-night candle-lit vigils, backed by hunger strikes demanding independence for Georgia. As tension mounted in the city, special Ministry of the Interior riot troops were flown in, while more and more ordinary citizens came out into the streets and squares to protect the hunger strikers. Early on the morning of 9 April – it is not known on whose orders – army and MVD soldiers dispersed the crowds forcibly, using clubs and spades. Some reports spoke of drunken troops 'butchering women and girls with military shovels'. It later transpired that some kind of gas was also used, more damaging and lasting in its effect than tear-gas. The authorities admitted that 19 people were killed, while Georgians maintained the figure was much higher; more than 200 people were injured.[14]

The then Soviet Foreign Minister Edvard Shevardnadze, doyen of Georgian Communists, flew in to take temporary charge of the situation. In a speech to the Georgian CP plenum, he condemned leaders of informal organisations who 'were quite deliberately leading those who trusted them to the slaughter', but also attacked the local party leadership for 'erecting a barrier' between themselves and the unofficial activists. 'An opponent can become a partner, but for this the minimum requirement is to talk with him and hear him out,' Shevardnadze admonished, tacitly recommending a more 'Baltic' strategy for assuaging public discontent and giving it a constructive political framework.[15] Dzhumber Patiashvili, Georgian party first secretary, accepted responsibility for the tragedy, and resigned.

Patiashvili's failure and Shevardnadze's advice throw the very different behaviour of the Baltic party authorities into strong relief. The peoples of the Baltic republics have the most recent memory of independence and of parliamentary democracy; and more than any other Soviet peoples they remain unreconciled to their incorporation into the Soviet Union. The experience of Stalin's brutality in the process of annexation in 1940 killed any positive support, even among most Communists, for rule from Moscow. A party leadership of nominal Balts (some barely able to speak their 'native' languages) had to co-exist with nations sullenly resentful of Soviet authority and determined to do their utmost to preserve their languages, customs and ways of life from external encroachment till a more favourable historical juncture. The Baltic became a discreet haven for experiments in the arts or in private economic enterprise which would not have been tolerated elsewhere.

In this soil a lively dissenting movement existed throughout the seventies, especially in Lithuania, where the disaffected Roman Catholic Church afforded it a semi-official shelter. In 1980, indeed, the Church succeeded in gathering no less than 148,000 signatures for a petition to have the closed cathedral in Klaipeda restored to believers: the largest petition, as far as I know, ever to have been presented in the Soviet Union up to that time.[16]

The Baltic peoples were, then, relatively well prepared for perestroika when it came. They have certainly been the most successful in taking advantage of it. Unlike the Armenians, they have not concentrated all their efforts on one overriding demand which Moscow cannot concede, but have chipped away at existing power relationships in a bewildering series of symbolic minor assaults. In the course of these, aspirations initially voiced only by dissenters were taken over first by scientists and cultural activists, then by broader public organisations, and finally – albeit hesitantly and incompletely – by the party itself. The pace differed somewhat in each republic, Estonia taking the lead, Latvia following closely behind, and Lithuania (less threatened in its national identity by foreign immigration) bringing up the rear.

As in the Caucasus, protests began over industrial projects, abhorred because they symbolised subordination to Moscow, because they degraded the environment, and because they brought in workers from outside to dilute the indigenous ethnic population. All of these concerns were felt especially keenly by Latvians, already a minority in their own republic. The plan to build a hydroelectric power station on the Daugava River, drowning an expanse of arable land and several villages, aroused opposition, first of all from writers, and then from a wider public writing in to the newspapers. 'Have those who sit in various Moscow planning institutes been but once to the places they so

nonchalantly propose to obliterate?' asked one indignant correspondent, expressing the helpless rage of millions of Soviet citizens at their subjection to economic decisions taken far away and
in complete ignorance of the people and places they would affect.
'For what will we use His Highness Electricity?' asked another
no less pertinently. 'Perhaps so that the First of May factory can
turn out a few more thousand defective pairs of shoes that no
one will buy?' A petition campaign in 1986 eventually attracted
30,000 signatures, the republican party authorities supported the
protests, and Gosplan in Moscow called off the project.[17]

This initial success encouraged further action. Under the weight
of the injustices inflicted on them in the past, Baltic protest naturally takes up history as its theme. Gathering momentum
throughout 1987 and 1988 demonstrations began to mark the
fateful anniversaries: Independence Day; the day of the great
deportations (14 June); the Nazi-Soviet Pact (23 August). Grimly
enthusiastic crowds demanded full glasnost about these events,
and a memorial to Stalin's victims.

Then came the stage of creating associations and formulating
programmes. As in Russia itself, the preparations for the 19th
Party Conference aided the process. In April 1988 secretaries of
the Estonian cultural unions (representing writers, artists,
musicians, etc.) drew up a comprehensive programme for the
Conference condemning the local party first secretary, Karl Vaino,
and denouncing the existing relationship between the Union and
the constituent republics for generating 'an unprofitable economy,
uncontrolled migration, increased risk of an ecological catastrophe, and failure to satisfy the population's social and cultural
needs'.[18]

Taking their cue from this declaration, the plenum of the Writers' Union in Latvia convened delegates from the other cultural
unions in June, and dispatched an even more specific and radical
programme. It asserted that political autonomy was required
to ensure the bare survival of the Latvian people, now being
swamped by immigrants in their own republic. They demanded

that Latvia should become a sovereign state – still within the framework of the Soviet Union, though offstage voices were already demanding secession – with its own citizenship, its own seat at the United Nations (on the model of Ukraine and Belorussia) and its own military units with Latvian as the language of command. The republic would run its own economy, have the right to restrict immigration, and declare Latvian its sole official language.[19]

In spite of initial resistance, the Communist Parties of both Estonia and Latvia soon registered that this programme had the support of the overwhelming majority of the population, and that it would be prudent to compromise with it, in order both to avert an explosion and to head off more extreme demands. This was the motive for the party's support of the formation of a Popular Front in Support of Perestroika, organised like the party itself, with cells in both workplaces and residential areas. It brought together the cultural, scientific and technical intelligentsia with party officials and ordinary workers.[20]

Its programme declared at the outset that the USSR was a 'union of sovereign states', whose interrelations should be 'regulated by treaty'. Underlying this assertion was the tacit claim that the secret protocols of the Nazi-Soviet Pact, which had given Stalin *carte blanche* for the annexation of the Baltic republics, were invalid, since they had been agreed contrary to the norms of international behaviour and without the knowledge of the sovereign states affected. 'It is necessary to acknowledge officially that the annexation of the Latvian Republic to the USSR was carried out by force and without consulting the people of Latvia.'

Repudiation of the Stalinist past led naturally on to rejection of Stalinist politics. The programme nowhere made the expected obeisance to the 'leading role of the Communist Party': on the contrary it envisaged the consolidation of 'socialist pluralism', such as would exclude 'the monopoly right of any political organisation to administer the state or social life'. Its constitutional recommendations were impeccably liberal, with complete separation of powers, a constitutional court, and guarantees of the full range of human rights. The most controversial points were the proposal to make Latvian the single official language, to terminate forthwith all immigration into the republic, and to establish the principle that Latvians should have a guaranteed majority in all local soviets within the republic, whatever the demographic situation in any given area.

The Popular Front programme said nothing (probably deliberately) about the conduct of foreign and military policy, and the demand for a separate Latvian army was toned down to 'the creation of a territorial military formation in which citizens of the Latvian SSR would discharge their obligatory military service, regardless of nationality'. This demand implied no more than the reintroduction of territorial units, which had been the norm in the Red Army up to 1938.[21]

To this forthright challenge the local Communist Parties, after some hesitation, reacted rather astutely. In Estonia, Vaino was dismissed and replaced by a first secretary more fluent in Estonian and more sympathetic to the aspirations of his fellow countrymen. Both Estonian and Latvian delegations adopted these Popular Front proposals as their official platform for the 19th Party Conference.[22]

In Lithuania events followed a similar course, if a little more haltingly. As late as August 1988, riot police were still turning out in force to disperse a demonstration being held in Vil'nyus's Gediminas Square to mark the anniversary of the Nazi-Soviet Pact. In the event, however, public indignation at this high-handedness was decisive in bringing about the downfall of the party first secretary, Ringaudas Songaila, replaced by the more acceptable Algirdas Brazauskas, who hastened to welcome the programme of the new Popular Front, known as Sajudis (the Movement).[23]

In all three republics the founding congresses of the People's Fronts, held during October 1988 turned into festivals of national rebirth. National flags, not displayed for nearly half a century, were once more hung from public buildings, anthems were sung by huge crowds, and in Lithuania a packed service was held in the Roman Catholic cathedral which had been a picture gallery for forty years and was only just being reconsecrated. As one visiting journalist put it, 'the Lithuanians march back on to the map of Europe after 48 years of darkness'.[24]

Even as these celebrations were proceeding, however, counterweights were being created. The non-indigenous (mainly Russian) population of the Baltic republics had initially displayed a remarkable degree of solidarity with the demands of their neighbours. By autumn, though, the prospect of having to deal with official documents in (say) Latvian became more real to Russians living in the Baltic. 'International fronts' or 'unity movements' began to spring up to protect the interests of the non-indigenous nationals. They protested against the planned restrictions on immigration and reasserted 'genuine bilingualism'; the new language law, they declared, in effect instituted a *Berufsverbot* against Russian speakers. They warned that the republics were questioning the leading role of the party and arrogating to themselves powers which undermined the constitutional integrity of the Soviet Union as a whole, and that this trend was encouraging 'extremists' intriguing to detach the Baltic from the Union altogether. They rejected what they feared would be a 'closed economy', and reaffirmed Latvia's need to trade within a federal market that would embrace the entire USSR.[25]

By the spring of 1989 the three 'Interfronts' were bringing quite large numbers of mostly Russian workers out on to the streets to parade with red hammer and sickle flags as symbols of devotion to the continued integrity of the Soviet Union. In March, for example, some 50,000 marched through Tallinn, protesting against 'creeping counter-revolution undermining socialism in Estonia': their banners read 'Down With Discrimination' and 'Give Russian the Status of an Official Language'. Strikes were threatened in the major utilities, to remind Estonians how dependent they were on their Russian working comrades.[26]

Compared with the Baltic, the formation of Popular Fronts encountered much more resistance from the Communist Party in Ukraine and Belorussia. There is good reason for this. The Ukrainians in particular occupy a key position in the constellation of Soviet nations. Whereas the others are in some sense 'peripheral' – that is, geographically and economically they lie at the edge of the multi-national empire – Ukraine is 'central'. Without Ukraine, something is torn from the heart of the Soviet Union.

This is partly a matter of economics. Ukraine contains most of the fertile black-earth soil of European Russia: indeed, its abundant production once justified for it the sobriquet of 'granary of Europe'. Much of the extractive, metalworking and machine-building capacity which is vital to Soviet industry and the armed forces is situated there. It is also a matter of population. If it were independent, the Ukrainian Republic would be the largest nation in Eastern Europe apart from Russia itself. Furthermore, without the 42 million ethic Ukrainians and the nine million Belorussians, the Russians number only one half of the Soviet population. Add them in, however, and the Russians become easily the dominant nation, numerically as well as politically. Since the Ukrainians and Belorussians are ethnically so closely related to them, moreover, the Russians have become accustomed to regard them more or less casually as co-nationals.

Rather like the English, the Russians have invested much of their ethnic awareness in the political structure they have created and sustained. They have, as a result, scant understanding for nations who possess no sovereign state of their own, and they expect Ukrainians and Belorussians to be content with the role of 'auxiliary Russians' in the vastnesses of the empire, in the same way that Englishmen would regard Scots as fellow-countrymen in the service of the crown. Russians tend to treat with good-natured but unmistakable disdain the idea that Ukrainians might be a separate nation: yes, they have their own picturesque customs and their own peasant dialect, but . . .

In some ways, Ukrainians' sense of their own nationhood is

the mirror image of the Russians'. Historically speaking their own native aristocracy has been inclined to assimilate to whichever state happened to be dominant in their area at any given time: up to the seventeenth century the Polish, thereafter the Russian. By the early twentieth century, Ukraine could easily be seen as a potential nation which had failed to achieve full nationhood because its élites, its cities and its cultures were dominated by others. But there is no doubt that the experience of independence in 1917–21, however beleaguered and precarious, followed by the cultural and educational flowering of the twenties, created a sense among all sectors of the population of belonging to a Ukrainian nation distinct from Russia. Many of the towns, into which newly literate peasants were streaming, became properly Ukrainian for the first time. The calamities which followed, the famine of 1932–4, the Stalinist purges, the Second World War and the German occupation, the partisan war against the Soviets, imparted to this national consciousness an embattled and heroic dimension. The Ukrainians have survived incredible adversities, some of them deliberately imposed by the Soviet government, and the heritage of 'blank spots' in their history is therefore a quite unusually sensitive one.[27] When I spoke to Ukrainian activists in the spring of 1988, I found them warm and outgoing as people, but imbued with a bitter sense that they had been betrayed, that their nation had deliberately been crippled.

This succession of renewal followed by repression underlies the remarkable upsurge of Ukrainian culture which took place in the late fifties and sixties, manifested especially in the poets who are today referred to as the 'sixties generation'. It also explains the response of the Soviet authorities, which has been more consistently repressive in Ukraine than perhaps anywhere else. Two great waves of arrests, in 1965 and 1972, engulfed those who sought Ukrainian independence, or even merely a greater degree of autonomy within a Soviet federation. Furthermore, under Gorbachev, long after personnel changes had shaken the leadership in all other union republics, Ukraine was still ruled by a Brezhnev appointee, Shcherbitskii, and repressive vigilance, though more sporadically applied, was still felt as an omnipresent threat. As a joker put it to me in 1988, 'You want a rest from perestroika? Then come to Ukraine!'

There existed more subtle and enervating dangers to Ukrainian nationhood than those directly posed by the authorities. Principal among them was the question of language tuition in schools. Since 1959 it had no longer been compulsory to teach a child's native language; the teaching of Russian, however, remained compulsory, and was vigorously promoted throughout the Soviet Union. This had weakened the position of non-Russian languages everywhere, but it had especially affected Ukrainian, because of its closeness to Russian. The problem was that, given the choice (as by law they had to be), many parents would send their children to Russian-language schools, or at least to mixed-language schools where Russian was in practice usually dominant. The reason is clear. Children who were used to thinking and speaking in Russian would find it easier to get into higher education and then to take up jobs outside their native republic. In practice, too, they would often find it easier and more convenient even within Ukraine to conduct their affairs in the imperial language. The result was that the number of Ukrainian-language schools, where Russian was taught only as a second language, had been declining sharply. In 1988, in Kiev, the capital of the Ukrainian Republic, only 34 out of 274 schools (12 per cent) were Ukrainian, while 152 (55 per cent) were Russian.[28] This decline meant that Ukrainian was gradually becoming a purely domestic and family language, while Russian was increasingly taken for granted as the natural medium for all public affairs, as well as for scholarship and culture.

In 1987 the Ukrainian Writers' Union took up the gradual atrophy of their language as a public cause. At a plenary meeting in June Dmytro Pavlychko warned that, if things went on as at present, the Ukrainian language 'would probably survive only in Canada'. He proposed a law making study of the language, literature and history of any republic compulsory in all its schools, including Russian ones. He also recommended that the republican Minister of Education, rather than parents, should have the power to decide any school's language of tuition.[29] A situation has been reached where Ukrainian patriots feel obliged to erect a defensive rampart round their vulnerable culture.

Ecological grievances had been gradually gathering momentum for many years because of the concentration of heavy industry and the growing use of intensive agricultural methods in Ukraine. They were brought to a head by the explosion in the nuclear power station at Chernobyl' in April 1986. Writers and scientists joined hands to protest at the evils which this disaster uncovered, the '*diktat* of producer over consumer' and the practice of taking decisions deeply affecting local people's lives without even informing them, let alone consulting them. The Writers' Union set up an Ecological Commission to monitor the situation, and the pages of its weekly newspaper *Literaturna Ukraina* became the best source of information in a press which, for the most part, remained dully conformist.[30]

I myself attended a meeting on the second anniversary of Chernobyl', organised by the Writers' Union and chaired by a writer, Yurii Shcherbak, who has written a novel about Chernobyl'. It was attended by several hundred people crowded into a modest-sized hall in the Union's Scottish baronial mansion just off the main street of Kiev. Here for three hours writers and members of the public cross-questioned officials of the Ukrainian Energy Ministry about radiation hazards, evacuation procedures, the pollution of rivers and agricultural land. The atmosphere was boisterous, though not disrespectful, and deeply sceptical. Meanwhile a demonstration was taking place in the main square not far away, with young people displaying placards calling for the closure of all nuclear power stations in Ukraine. It was swiftly broken up by police and the demonstrators were bundled into buses. A woman whose son had been arrested came to the writers' meeting and challenged them: 'You writers are the conscience of the

people: it is up to you to do something to help those detained.'
Reaction to her was mixed, some in the audience evidently feeling
that public demonstrations were not the best method of dealing
with a complex problem like nuclear energy.

The organisers of that demonstration were the Ukrainian Culturological Club, which has been at the vanguard of the unofficial
public movement in Ukraine. Set up in August 1987, it continued
the work of the Ukrainian Helsinki Group of the seventies, bringing out a *samizdat* journal, *Ukrains'kii Visnik (The Ukrainian
Herald)*, and organising public meetings on ecology, historical
monuments, culture and on the 'blank spots' of recent history.
They sponsored, for example, a memorial gathering for Vasyl'
Stus, one of the leading sixties generation poets, who died in a
labour camp in 1985; and they organised evenings of testimony
and discussion on the famine of 1932–4. The Culturological
Society was far from being the only informal association to promote awareness of Ukrainian language, culture and history: the
Hromada (Community) Society at Kiev University, the Lion
Society in L'viv (called after the name of the city) and the Ukrainian Helsinki Association (monitoring the treatment of political
prisoners) were further examples.[31]

The Ukrainian informal associations experienced much more
difficulty than their Baltic counterparts in creating a Popular
Front. When they first tried to do so in summer 1988, the authorities forbade meetings and detained known activists, even driving
some of them out of town and dumping them in the countryside
on the days of planned occasions.[32]

The turning point came, as in so many national republics, with
a big meeting on ecological issues, held in Kiev. Ten thousand
people gathered in Kiev Stadium in freezing weather on 13 November. The authorities permitted the assembly, but insisted on
the removal of placards saying 'Hiroshima, Nagasaki, Chernobyl" and even 'A Nuclear free Ukraine'. Dmytro Pavlychko, Yurii
Shcherbak and others called for the establishment of a Popular
Front, and on 4 December an Initiative Group met, including

representatives of the Writers' Union and many of the informal associations.[33]

The programme of the Popular Front was at last published in the Ukrainian Writers' Union weekly (presumably the only paper that would carry it) in February 1989. It was similar to the equivalent Baltic documents, expressing support for the Communist Party's programme of perestroika, and calling for 'genuine sovereignty for Ukraine', the full range of human rights, a self-managed economy and 'the granting of the status of state language in the Ukrainian SSR to Ukrainian'. 'The practice of parental free choice in the language of education ... leads,' it warned, 'to national nihilism.'[34]

No sooner had this programme appeared than a riposte was published in the organ of the Ukrainian Communist Party, signed by a number of scholars in the Ukrainian Academy of Sciences. They dismissed the Popular Front as no more than an 'initiative group of the Kiev branch of the Writers' Union', and attacked it for trying to drive a wedge between the party and the people and for denying parents' constitutional right to choose the language in which their children should be educated.[35]

In Belorussia, too, the formation of a Popular Front encountered determined opposition from the republican Communist Party. Much of the impetus for the expression of national feeling derived from the discovery of a mass grave of Stalin's victims in the Kurapaty Woods outside Minsk, the Belorussian capital. An informal society called 'Martyrology' was set up to promote the idea of a memorial and to call for a public commission to carry out an independent investigation of Stalin's crimes in Belorussia. This led on to the idea of a Popular Front to articulate the Belorussian national interest over the whole range of politics, As ever, scholars and writers were in the forefront of the movement, notably Belorussia's leading writer, Vasyl' Bykau. So too were the patriotic youth associations, Talaka (the Belorussian word for a peasant community) and Tuteishya (People from Here).

When these groups held an anti-Stalin demonstration in Minsk on 30 October 1988, the authorities sent in riot police with truncheons, tear gas and water cannon to disperse it. This outrage prompted Bykau to write an article of protest in the Moscow magazine *Ogonyok*, and the Belorussian Writers' Union announced that it would receive signatures from those who wished to register as members of the 'Renewal' Popular Front. The programme of the new movement, which is very similar to that of its Ukrainian counterpart, has not, as far as I know, been published in the republic's press.[36]

One intriguing development in Belorussia is that, in the face of official refusal to rent them a hall, the unofficial groups promoting a Popular Front held one of their meetings in premises provided free of charge by Sajudis in Vil'nyus. The Belorussians are closely linked by their history with Lithuania, but this is only the most conspicuous example of a growing willingness among non-Russian national movements to work together. A co-ordinating committee was set up in June 1988, representing the national movements of Armenia, Georgia, Ukraine, Lithuania, Latvia and Estonia. It issued declarations in September, some of which were addressed to the signatories of the Helsinki Final Act and expressed concern about political prisoners, about the Soviet nuclear power industry, and about the authorities' continued failure to satisfy the national aspirations of the Crimean Tartars and the Armenians in Nagornyi Karabakh.[37]

Conspicuous by their absence were the Russians and the Muslim nations. The Muslims are presumably distrustful of *all* Europeans, especially perhaps the Armenians, and so (except for the Crimean Tartars) are not prepared to work with them. The Russians, however, were absent either because they did not appreciate the importance of the national liberation movements within the Soviet Union, or because they were opposed to them.

When the non-Russian co-ordinating committee met again in January 1989 (joined by representatives of the Belorussians and Crimean Tartars) it addressed an appeal 'to the Russian Intelligentsia', warning: 'Many of the activists of the Russian democratic opposition have not yet grasped the primary axiom of democracy: nations cannot be free if they oppress others, or if they serve as instruments of such oppression.'[38] They were, I believe, justified in this reproach. At that stage, with few exceptions (one of whom was Solzhenitsyn, in Vermont), the Russians had not yet realised that they had a common interest with the non-Russians in resisting a totalitarian apparatus which had oppressed them all.

In the Central Asian republics Brezhnev's benign policy of 'stability of cadres' permitted the entrenchment of local party leaders adept at achieving a *modus vivendi* with local communities. In the year of Brezhnev's death, 1982, four out of the five republican first secretaries (those of Uzbekistan, Kazakhstan, Kirghizia and Tadjikistan) had been in office for twenty years or more, while the exception (the first secretary of Turkmenia) had already lasted thirteen years. During this time they had used the *nomenklatura* system to build up networks of patronage, promoting their own acquaintances, local favourites or extended families, while keeping Moscow happy by reporting impressive figures for the learning of Russian and the output of cotton. They also became increasingly tolerant of Islam (see next chapter).

Over the years, old-style nepotism combined with the chicaneries of the planned economy to generate a formidable edifice of corruption which some have compared to the Mafia. Embezzling funds from Moscow by exaggerating cotton production figures, local party leaders used the proceeds to stimulate whole branches of the 'black economy', to remedy shortages of goods and services, and to provide lucrative jobs for favourites. If the state procuracy got wind of these operations, it took no action, for, as a later investigation explained, 'everything was excused and camouflaged by traditional hospitality and the need to fulfil the plan'.[39] Russians living in the Central Asian republics were generally excluded from these arrangements, except where they needed to be bribed, and so felt discriminated against or even victimised.[40]

Although the region was kept quiet by this tolerated particularism, its results were quite damaging to the Soviet system as a whole. It contributed less than nothing to the *rapprochement* of the Soviet nations which was the official policy of the CPSU. On the contrary, the censuses of 1970 and 1979 showed that intermarriage and the settlement of outsiders in Central Asia were beginning to decline, while Central Asians themselves were becoming extremely reluctant to quit the relative security of ethnic protectionism to take up jobs going begging in other parts of the Soviet Union. Besides, the rapacious use of water for the irrigation of cotton plantations was drying up the Amu-Darya and Syr-Darya rivers, lowering the water level of the Aral Sea and causing it to shrink by more than a half. The rapid encroachment of salty marsh and even desert on its banks endangered the public's supply of drinking water and threatened to alter the whole climate of the region, creating hotter summers and shorter winters, and jeopardising the whole cultivation of the cotton for which the irrigation had been undertaken in the first place. One Uzbek writer, visiting a fishing village which used to sit astride a neck of land with fishing boats moored on both sides, wrote that now desert stretched out in all directions as far as the eye could see. The Central Asian party leaders had been hoping to stave off disaster by receiving water diverted from the north-flowing rivers of Siberia, but this project was, as we have seen, cancelled in 1986.[41]

Moscow's attempt to regain control of the region began under Andropov in 1983, when a special investigation team was sent to Uzbekistan. Among other things it precipitated the fatal heart attack of Sharif Rashidov, party first secretary there since 1959, who was soon shown up as a past master of the skills needed to run a semi-criminal barony. By the end of 1986 all five republican secretaries had been replaced, and criminal proceedings had been set in motion against their subordinates. What the investigations disclosed may be exemplified by the case of one Uzbek state farm director, a certain Adylov, who had turned himself into a local tycoon, maintaining several luxurious villas, stocked with racehorses and concubines. He loved to sit on a granite podium by a fountain at one of his villas, under a statue of Lenin raising his arm as if in blessing: there Adylov would sip Napoleon brandy, issue his orders, hand out reprimands, and, if the mood took him, have recalcitrant vassals whipped.[42]

The procuratorial investigations in Uzbekistan proved very sticky. It is not clear whether the main explanation for this was obstruction by local officials and underground businessmen beholden to the old regime, or widespread popular resentment at external interference in local affairs. One reason for the difficulties was revealed when the man sent in as Rashidov's successor to clean up the show, Inamzhon Usmankhodzhaev, abruptly resigned in January 1988 and was himself subjected to criminal charges. The trial for corruption of Brezhnev's son-in-law, Yurii Churbanov, also prompted a string of further press revelations about the Uzbek mafia.[43]

The first open resistance to outside intervention came, however, in Kazakhstan, when Dinmukhamed Kunaev, party first secretary, was replaced in December 1986 by a Russian, Gennadii Kolbin. This was an exceptional violation of the custom that republican first secretaryships should be held by a member of the indigenous nation. Why Gorbachev overrode local susceptibilities in this conspicuous manner is not clear: perhaps he could find no suitably qualified Kazakh who could be trusted to root out corruption. At any rate the affront provoked two days of rioting in the Kazakh capital, Alma Ata, when a student demonstration apparently got out of hand. Students are probably the most nationally conscious element of the whole Kazakh population, and, being systematically preferred over Russians in admission to college, had the most to lose from the undermining of existing ethnic protectionism.[44]

In June 1989 a problem left by Stalin erupted into a savage outburst of ethnic violence. Uzbek youths in half a dozen towns attacked the homes of Meskhetian Muslims from the Caucasus, who had been deported there in 1944 and never permitted to return home. The combination of a high Central Asian birth rate with economic uncertainty, aggravated by the abandonment of the Siberian rivers diversion project, had intensified the competition for jobs and official favours, and revived old resentments among Uzbeks about having an alien people dumped in their midst. The violence was unleashed by a dispute over the price of strawberries in a local market: it exemplified the way in which economic and ethnic resentments can easily become superimposed on one another. In the end special MVD troops had to be flown in to restore control after pogroms in which a hundred or so people are said to have lost their lives.[45]

While conducting old feuds and maintaining, even extending, semi-feudal social institutions, the Central Asian people were strikingly slow to create civic associations of a more modern type such as had emerged in most other regions of the Soviet Union. Where such associations made their appearance, they were stimulated by writers and scholars as the individuals most likely to have contacts outside Central Asia.[46]

One nation in the Soviet confraternity is in a very singular position, and that is the Russians. They are to all appearances the imperial nation, the 'elder brother', in Stalin's words. They have no worries about their territory, or language, or alien immigration: in fact, other nations feel threatened by *them*. Yet, curiously enough, in some respects the Russians feel like a national minority discriminated against in their own country. They know that the non-Russians are often more prosperous. And they can see that since 1917 their church has been undermined, their rural way of life mortally enfeebled, their finest writers, artists and thinkers banned, driven into the underground and emigration.

As an imperial nation, the Russians, like the English, tend to invest their ethnic consciousness in the state structures they have created. But what happens when those structures turn round and victimise Russians? Whom are they to blame for that? Actually it was the Communist Party, especially but not only in its Stalinist guise, which inflicted these injuries, but not all Russians have the detachment to appreciate that fact. And since there is no ethnic 'elder brother' to reproach, it is easier to heap imprecations on the Communist Party's traditional targets, on international imperialism and on unspecified 'rootless cosmopolitans', which usually means the Jews.

The advent of perestroika has in many ways intensified the paradoxes of Russian national consciousness. The vague and brooding sense of being victimised has been much sharpened both by the revelations of glasnost and by the surge of national liberation movements in the non-Russian republics. Conflict is most acute in the Baltic, where, in reaction to the self-assertion of the Estonians, Latvians and Lithuanians, 'unity' movements or 'international fronts' have been created to protect the interests of non-local nationals. The driving force in these movements consists of Russians suddenly faced with the prospect of having to learn (say) Estonian in the next few years in order to cope with everyday life. They have protested against planned restrictions on immigration and have asked for legislation granting supremacy to local languages to be suspended, and genuine bilingualism to be consolidated. They have warned that the Republican Supreme Soviets, especially in Estonia, are arrogating to themselves powers which call into question the constitutional integrity of the Soviet Union; and that the situation is encouraging extremists who are intriguing to detach the Baltic republics from the Union altogether.[47]

This warning casts the shadow of what I believe may well prove to be the most serious threat to the whole reform process, certainly in the form which it assumed during 1987–90: that is, an alliance between the Communist Party's conservative *apparatchiks* and a militant Russian nationalism spearheaded by the beleaguered Russians living in the non-Russian republics.

In the last few years an informal association has also arisen inside Russia itself to articulate the sentiments of Russians who feel threatened by the separatist forces which perestroika has unleashed. Known as Pamyat' – Memory – it orginated, like its non-Russian counterparts, as an action group of those concerned about the protection of the environment and historical monuments. Some say it was founded by V. Chivilikhin, the writer who first raised the alarm about the pollution of Lake Baikal. Whatever its origins, it has broken far away from them.

In many ways, we are poorly informed about Pamyat'. We know next to nothing about its numbers, its membership or its organisations. We have accounts of its members parading at times in black shirts, embroidered with a bell, the symbol of the ancient Russian *veche*, the folk assembly. Its manifesto poses assertively the questions which bother many Russians: 'Who has defiled our history and culture? Who has been undermining our economy and destroying our agriculture all this time? Who has been destroying the nation with ideological and alcoholic drugs?' Its answer is 'the cosmopolitans', and it warns that 'international imperialism, sustained by Zionism and by its servile, mercenary lackey, Freemasonry, is attempting to plunge the world into the vortex of a new global catastrophe'. Among its enemies it identifies prominent reformers, like Aganbegyan, Zaslavskaya, Vitalii Korotich (editor of *Ogonyok*) and Aleksandr Yakovlev (Gorbachev's principal ideological adviser).[48] To such people it sends threatening letters: 'We shall get even with you. Signed: warriors of the patriotic union Pamyat'.'[49]

An Italian who chanced across a Pamyat' meeting in Leningrad commented: 'A whole week has passed, but I haven't shaken off the feeling of horror. I felt as if I were attending a real Fascist meeting of the 1930s.'[50] Although its programme also contains unobjectionable demands, such as freedom of speech, temperance and the revival of the Orthodox Church, its language and methods leave no doubt that this judgement is essentially correct. Pamyat' represents a throwback to the sentiments cultivated by Stalin in his last years, anti-imperialism, Russian chauvinism and anti-Semitism, now reawakened by the unfamiliar and unsettling conflicts of perestroika.

This would make it the natural ally of the conservative wing of the party-state apparatus, of those who have most to lose by perestroika. Such an alliance would be nothing new. Ever since the thirties the Soviet Communist Party has sometimes made use of Russian nationalism as an auxiliary ideological force with more mass appeal than Marxism.[51] In the turmoil generated by perestroika it may be tempted to do so again now.

For the moment, however, the signs are that Pamyat' is not considered respectable enough for such august fraternisation. Its meetings proceed relatively unimpeded – compared with those of, say, the Democratic Union – which indicates that there is a degree of official support for it. But it is not given space in the Soviet press, probably justifiably, since some of its utterances would fall foul of the law prohibiting the propaganda of racial hatred.

The more 'respectable' face of Russian nationalism, and one with considerable political potential, is the Writers' Union of the RSFSR. The writers and journals grouped round this organisation can by no means be dismissed as Stalinist, chauvinistic or dema-gogic. During the 1970s, indeed, *Nash sovremennik*, the most successful of the Russian national journals, took the lead in expos-ing Stalin's crimes, and especially the brutal collectivisation of agriculture, in a manner which anticipated (though it fell far short of) the revelations stimulated by recent glasnost. Some of its leading authors, like Sergei Zalygin and Vasilii Belov, had orig-inally made their name in Tvardovskii's *Novyi mir*, and they continued his tradition of truthful investigation of the life of ordinary people, especially peasants, throughout the upheavals of Soviet history.

In the spring of 1988 I had the opportunity to interview Sergei Vikulov, the chief editor of *Nash sovremennik*, who is a vigorous and forthright, sometimes even overbearing man. He told me how, on taking over the journal in 1968, he had decided not to try and attract the fashionable intelligentsia of the capital city, but rather to back writers from the Russian provinces. He claimed that Tvardovskii himself, after leaving *Novyi mir* in 1970, had encouraged his former protégés to go over to Vikulov.[52] At any rate, the move was an astute and fortunate one, and *Nash sovremennik* became the most interesting literary journal of the seventies, specialising in the 'village prose' school of writing.

To understand its orientation, one must appreciate that there is more than one kind of Russian national consciousness. To polarise the various sub-species somewhat, one may say that at one extremity there are the National Bolsheviks, those who see the Communist Party and the Soviet state as the best guarantors of the integrity of the Russian Empire and the continuity of Russian national traditions: such people tend to be atheists, and to worship Stalin as a hero. At the other pole are the 'revivalists', those who care most about Russian culture, the Orthodox Church and the way of life of the peasant village; they are usually Orthodox believers, and they execrate Stalin as the destroyer of that culture. In the era of glasnost they are moving closer to expressing their doubts not just about Stalin, but about the October revolution and the whole Communist enterprise as forces which have undermined the Russian national essence.[53]

As a result of the efforts of the revivalists, something of a *Historikerstreit* is developing in the Soviet Union – though characteristically not among historians, but among writers and critics – which might in the end become more important than its analogue in West Germany. Some of the participants in the controversy feel that the revelations of the glasnost era, by concentrating so much on the crimes of Stalin, fail to penetrate to the fundamental causes of the Soviet Union's problems. The point at issue was dramatised by the writer Vladimir Soloukhin late in 1988, when he refused to sign a letter calling for a worthy memorial to the victims of Stalin's purges. The motive for his refusal, he explained, was not sympathy for Stalin, but rather the absence of any answer from *Memorial* to his question 'From which year must we consider repressions illegal and unjustified, and up to which year should we consider them legal and justified?' What about the millions of victims of the forced collectivisation and 'dekulakisation'? What indeed about the lawless mass killings of the Cheka in the very earliest years of the Communist regime, when (although Soloukhin did not mention it) Lenin was still heading it?[54]

The critic Vadim Kozhinov made the same point on a broader scale when reviewing Anatolii Rybakov's novel *Children of the Arbat*, whose subject is the lead-up to the murder of Kirov in 1934. Kozhinov reproaches Rybakov with placing all the blame for the evils of Soviet society on Stalin and a clique of close advisers. He points out the enormous population losses of the years 1917–35, before the start of the famous 'purges', and, like Soloukhin, dwells on the suffering of the peasantry. Lenin, he reminds his readers, made no secret of his belief that the dictatorship of the proletariat was 'a government resting directly on violence and unrestrained by any rules or regulations'.[55]

The real responsibility for the current devastation of Russia Kozhinov attributes to those who in the twenties and early thirties stood for 'a complete break with the past' (*velikaya lomka*). By this (though he produces a few quotations to show that Lenin urged restraint) he must mean the leaders of the Communist Party. And to forestall the accusation of targeting only the Jewish members of the Communist leadership, he explicitly concentrates his attack on Bukharin, recently rehabilitated and now much officially praised for having set forth an alternative model of socialist construction in the late twenties, which might have enabled the Soviet Union to continue the mixed economy of the twenties and avoid the violent upheavals of the Stalinist model. Not at all, asserts Kozhinov: Bukharin was an ally of Stalin on almost every point, and different from him only on minor tactical questions. Kozhinov's argument is in fact an implied rejection of the October revolution and a plea for a return to pre-revolutionary traditions; significantly, all he can find to say in respect of the October revolution is that it *happened* and that there is no point in discussing alternatives to it.[56]

What the Russian nationalists propose is an alternative model of economic development designed to avoid the twin dangers of the command economy and unregulated capitalism. This is the tradition of what the critic Mikhail Antonov calls the 'civilised co-operative', by which he means a modernised version of the peasant land commune and the *artel'*, which I described in Chapter 2. Antonov criticises the principal reform economists, such as Aganbegyan, Zaslavskaya and Shmelyov, for remaining bogged down in the long-discredited economic categories of bourgeois society, for treating economics as a 'science of production relations, which ignores the human being and the whole moral and spiritual sphere of social life.' His own proposals are close in spirit to the ideas of Schumacher or the West German Greens.

How far the newly grown Soviet co-operative movement can or will evolve in this direction remains to be seen. But one of the pre-conditions of its doing so is a much less rigidly regulated economic environment: Antonov, in spite of his attacks on Stalin, inconsistently hankers after official maintenance of the 'just price' and other features of the indigent egalitarianism which the command economy imposed on the Soviet peoples.[57] The danger is that in order to restrain the operation of the market, especially as it may develop in the non-Russian republics, the protagonists of the 'civilised co-operatives' will throw themselves into the arms of an already hypertrophied party-state apparatus. The danger is aggravated by the Russian nationalists' habit of attributing the root of all evil — whether of the capitalist or Communist variety — to the Jews, for this renders them susceptible to the anti-Semitism and great power chauvinism of the late Stalin years, a combination which made possible the very administrative distortions they deplore. From that point of view, the failure of a reputable writer like Valentin Rasputin to distance himself from Pamyat' is a political mistake of major proportions. Russian national feeling always risks degenerating into an overbearing imperialism, which oppresses the Russians themselves as much as it does any other Soviet nation.

6

Religion and the atheist state

As I was leaving Tbilisi at the end of April 1988 I witnessed from the taxi an extraordinary event. On the Mekheti Church, high up on the crags which overlook the River Kura, two men were clambering over the roof, using an arrangement of ropes and pulleys to haul a golden cross on to the pinnacle. Inside, a service of dedication was being held: a church which had not seen divine worship for nearly seventy years was being returned to the faithful.

The day before in Moscow, Gorbachev had received Patriarch Pimen and five senior bishops. 'Believers', he told them, 'are Soviet working people and patriots, and they have every right to express their convictions in a fitting manner.'[1] This uncharacteristic statement was just the prelude to a series of festive occasions by which the leaders of state and church celebrated a millennium of Christianity. One of the high points was the restoration to the church of the Kiev Monastery of the Caves, on the site where the first baptism of the Russian peoples was reputed to have taken place a thousand years before.

It is not just the happy chance of the calendar which has brought Church and State together. Many of the social problems Gorbachev is tackling today – corruption, alcoholism, slovenly work discipline, unstable family life – are moral rather than political in character. They have not responded to repeated campaigns of ideological exhortation mounted by the party's zealots.

The party seems to have decided, doubtless reluctantly, that it might as well enlist the help of the established Churches. Many of the country's best writers have been saying for years, even in the teeth of censorship, that faith was an antidote to demoralisation. In any case, why alienate millions of believers – perhaps a third of the population – who would mostly be loyal and patriotic citizens were it not for the party's ingrained disdain for them?

The party, in short, is looking to the Churches as a source of social solidarity which by itself it is poorly equipped to inspire. The Orthodox Church, which has long regarded *sobornost'* – the spirit of community – as its distinctive strength, ought to be ideally fitted to supply this deficiency.

Today, however, one can no longer be confident of its ability to do so. The trouble is that the Church has been seriously, perhaps fatally, weakened by the party's own past treatment of it. Decades of active persecution alternating with contemptuous manipulation have left it not only numerically reduced but spiritually debilitated to the extent that it may no longer be able to play the role the party now envisages for it.

The heritage of bad, at times murderous, Church-State relations is a grievous one. From the very beginning the Soviet state expropriated the Church, and declared the clergy more or less outcasts. The Law on Religious Associations limited religious worship strictly to designated churches and prayer houses. It forbade Sunday schools or any form of religious instruction, pastoral visits, or charitable work. In other words, the state tacitly outlawed any religious activity other than the performance of divine service. Normal parish life was rendered impossible, and religion became, as one might say, a matter for consenting adults in private. Those provisions have remained in force to the present day.

The Orthodox Church eventually accepted this situation, though not without damaging internal rifts. In 1927 Metropolitan Sergii, locum tenens for the vacant Patriarchate, proclaimed, 'We wish to be Orthodox believers, and at the same time to acknowledge the Soviet Union as our civil motherland, whose joys and successes are our joys and successes, and whose misfortunes are our misfortunes.' Asked privately how he could accept such a humiliating predicament, he replied, 'We must preserve the Church for the people; after that, the Lord will show us what we must do.'[2] Survival at any price has become paramount in the Russian Orthodox Church. This caution derives not just from difficult relations with the state, but also from the uncertain allegiance of the people. Russia's élites and intellectuals have a long history of heresy and unbelief. As for ordinary people, the Church was worried long before the revolution that they would fall prey to the numerous non-conformist sects, or indeed to the other religions which perforce coexisted in the multi-national Russian Empire: Catholicism, Lutheranism, Judaism, Islam. Against this background, and with the added threat of the militantly atheist Communist Party, simply keeping the Church in being was a daunting challenge, and doubtless it was in that spirit that Sergii made his gesture of reconciliation.

Unfortunately, though, Sergii's declaration of loyalty to the Soviet state induced no reciprocal concessions. The 1930s were the grimmest period the churches – and not just the Orthodox Church – had ever experienced. The collectivisation of agriculture often meant the closure of the village church, and sometimes its physical destruction, though more usually it would be turned into a storehouse or club room. Priests were arrested and sent to labour camps or driven into exile along with the 'kulaks'. Of more than 50,000 churches open before the revolution, only some 4,000 remained by 1939. Of 163 bishops, only four were still at liberty.[3]

At that juncture, in spite of all its concessions to a brazen atheist state, the very survival of the Orthodox Church was in doubt. Yet Stalin never completed its destruction. In 1939, when the Soviet Union annexed what had formerly been Eastern Poland, he decided that the Church could help to assimilate the region's largely Ukrainian and Belorussian population. During the war, he was glad to co-opt the Church as an ally in the patriotic struggle, and encouraged the faithful to raise the money for a tank column named after the medieval prince Dmitrii Donskoi. In 1943, when he was beginning to envisage taking control of Eastern Europe, Stalin received Metropolitan Sergii in audience (the only such occasion in Soviet history till Gorbachev repeated it in 1988) and he allowed the Church to re-establish an ecclesiastical administration, to publish a journal, to reopen some of its parishes and to resume training recruits for the priesthood. Thereafter – and right up to the present – the Orthodox Church has been a useful ally of the Soviet state in its diplomatic relations throughout the world, and especially in the international peace movement.

At a certain stage, then, the Soviet leaders decided that the Church would be more useful to them alive than dead, or perhaps one should say open than clandestine. That was a fateful decision, and maybe in a sense it justified Sergii's act of submission. In spite of renewed persecution by Khrushchev in the sixties, under which at least half the existing parishes were closed down, the Church *has* survived as a recognisable entity to the present more favourable juncture, when the Soviet intelligentsia is displaying renewed interest in religion and the state seems inclined to make concessions.

On the other hand that survival has been secured at a very high price. Enfeebled by subservience to an atheist state, the Church is no longer well fitted to act as vehicle for the religious revival or to promote social solidarity. New converts feel acutely the absence of any normal parish life. As a lay Soviet believer commented a few years ago, 'In the Church there is almost no Christian interpersonal sociability, no activity in fulfilment of the second commandment. How many lonely old people are too weak to leave their homes for bread or medicine, but the people with whom they have prayed together for years don't even know of their plight.'[4] If this is so, then the Church is not fulfilling the very ideal of *sobornost*' – the spirit of congregation – which it used to claim as its distinctive strength.

Besides, the system of ecclesiastical appointment ensures that priests and bishops are chosen, as far as possible, for their deference to the party. Patronage is ultimately in the hands of the Communist Party Central Committee, like all other serious personnel questions in the Soviet Union. It is delegated through a state committee called the Council for Religious Affairs, which reports regularly on the comportment of every priest and bishop. A few years ago the text of one of these confidential reports reached the west. It divided bishops into three categories, according to the degree of their compliance with party policy. The first, most favoured category, consists of those who 'realistically understand that our state is not interested in proclaiming the role of . . . the Church in society and accordingly do not display any particular zeal in extending the influence of Orthodoxy among the population'. Less favoured is a second category: those bishops who correctly observe the law on cults, but nevertheless 'stand for the heightening of the role of the Church in personal, family and public life', who 'select for priestly office . . . zealous adherents of Orthodox piety'. Third and last, the Council deplores those bishops who 'have made attempts to evade the law on cults' and who slander the Council's commissioners, 'falsifying the position in their dioceses'.[5] Presumably they have been doing something like sanctioning unauthorised Sunday schools and then misleading official informers.

This report prompts mixed reflections. On the one hand, any appointments system adopting these criteria is likely to produce a submissive church hierarchy. On the other hand, I am intrigued by the intermediate category – the largest numerically. It suggests a substantial contingent of bishops who, under the mask of outward conformity, are discreetly doing what they can to extend the Church's influence and to prepare for its future. One is reminded that, even in the most abject times, the Orthodox Church has remained a source of spiritual strength for many, partly through its liturgy, partly through the ascetic, contemplative tradition of its elders and holy men, whose effect on believers derived not least from the fact that they had no institutional place in the church, but acted by virtue of their personal charisma. Father Zosima in Dostoevskii's *The Brothers Karamazov* was based on a real-life model of this kind. Today the monastic heritage has been almost completely destroyed, but there is still fitful evidence that a few such holy men have helped to keep alive the faith through the recent bleak decades.[6]

Because of its enserfed position, the Russian Orthodox Church has had little opportunity to adjust to the huge social changes of the twentieth century. It remains essentially the same Church which used to tend an overwhelmingly peasant congregation. Now the faith of peasants was very different from that of the contemporary urban intellectual. The Russian peasant's religion was a largely illiterate one – a rustic faith based on the liturgy and icons. It followed the rhythms of the agricultural cycle, and it was interwoven with a rich overlay of pagan elements, especially those associated with the peasant hut and the ancestors.[7]

In the early twentieth century ecclesiastical reformers did try to modernise the liturgy, improve religious education, encourage a livelier parish life and break down the social divisions within the Church. But the tsarist regime resisted them and then – even more lethal – the Bolshevik one favoured them, laying reformers open to the charge of serving as the agents of atheism in splitting and undermining the church from within. Today's Orthodox Church has not forgotten the experience and has drawn from it the lesson that reform is divisive and therefore mortally dangerous to a church under siege.

Today, however, the old peasant faith is more or less dead – its passing mourned in Valentin Rasputin's magnificent novel, *Farewell to Matyora*, published in 1976.[8] The educated young people of the modern city are seeking something very different: a highly literate faith, based on a knowledge of the Bible and the

Church fathers, of ecclesiastical history and theology, a faith capable of holding its own in the intellectual contest with Marxism and other secular philosophies. Soviet intellectuals are, I think, peculiarly prone to the religious urge. After all, they have been brought up to an ideology which demanded submergence of the ego in the collective for the sake of an exalted aim, the building of an earthly paradise. Not only have they thoroughly imbibed the catechisms of that doctrine, but they have participated in public rituals designed to consolidate it, and they have made their obeisances to its icons. Communism has never been a religion in the full sense of the word, but it has adopted many of the outward appurtenances of one. When its conviction fades, therefore, as it certainly has in the Soviet Union, it is natural that many of its adherents should seek a genuine religion to put in its place.

They come, moreover, from a faith whose teachings are expounded in a comprehensive and reasoned manner. They will expect a church to present its doctrines no less convincingly. This is where the Russian Orthodox Church often fails to live up to their expectations.

Some have dealt with this vacuum in their own way, by setting up study groups and seminars, putting together small libraries of religious works, which are otherwise so difficult to obtain in the Soviet Union. They hold regular meetings to exchange ideas or even simple information. This is the *kruzhok* again – the cohesive little circle which is the natural habitat of the Russian intelligentsia – and it not only fills the intellectual deficiency, but also compensates for the absence of a proper congregational life within the Church. One such *kruzhok* was established in Moscow in 1974 by a cinema student, Alexander Ogorodnikov. He brought together friends who had grown up in atheist families and then gone through a complex, sometimes agonising process of spiritual questing. 'From Marxist convictions, via nihilism and the complete rejection of any ideology,' Ogorodnikov later recalled, 'via attraction to the "hippy" lifestyle, we came to the Church.' Even there, they found no secure haven, partly because of what they called their 'pagan intellectual pride', but partly because of the 'lack of a flourishing community life within the Orthodox Church'. As Ogorodnikov said: 'Our thirst for spiritual communion, religious education and missionary service runs up against all the might of the state's repressive machinery.'

The seminar met irregularly, with a fluctuating membership whose only qualification was readiness to join in what under Soviet conditions was a hazardous enterprise, but it recreated for some of its members the *sobornost'* – that spirit of community – which they felt they had not found in the Church itself. 'We loved that little flat,' one of its members has testified, 'for the spirit of freedom which filled it . . . Those conversations, that way of life, took hold of me completely: it was all . . . so full of meaning and depth, so full of the warmth and genuine feeling which you cannot confuse with anything else; it was so different from vulgar Soviet life . . .'[9]

Well, 'vulgar Soviet life' supervened. Members of the seminar were searched, interrogated and harassed. Ogorodnikov was deprived of his residence permit for Moscow, then arrested for 'parasitism' and sent to a labour camp. Other members were charged with disseminating the journal, *Obshchina (Community)*, which they had started to bring out. The Soviet state in the late seventies was not prepared to tolerate this kind of religious seeking.[10]

The church hierarchy is vulnerable to the charge that it did not do enough to intercede for young people like these endeavouring to take up a Christian way of life. When I asked Metropolitan Filaret, a senior bishop, about them a few years ago, he replied that, since they had never entered the Church, he could do nothing for them. Besides, he added, they criticise irresponsibly, bringing conflict and disharmony into our church and sowing hatred where there should be love. The leaders of state and party are our flock, and for the sake of the Russian people as a whole we should approach them in a spirit of dialogue, not one of rejection.[11]

Fair enough, if the state had not taken the lead in sowing the disharmony. But Filaret's attitude also reveals a very understandable aspiration: the desire to play once again a full role in society, to be part of the Russian people, coexisting in dialogue with a ruling party which has a very different philosophy. The Church could not, however, be a full partner in such a dialogue unless it was able to stand on its own feet as a self-governing legal entity, with structures which would enable it to elicit and articulate the views of its own members, clergy and laity. The *sobor* (synod) which accompanied the millennial celebrations began the work of disentangling the Church from the embraces of the atheist state, and giving it back to its congregations.

The first task was to start at the base and regularise the position of the parish priest. Under current legislation he was excluded from all executive responsibilities in the parish, which made it easier for the Council for Religious Affairs to manipulate parish councils. The statute passed by the *sobor* now reinstated the priest as chairman of the parish assembly. It restored long defunct parish and diocesan assemblies; above them, the Council of Bishops was henceforth to gather every two years, and the *sobor* itself every five (previously it had never met except on the death of a Patriarch).[12]

The new procedures had their first serious test in the summer of 1990, when Patriarch Pimen died. The *sobor* which met to appoint his successor consisted for the first time of elected representatives of clergy and laity: they were not hand-picked by bishops, as on previous occasions. On the other hand, the elections were held in great haste, and some church activists complained that insufficient time was granted for believers to participate fully in the process. The man chosen to be the new Patriarch, Alexii of Leningrad, had been characterised in the report quoted above as one of those who 'do not display any particular zeal in extending the influence of Orthodoxy among the population'. Of course, individuals can and do change their opinions at times of crisis like the present, but on the face of it, the Church's more democratic structure does not promise a swift renewal of its compromised hierarchy.[13]

Apart from the Church's internal reforms, there remained the question of its relationship to the rest of society, and above all to the political system. This was the subject of controversy long after the millennium. A law on freedom of conscience and worship was being prepared in the Supreme Soviet, affecting of course not just the Orthodox Church, but all religious associations. It became evident in the course of drafting it that the state was reluctant to yield its instruments of pressure on believers. There was bitter controversy especially about the legal status of the Church and its member congregations, the role of the Council of Religious Affairs and the right to religious education.[14]

The law eventually enacted in September 1990 made more concessions to believers than had earlier appeared likely, but still left the Church a partially handicapped institution. The Church as a whole was not given the status of legal person, only the parishes or 'religious associations' within it. Even the 'associations' were required to register with the local soviet if they wished to receive full legal rights, but the soviet was now bound to reply to any application within one month, and, if it refused, to state the precise legal grounds for the decision. Refusal of registration could be appealed in the courts. Associations now had the right to own immovable property and all the effects they needed to carry on their business; it was even stated that they had a 'preferential right' to have 'cultural buildings' (meaning presumably old churches) transferred to them gratis by the state. Religious education was once again to be permitted, though not within state schools, even after hours. Religious discrimination was outlawed, and most restrictions on religious activity were withdrawn, so that it now became possible to organise open air processions and pilgrimages, conduct services in army units, hospitals and old people's homes, hold public funerals, raise funds and undertake charitable work. One result of this provision is that, for the first time within most people's living memory, church bells can sometimes be heard in Russian towns and villages announcing divine service (few churches, however, still have serviceable bells). The Council for Religious Affairs was replaced by an unspecified 'state body for religious affairs', which would have no executive or judicial functions (such as confirming registrations) but simply act as an 'informational, consultative and expert centre'.[15]

The man who conducted the Church's side of the drafting of this law was Archbishop Kirill of Smolensk, who is a young man, open to modern intellectual currents and aware of the problems of the secular world. In 1988 he gave a lecture in London, in which he acknowledged that the Church had not been able to play its proper role in Soviet society. Much of the task of transmitting the Christian spirituality of the past had, he pointed out, been accomplished by *writers*, even by writers who were not themselves believers, but who derived their inspiration from Russia's cultural heritage. Now, he said, the priority of 'all-human values' was at last recognised once again by the political leadership, and therewith the Church faced the opportunity and the challenge of resuming its proper role. Whether it could respond successfully to this challenge he left an open question.

It is the vital question. Can a hierarchy brought up under the tutelage of the atheist state find the spiritual and organisational strength to guide the Church in meeting the needs of its potential flock today? Already the expansion in the Church's activities has been considerable. Many church buildings have been handed back to their congregations: according to Yuri Khristoradnov, head of the Council for Religious Affairs, 809 in 1988, and 2,039 in the first nine months of 1989. Among the churches reopened for worship were the Kazan' Cathedral in Leningrad, long an atheist museum, and the Uspenskii Cathedral in the Kremlin, while Optyna Pustyn', the great hermitage visited by Gogol', Tolstoy and Dostoevskii, became a monastery once again.[16]

Not that all such transfers passed off smoothly. In Ivanovo, for instance, the local soviet refused to hand over the Church of the Presentation of the Mother of God to a congregation, in spite of a favourable ruling from the Council of Religious Affairs. It took hunger strikes, a demonstration in Moscow, and several articles in the central press before success was achieved.[17]

Opening churches, of course, is only the start. The Church is desperately short of both priests and lay people with the diverse skills needed to run a parish successfully: the provision of Sunday Schools and Bible reading classes, youth work, visiting the sick, lonely and unhappy, pastoral counselling, charitable work and fund raising. For decades, parishioners have met only at the weekly divine service, to disperse immediately afterwards, so that even priests, deacons and churchwardens have minimal experience of community work. This has been one of the most debilitating effects of the atheist yoke.

Equally, the level of religious knowledge is low. Decades of suppression of religious education and literature have left even most priests, let alone lay people, with poor knowledge of the scriptures, the liturgy, church history and theology. Seminars like Ogorodnikov's were set up to fill this gap. One or two priests have also done their utmost to spread religious enlightenment. Father Alexander Men', for example, began in the late sixties to hold open house on certain days of the week in his home village of Semkhoz, near Zagorsk. The discussions held then would turn into informal seminars on all aspects of the Christian faith, as well as literature, art and politics, and Father Alexander would lend books freely from his personal library, so that attenders could follow up their interests and extend their knowledge.[18] For a long time he had to curb his spiritual pedagogy under political pressure, but now he was able to resume it in full. He continued to have his enemies, however, and in September 1990 he was killed with an axe by unknown assailants outside his house as he was setting off for early morning service. As he was Jewish by origin, and a proponent of Jewish-Christian reconciliation, it is possible that his murderer's motive was anti-Semitic. A 'Sunday

Orthodox University', which he was to have headed, opened in October 1990, and has been named after him.[19]

In some ways the most difficult issue which the Russian Orthodox Church has had to face has been the revival of the Ukrainian Catholic Church. This, the old 'Uniate' church set up by the Poles in the sixteenth century, was forcibly merged with the Russian Orthodox Church at an illegally convened Synod of L'viv in 1946. Some of its followers became more or less reluctant communicants of the Russian Church, but many refused to surrender their distinct identity, and attached themselves to unregistered priests or itinerant monks. In the intervening decades, the Church flourished underground because it offered Ukrainians a way of celebrating their faith in their own language, and of marking their alienation from a Russian-dominated atheist system.[20]

The election of Pope John Paul II, who explicitly supported the Ukrainian Catholics, brought renewed hope of legalisation, and 1982 saw the creation of an Initiative Group for the Defence of the Rights of Believers of the Church in Ukraine, which began to bring out a journal to publicise violations of freedom of conscience and worship. Its leading members were soon imprisoned or driven into exile. Popular support for the Church was further intensified by the appearance of the Virgin Mary to a twelve-year-old peasant girl in the village of Hrushevo in April 1987, on the first anniversary of the Chernobyl' explosion. Pilgrimages and processions followed, in which other believers claimed to have had visions of the Virgin Mary telling them the Ukrainians were a 'chosen people' and should break free of the Soviet yoke.[21]

A few months later a synod of Ukrainian Catholic bishops in Rome announced that their Church had, after all, a primate inside the Soviet Union: Bishop (later Metropolitan) Volodymyr Sterniuk, then eighty years old and living in a communal apartment in L'viv. He had, it transpired, been secretly consecrated eleven years earlier. The announcement encouraged Ukrainians to hold religious processions and open-air services. The following year, there were a number of 'alternative' Uniate celebrations of the millennium in streets and squares.[22]

It was natural that, with church buildings being returned to believers, the Ukrainian Catholics should request their fair share. Here there was a serious difficulty, however: the Russian Orthodox hierarchy did not even acknowledge the separate existence of the Uniates. Furthermore, for historical reasons, some two-thirds of Orthodox parishes are in Ukraine, so that the loss of large numbers of them would seriously weaken the Church as a whole. The Ukrainians took their cause to Moscow, where they held a vigil on the Arbat lasting for five months and written up in the popular weekly magazine *Ogonyok*.[23] Gradually parishes and their priests began to declare their defection to the Uniates.

When Gorbachev met the Pope in December 1989, the state swung its support for the first time behind the Uniates. To coincide with the visit, the Council for Religious Affairs announced that, in tacit contravention of the L'viv synod, Ukrainian Catholic parishes would be allowed to register officially. More than a thousand parishes applied almost immediately, while a *sobor* of their bishops met to declare the Synod of L'viv null and void. A Russian Orthodox Council of Bishops countered by accusing the Uniates of 'acts of violence and the capture of churches in which the Orthodox worship'. A Russian archbishop even went on hunger strike in his cathedral at Ivano-Frankivsk, to protest.[24] The accusations of 'violence' have never been substantiated, though it is possible that the Uniates were sometimes unceremonious in occupying church buildings.

A joint Orthodox-Uniate commission met, with Vatican participation, to try and agree how the new parish registrations and the division of property should be handled, but it fell apart, reportedly because the Orthodox would not recognise the Ukrainian Catholics as a proper Church, merely as an assortment of religious communities.[25] The Uniates' position was being strengthened by the election of new radical soviets in the western Ukraine. The

L'viv City Soviet ordered the transfer of St George's Cathedral to them, but the Orthodox delayed for several months. Finally, on 12 August 1990, after a service elsewhere, thousands of Uniates marched on the cathedral and occupied it, remaining there round the clock, till soviet officials arrived to complete the hand-over. Orthodox bishops complained of 'Stalinist methods' being used against them, but the following Sunday 300,000 people crowded round the cathedral under Ukrainian banners, while young people dressed in traditional festive costume greeted Metropolitan Volodymyr on the threshold with bread and salt.[26] This was a remarkable example of a national and religious revival taking place simultaneously.

It is difficult sometimes to avoid the impression that the hierarchs of the Russian Orthodox Church, in fighting to survive, have become so wedded to the imperial Russian state, even in its Soviet atheist form, that they fear a genuine spiritual revival, especially among the intellectuals and the diverse nations inhabiting 'their' territories. As the lay believer Evgenii Pazukhin has commented, 'The state is encouraging Christian activity; priests are doing all they can to obstruct it.'[27] This is unfair, as the case of Father Alexander Men' shows, but it is not a travesty of the truth. It will take years, even decades, before the heritage of the 'nomenklatura bishops' is overcome. In the meantime, will the religious revival flow into other channels?

There are certainly formidable rivals waiting among the other Christian denominations. The fastest growing Church in recent decades has been the Union of Evangelical Christians and Baptists, formed during the war under state supervision to bring together a variety of Protestant sects.

The reason for its relative success is partly that, like the nonconformist chapels of Victorian Britain, it has filled the gaps left by the official Church in the cheerless new industrial towns. Where the Orthodox Church has been forbidden to build, the more informal congregations of the Baptists have inconspicuously taken root, using temporary prayer houses, or even each other's apartments. Their presbyters are mostly unpaid, with full-time jobs in the secular world, and they devote their spare time to pastoral work. They are overworked but flexible, able to adapt readily to Soviet life.

Perhaps most important of all, the Baptists offer a warm and supportive community, which, by all reports, rallies round its own needy members, helping the old and sick, giving relief and sometimes financial aid to one-parent families. This may be why they were the first to practise a form of social solidarity later adopted by secular dissenters. In 1964 families of persecuted Baptists set up a Council of Prisoners' Relatives, to obtain data about co-believers imprisoned for their faith, to collect funds for their aid, and to write appeals to the authorities.

In a sense the Baptists practise what the Communists preach. They live lives of hard work, sobriety, moderate asceticism and mutual aid; they are patriotic and law-abiding. They have inherited the best qualities of the old peasant community. Yet with all that theirs is a religion of the literate, in which sermons and the study of the scriptures occupy a paramount place, and it is natural that it should attract so many people in a society which has been moving fast towards universal literacy.

All the same, some elements of their faith are in direct tension with the atheist state. Close study of the scriptures is difficult to keep up when the authorities permit very few Bibles to be printed. The Baptist ideal of the autonomy of each congregation and the separation of Church and State is incompatible with strict official supervision of the churches. Above all, the duty to evangelise, to bring up children in the faith and to convert unbelievers, runs directly counter to the party's religious policy.

Disagreement over how to react to this incompatibility split the Baptists in the sixties. Whereas the leadership of the Baptist Union took the line that they must preach the gospel only within permitted limits, some congregations denounced this policy as 'rendering unto Caesar that which is God's', and insisted on their right and duty to bring children to services, and to seek converts in the world.[28] These non-conformists, calling themselves Initsiativniki or reform Baptists, suffered heavily from persecution during the Khrushchev and Brezhnev periods. In 1966 they managed to organise the first unofficial public demonstration to be seen in the Soviet Union for forty years, when 500 delegates came from 130 cities to present a petition to Brezhnev. Not being received, they sat in the courtyard of the Supreme Soviet's Presidium, and eventually had to be bodily carried away, singing hymns, by the police.[29]

So the Baptists have been a major force. They do not on the whole attract intellectuals, for their theology is unsophisticated, but they have done much to provide for the religious aspirations of workers and employees, especially perhaps those recently uprooted from a traditional rural way of life. With perhaps a million and a half members,[30] they are not all that numerous, but they are still growing, and they have been political innovators, offering an example of solidarity under pressure from which others have learnt. Their conflicts with the authorities show how a religious movement with an effective community spirit can make life difficult even for a reformist atheist state. If the Orthodox Church disappoints the party's hopes through insufficient *sobornost'*, the Baptists may prove to have an excess of it.

Although Islam springs from a very different origin, it does in some ways resemble the Evangelical faith: it is fiercely committed and egalitarian, but also flexible, able to accommodate itself to Soviet life. In the early years of the Soviet regime Islam and communism had much in common: a commitment to equality, the brotherhood of nations and the struggle against western imperialism. But the temporary alliance between them soon split apart: the atheism of Moscow fitted ill with the fervent theism of Islam, and Asiatic ties pulled Muslims away from the orbit of European Russia.

We know relatively little about Islam in the Soviet Union today. Few Sovietologists command the necessary languages, and we receive scant information from the relevant geographical areas.

Except among the Crimean Tartars, there appears to be little or
no dissent as we understand that term. What evidence we have
suggests that Muslims quietly distance themselves from the Soviet
mainstream, discreetly maintaining their traditional way of life
in its essentials, while conceding inessentials to secular society.
People stay in villages and small towns, with their social round
centred on the tea-house, their religious life on the mosque or
Sufi brotherhood, rather than move into the large cities with their
more anonymous lifestyle. One consequence of this tendency is
that the birth rate remains much higher than in the European
parts of the Soviet Union. Large families, encouraged by both
religion and custom, are the norm, and the Muslim peoples,
already at least a sixth of the Soviet population, are steadily
increasing their share. But they are too attached to their homeland
to move to European Russia or Siberia to fill the labour shortages
there.

Soviet Muslims are reluctant, then, to leave their small towns
and villages. They accept what socialist society has to offer them:
broader education, relative prosperity and greater freedom for
women, while at the same time they adapt their religious practices
to the work patterns imposed by the planned economy. There is
not in any case the sharp distinction between the sacred and the
secular in Islam that we are used to in Christianity. To say 'I am
a Muslim' is more to acknowledge membership of a specific
community or to deny being European than it is to assert a
conscious confessional choice. In other words, it may be an ethnic
as much as a religious statement. This means that custom and
worship can mingle in a relatively relaxed manner. If a month's
fasting at Ramadan is too demanding for a Soviet production
worker who must keep up his bodily strength, then it can legit-
imately be curtailed to as little as three days. Or the requirement
to pray five times a day prostrated in the direction of Mecca can
be modified to once or twice in a posture more suited to the
layout of office or factory floor. In general, the customs which
have survived best are those connected with family and com-

munity life, such as circumcision, marriage and burial, rather than with religion *per se*.[31]

It is important to remember, though, that beyond official Islam, sanctioned by the Soviet state, lies the forbidden milieu of the Sufi brotherhoods. Descendants of the holy orders which headed the resistance to Russian colonisation in the nineteenth century, they preserve the Islamic faith in its purest, most uncompromising form. By their very nature we know little about the brotherhoods, but it seems certain that they are abiding sources of unofficial education, spiritual guidance and cultural transmission in a society torn between the sacred and the secular.[32]

Some scholars would maintain that a Muslim explosion of some kind is imminent. It is true there *have* been isolated outbursts in recent years, but not quite the sustained unrest one might have expected following the Iranian revolution and the Soviet invasion of Afghanistan.[33] On the other hand, there is evidence that in the current re-evaluation of all values, Islam is gradually strengthening its position to the point where local political leaders have to take it very seriously. The westernised and secular programmes of the intelligentsia evidently do not satisfy the mass of the people. The Tadjiks, perhaps because, unlike the other Central Asian nations, they are not of Turkic stock, seem especially susceptible to the appeal of Islam: some Tadjik intellectuals have actually called for the establishment of an Islamic republic. In other republics, too, Communist leaders have quietly been legitimising Islam as a source of social stability and public morality in a period of turmoil. It seems likely, then, that the national self-assertion of the Central Asian peoples will be increasingly tinged with Islamic motifs. Perhaps this trend offers the best prospect for the re-establishment of civil peace in the region.[34]

Spiritually, the Soviet Union today is in an extraordinarily labile state. A secular Utopia has finally and completely collapsed, leaving many bewildered and bereft of hope or belief. Man-made disasters and a blighted environment testify to a fundamental disharmony between human beings and nature. Nations long oppressed (including the Russians) are struggling to emancipate themselves from the imperial colossus, but cannot quite manage the final heave. And underlying these convulsions, the long delayed transition from rural to urban mentalities, from traditional to modern communities, is being accomplished in conditions of economic breakdown and political confusion. A strong Church might be able to absorb and direct the spiritual searching which must arise in these conditions. Now, some of the Soviet Churches *are* strong: usually those which have identified themselves with an oppressed nation. But, for reasons I have indicated, the largest Church of all, the Russian Orthodox, may not be able to cope with the sheer pressure of people's need for it. In that case, we may well see new religious movements and leaders appear, with visions and appeals yet unformulated, and with unpredictable results for the future of Soviet society. The Hrushevo episode may prove to be but a harbinger of what is to come.

7

The paradox of Gorbachev's reforms

In the foregoing chapters I have shown how civil society began to emerge, in very diverse forms, from beneath the totalitarian carapace, and to make itself felt in the political system still dominated by the Communist Party. Having thus, as it were, put the cart before the horse, I should like to continue where most observers would start, by examining what the political leadership was trying to achieve.

Most observers of the contemporary Soviet Union put the figure of Mikhail Gorbachev at the centre of their accounts, as the man responsible for the recent changes. I have adopted a different procedure, believing that the current upheavals have their roots deep in the nature of Soviet society, and that Gorbachev, important though he has been as a catalyst, soon found himself grappling with forces that he had had no idea he would unleash. As a member of a complacent totalitarian leadership, he seems to have had no conception of the depth of the country's crisis, even though he was evidently more aware than most of his colleagues that something was wrong with 'developed socialism'.

What is impressive about Gorbachev is the flexibility, intelligence and manoeuvring skill he has displayed in responding to the unexpected consequences of his own reforms. These qualities in him are not inexhaustible, as we shall see, but they have enabled him to cope with situations that would surely have engulfed most of his predecessors. He has harnessed the ideas of reformist advisers in the Central Committee apparatus, he has treated his adversaries firmly but without brutality, he has accustomed the public to open political debate, and has made the Soviet Union part of European civilisation again as it has not been since shortly after Lenin's revolution. How could such a man appear in the midst of what we are used to regarding as the faceless Communist Party apparatus?

One manifest difference between Gorbachev and his predecessors is that he is younger and much better educated. That is, he is more representative of the urban and sophisticated society that the Soviet Union is becoming. But that alone is not to say much. It is the *kind* of education and early experience which is crucial. Gorbachev comes from the fertile southern region of Stavropol', an area of Cossack traditions and rich peasant farming, which underwent severe famine after collectivisation in the first year or two of the young Mikhail's life. When he became party first secretary in Stavropol' nearly forty years later, he devoted a lot of attention to agriculture, which, as elsewhere in the country, was in a grossly demoralised state. He even took a correspondence course in agricultural economics. His studies as well as his direct observations led him to promote an experiment for motivating collective farmers which was currently out of favour in Moscow: the farm labour force was divided into brigades of 15 to 30 people, each of them was assigned a fixed area of land, together with seeds and equipment, and was then paid according to the results achieved. Under this regime, wheat output rose 30–50 per cent over a few years, and Gorbachev was permitted to continue the practice, even though many *apparatchiks* worried that the brigade system meant the beginning of the break-up of the collective farms and a reversion to private agriculture.[1]

The other major component of Gorbachev's formative experience was his law course at Moscow University in the early fifties. In the west, to say that a budding politician studied law sounds unremarkable. Most Soviet politicians, by contrast, start their careers with technological studies rounded off by a course at a

Higher Party School. Law has been looked down upon as faintly 'bourgeois'. Gorbachev, then, set out in a distinctive way. Now jurisprudence in Stalin's time was far from liberal in spirit, but all the same he will have had to familiarise himself with Roman law and western constitutional law, and it is fair to suppose that this may have given him the makings of a rather different outlook on the problems of Soviet society from that held by his colleagues. This was important to a leader who was to come to power at a time when social groups with their own distinct interests and aspirations were beginning to assert themselves and to interact; for if there was to be peaceful mediation between them, then it could only be through the processes of the law.

At the same time Gorbachev was secretary of the Komsomol in his faculty, and subsequently spent nearly thirty years in the party apparatus – sufficient, one might suppose, to obliterate any trace of nostalgia for what he had learned in law school. He achieved the highest office in 1985 as the candidate of those who wanted change, or at least realised it could no longer be postponed. His mentor was Brezhnev's immediate successor, Andropov, also an intelligent and by all accounts uncorrupt figure determined to bring about change, but so moulded by fifteen years of heading the security police that his thoughts turned naturally to discipline and the eradication of corruption as the principal instrument of regeneration. It is true that he was open to the possibility that some decentralisation of the economy was required, but he was already too old and ill on attaining office to undertake any serious steps in this direction.

This was Gorbachev's immediate inheritance. He became General Secretary of the party in March 1985 with the support of the KGB, among others, and for his first year or so in office he could be plausibly seen as Andropov's disciple. He tightened labour discipline, invoking the legendary feats of the Donbass coalminer Alexei Stakhanov; he established an official quality control inspectorate, Gospriyomka, which was instructed to reject shoddy manufactured goods and dock the pay of those responsible; he continued and even stepped up the dismissal and criminal investigation of corrupt officials; notoriously, he sharply restricted the sale of vodka and banned its use in official institutions, even for celebrations. Henceforth mineral water had to be substituted, an affront to Russian traditions of sociability and hospitality which earned Gorbachev the none too affectionate nickname of 'Mineral Secretary'.

This, if you like, was perestroika Mark 1, the fruit of Gorbachev's long experience in the apparatus. It was launched with a new and lively style of presentation, television interviews, question-and-answer sessions with workers on the shopfloor, during which Gorbachev *talked* about technological innovation, about greater openness or glasnost, about encouraging personal initiative in the economy, but made very little progress towards these goals.

Then, some time in the summer or autumn of 1986 there was a real change, partly in words but even more in substance. Perhaps this was a transition to a more radical transformation which Gorbachev had long intended to carry out; more likely it was the result of learning on the job just how deep the crisis was, and therefore how far-reaching were the measures needed to grapple with it. The explosion at the Chernobyl' nuclear power station in April 1986 certainly dramatised the defects of the system, revealing as it did the mortal dangers of handling awesome technological power with such secretive and slovenly irresponsibility. The aftermath of Chernobyl' underlined the shortcomings of restricted glasnost in creating hostility abroad and panic at home. Foreigners were indignant at Soviet obfuscation in a matter affecting public health all round the world. As for Soviet citizens, thousands of them were besieging the railway stations to flee from unknown dangers they could only learn about from foreign broadcasts. Chernobyl' might have been calculated to reawaken Gorbachev's interest in the legal studies of his youth; and he had many advisers on hand to tell him that freedom of speech and the rule of law were prerequisites for any lasting improvement in society. In December 1986 he released from exile one of the earliest protagonists of this doctrine, Academician Andrei Sakharov.

This was the onset of Gorbachev's perestroika Mark 2, which soon led him into uncharted territories, awakening suspicion and resentment among some of those who had helped him to come to power. Above all it alarmed the medium and lower level party-state officials, those sufficiently well placed to enjoy a modicum of power, privilege and the 'emoluments of office' under the existing system, but not high enough to realise or perhaps care about the depth of the crisis. Gorbachev was strengthening the supervision of the *apparatchiks* by affecting it from below as well as from above: that is by encouraging ordinary workers to report on the shortcomings and transgressions of their managers, their trade union officials and party secretaries. Stalin had of course encouraged this too back in the thirties, but his chosen vehicle, the anonymous denunciation – the infamous *donos* which sent so many innocent men and women to their deaths – was utterly discredited. Instead of the *donos* Gorbachev proposed increased openness and democracy: public meetings, letters (signed) to the press, and the election of responsible officials by their subordinates.

An intriguing theme began to make an occasional appearance in his speeches at this time: that is that the absence of an opposition party obliged party officials to be especially searching in their self-criticism, and to respond with alacrity and probity to criticism from others. In a televised speech at Khabarovsk he warned that 'officials who react to criticism by persecuting their critics lay themselves open to criminal prosecution'.[2] Significantly, these words, which were clearly heard on television, were omitted from the newspaper version of the speech, for they enunciated a novel and unwelcome principle: that in certain circumstances the law ranks higher than party hierarchies. This is where the perestroika Mark 1 practice of cleaning up corruption began to intersect with the Mark 2 theory of the rule of law. Gorbachev was beginning to see how a legal system with real teeth could strengthen Soviet society.

He was talking now, furthermore, not just of 'restructuring', but of a transformation of social consciousness, of a 'revolution . . . in the hearts and minds of the people'.[3] This implied opening up the whole field of culture and education. If he was going to take on the party-state apparatus, then he needed an alliance with the cultural and scientific intelligentsia, whose importance, as we have seen, is out of all proportion to their fast growing but still relatively limited numbers. In June 1986 he met a delegation of writers and appealed to them for help. The people want change, he declared, and the leadership wants change, but in between stands 'a managerial stratum, the ministerial and party apparatus, which does not . . . want to give up its . . . privileges'.[4]

The writers, despite divisions among themselves, responded to his appeal with their own brand of public spirit. Their congress spearheaded a public campaign against the diversion of the northern rivers, they called for the abolition of censorship and they turned some of their journals into bastions and exemplars of glasnost. Joined by a few campaigning newspaper editors, film directors and courageous historians, they published hitherto forbidden authors, and opened up Soviet history once more as a serious subject of study. Stalin's crimes were exposed as never before, even in Khrushchev's thaw: his vilification and hounding of the opposition, the brutal collectivisation of agriculture and the consequent famine, the arrests and executions, the deportations of whole peoples, the costly mistakes in wartime leadership – all these half-suppressed and wholly suppressed topics were exposed week after week to a public that seemed insatiable. People would come weeping out of a film like *Repentance*, which was a vivid allegorical representation of Stalin's repressions. Nothing could be more revealing about the profundity of the trauma the Soviet people have undergone than the stunned and fixed attention they accorded the revelation of fifty-year-old crimes. 'It's as if we can breathe again freely,' a friend said to me. Even many young people, not directly affected by Stalin, seemed to sense relief at this exorcising of his ghost.

By the second half of 1989 this re-examination of the past was beginning to extend to a serious questioning of what had hitherto always been sacrosanct, the heritage of Lenin and the October revolution. The process began when the literary journal *Oktyabr'* published a posthumous work by Vasilii Grossman, *Forever Flowing*, which accused Lenin of having created the essentials of the system Stalin later employed for mass murder. Grossman portrayed Lenin as a courteous and considerate person in his private life, but as a ruthless fanatic in politics, poisoned by Russia's 'thousand-year tradition of slavery', which he had restored after the tsars had begun to introduce elements of civil freedom.[5]

This publication provoked a storm of controversy, though, significantly, that controversy raged not around the disparaging reassessment of the October revolution, but the alleged slander on Russian history. It was as if the reading public already took for granted the negative evaluation of Lenin, and was interested only in the ethnic slur. This was typical of the way all political questions were being reduced to ethnic issues. At any rate, Grossman prepared the way for the complete rehabilitation of Solzhenitsyn. During 1990 Soviet journals were full of his long prose works, including *The Gulag Archipelago*, which was not just an exposé of Stalin's crimes, but analysed the process by which they had grown out of Lenin's drive to total power and his disdain for legality. By this time, it had become not only possible, but almost de rigueur for self-respecting intellectuals to trace the current deficiencies of the Soviet system directly back to Communist intransigence and brutality from 1917 onwards.

Glasnost embraces not only the past, but also the present. The media comment with considerable freedom on the evils of today, which, moreover, they usually present not as regrettable aberrations, but as failings inherent in the system itself. The housing shortage, poor work discipline, shoddy consumer goods and lamentable medical care are described in vivid detail. Statistics are published on alcoholism, suicide, disease and mortality. Policies and decisions of the leadership are discussed uninhibitedly and often critically. A remarkable example of current frankness was the forthright exposé of the activities of the KGB by its recent member, Major General Oleg Kalugin, who accused it of having 'preserved virtually intact the huge apparatus which for decades had been the main buttress of the Soviet dictatorship'.[6]

Some subjects are treated in a more gingerly fashion, especially foreign and military policy. The non-Russians feel that the central press does not present their case with sympathy, but then they usually respond in kind. More serious was the slowness to publish full information about the dangers of radiation around Chernobyl', a delay which posed serious risk to life and health, and certainly fuelled separatist sentiment in Belorussia and Ukraine.[7] But this was not special to Chernobyl': the gradual and tardy release of data matched the progress of glasnost in other areas of information.

By 1990, in fact, it became possible to argue that we were no longer dealing with glasnost, but with freedom of speech as we understand it in the west, with analogous limitations and problems. The process was sealed by a law on the press and mass media which, though far from impeccable, at least gave journalists and editors a base from which to fight for their rights. It forbade censorship of mass information and guaranteed 'the right to express opinions and beliefs, to seek, select, receive and disseminate information and ideas in any form', except for 'state secrets', incitement to crime, and calls for violence or 'racial, national or religious exclusivity'. All organisations and individuals were given the right to found an organ of the mass media; official refusal to register one must be clearly explained according to the law and can be appealed in the courts. Problems arise with the concept of information: while journalists and editors can be prosecuted for the publication of false information, there appears to be no procedure by which they can enforce their right of access to correct information.[8]

Another potential problem of the law is that it accords considerable power to the 'founder' of a press organ, meaning the organisation of which it is acting as the mouthpiece, or which provides it with premises, finance and equipment. The founder has the right to determine editorial policy and to appoint and dismiss editors. Doubtless this is the reason why promulgation of the law was swiftly followed by attempts on the part of some newspapers and journals to break with their 'founders' and set up as self-governing editorial collectives. The popular weekly *Literaturnaya gazeta*, for example, announced that it was disavowing the Union of Soviet Writers, whose organ it had been since 1932, as an institution which 'for decades had stood guard over the interests of the totalitarian state'. Its 'founder' would in future be its own working collective.[9] The problem is a serious one, for in some circumstances the 'founder' might readmit the authoritarian state through the back door, but at least this danger is one not unfamiliar to western readers concerned about overmighty press barons.

Altogether, the conquest of freedom of speech counts as the greatest achievement of the recent Soviet reforms and the greatest single advance towards civil society. It was not brought about solely from above, but depended on the skill and courage of individual editors and journalists, who expanded the officially proclaimed policy of glasnost far beyond what its framers intended or anticipated. The public responded well, especially in the early years, queueing from early in the morning to buy journals and newspapers which had acquired a reputation for honesty and liveliness. Later a reaction set in, as publications became more expensive under commercial pressure, and as the constant flood of bad news induced a certain weariness.[10] But no one would wish a return to the deaf-mute mass media of only five years ago.

By contrast, in the economy, the legacy of the past weighs

implacably and heavily. Traditional practices have corrupted producers and reduced consumers to a state of resentful but helpless apathy, so that serious change, if it happens at all, is bound to be prolonged and painful. The economic system established by Stalin has proved, despite all its conspicuous deficiencies, to be forbiddingly stable and self-reinforcing. As I pointed out in the first chapter, it provides for most of the population job tenure and a guaranteed minimum sufficiency of material provision in return for a low standard of living and absence of control over workplace decision-making. This is a bargain which the majority of the Soviet population has tacitly accepted and they are apprehensive of seeing it violated, for fear of the disruptions that might well follow.

In some ways, in fact, the Soviet state has perpetuated the attitudes of the pre-1930 Russian village community. The expectation is still prevalent that the community will guarantee essentials in a context of comradely indigence just above the poverty line. This shared privation generates natural fears about what economic reform might entail, as well as resentment of those who benefit from the new atmosphere to indulge in some newly legalised private enterprise. How many times over the last three or four years have I heard Soviet citizens use the word 'speculator' to disparage private traders or co-operatives providing at high prices goods and services seldom available at all in the state sector?

This sullen egalitarianism dovetails neatly with the interest of the party-state apparatus in retaining their network of controls and hence their grip on the economy. It is also especially common in Russia, as distinct from the other nations of the Soviet empire, maybe because the village community was more cohesive and lasted longer there than elsewhere. However that may be, most observers would agree that private enterprise is likely to be both more successful and more socially acceptable in the Baltic or the Caucasus, even perhaps in Central Asia, than in Russia itself. Such ethnic discrepancies harbour considerable dangers, for they mean that effective economic reforms may intensify conflicts between the various Soviet nations, with their different levels of economic achievement and expectation. The damaging rivalries between the various republics of Yugoslavia are a warning; and in the Soviet Union the situation would be aggravated by the fact that the nation which may prove economically most backward is also the largest and most powerful.

This resistance, or at any rate, inertia, is reinforced by the practical difficulties of implementing reform. So many institutions and so many attitudes have to be changed that it cannot be done at one blow. For instance, it is virtually impossible in conditions of scarcity and imbalance simultaneously to abolish the system of centralised supply allocation (*Gossnab*), and also to carry out a comprehensive price reform, letting goods find their own level on the wholesale market. Nor is it easy for enterprise managers to break away from dependence on the state to find their own suppliers and customers, a task to which they are entirely unaccustomed, and for which in any case normal market information is largely lacking. Yet if these changes are not carried through, then enterprises cannot in any meaningful sense exercise the autonomy they have been granted by the law of July 1987. They continue to rely on the state for raw materials, spare parts and fuel, and their negotiations with potential customers are still distorted by administratively determined prices which may bear no relation to supply and demand. One has to agree with the British economist Alec Nove that 'To change everything at once is impossible, but partial change creates contradictions and inconsistencies.'[11]

The inherent difficulties of reform are further aggravated by the inconsistencies of the leadership. Perestroika Mark 1 persists and interferes with perestroika Mark 2. When Gorbachev came to power, he began by continuing Andropov's policy of trying to reinvigorate the economy by tightening up and disciplining the existing system. He proclaimed the need for technological innovation and 'acceleration' (*uskorenie*). He established Gospriyomka. He cracked down on alcohol consumption. He shut down some of the old ministries and set up super new state agencies to run whole branches of the economy, like machine building, energy and agriculture. He imposed new penalties for receiving 'non-labour income', to try and restrict the black economy.[12]

It is true that from the outset Gorbachev also proclaimed his intention to decentralise the economy by offering individual enterprises more autonomy. But by the time the new enterprise laws came into effect, on 1 January 1988, the new institutions of centralisation and discipline were already thoroughly in the saddle, their strength bolstered by decades of custom and self-interest. Not surprisingly, then, enterprises required to cope with 'self-financing' found it simplest to continue fulfilling imposed production targets, now renamed 'state contract orders' (*goszakazy*), which account for all or nearly all of their output. As the economist V. Selyunin says: 'Either you can have *uskorenie*, or you can have perestroika. You cannot have both.'[13]

In this way too, increasing aggregate growth has the paradoxical effect of exacerbating shortages, since it enfeebles enterprise autonomy and thwarts the working of the market. It does not even result in more goods that people can use. In the words of Premier Ryzhkov: 'We produce more tractors in this country than all the capitalist countries put together. And yet we don't have enough tractors.'[14] Or as the reform economist Otto Latsis puts it: 'They build irrigation channels which bring no increase in agricultural production. They produce machine tools for which there are no operators, tractors for which there are no drivers, and threshing machines which they know will not work. Further millions of people supply these superfluous products with electricity, ore, oil and coal. In return they receive their wages like everyone else, and take them to the shops. There, however, they find no goods to buy, because their work has not produced any.'[15] So the economy grows, and the shortages grow with it.

Agriculture is a special problem. The villages have never recovered from the demoralisation of the brutal and humiliating collectivisation imposed by Stalin. Whatever experiments Gorbachev may have tried in Stavropol', since coming to power he has been hesitant about tampering with the collective and state farms as the keystone of the system of agricultural production and delivery. Indeed he strengthened the existing system in some ways by the creation of a new super-ministry for agriculture and food-processing, Gosagroprom. This characteristic brainchild of perestroika Mark 1 soon established its deadening grip, and by 1989, according to *Pravda*, was 'flooding the collective farms with instructions and regulations', while its offices churned out more than five thousand categories of forms and bulletins, containing eight million planning indicators.[16]

Unabashed, Gorbachev soon began to move smartly in the opposite direction, towards the principle that 'small is beautiful', by encouraging the creation of contract brigades from units as small as the individual household or family.[17] He went on from there to urge collective farm chairmen to offer such miniature 'brigades' long-term leases of land, up to fifty years at a time. This campaign was accompanied by the rehabilitation of Bukharin, who in the twenties had argued for a gradual 'co-operatisation' of farms as an alternative to full-scale collectivisation. These moves seemed to presage a transition to an essentially private agriculture, with former collective and state farms acting as co-operatives to provide bulk purchasing, agrarian expertise and marketing services.[18]

Gorbachev has hesitated, however, to take the final step, presumably because of fears in the rural party apparatus of losing its authority and indeed the lion's share of its current function. At the long-awaited Central Committee plenum on agriculture in March 1989, Gorbachev abolished Gosagroprom, but reaffirmed that the collective principle would stay and that there was no intention to return to private property in land. Otherwise he merely reiterated his commitment to changes already announced, that is to a mixture of collective and private leasehold farming.[19]

These changes have not generated a marked increase in food

production, and they are unlikely to. Land is available to be leased, but both the collective farms, as its current owners, and the peasants, the potential lessees of it, are proving reluctant to take up the opportunity. Some commentators attribute this reluctance to the 'depeasantisation of Russia's countryside': as sixty years have passed – at least two whole generations – since private agriculture was the rule, the basic skills needed to run a small family farm have been lost, and even the will to resuscitate those skills is absent. There is undoubtedly some truth in this diagnosis. Yet one feels that if the right framework were created, both enterprise and skill could be recovered. This will happen only when villagers are convinced that the party leadership is permanently committed to private farming, and that there will be no more lurches and turn-abouts in policy. Such commitment would require explicitly slimming down collective farms and turning them into co-operatives, while freeing food prices and making cheap credit available to smallholders, as well as investing heavily in rural roads, schools and other services. Only such a demonstrative package of measures would halt the exodus of the best people from the villages and even perhaps promote something of a reverse flow. Gorbachev is still some way short of this kind of commitment. He has shown flexibility and a willingness to learn, but even so, this failing is ominous in a policy area which is crucial if he is to regain the faltering confidence of the public at large, who will assess perestroika not least by what they can buy in their groceries.

The one economic innovation that began to produce results fairly quickly was the legalisation of co-operatives in May 1988. A co-operative is essentially a private enterprise, owned by a group of people, all of whom, at least nominally, work for it – hiring labour in the private sector is still illegal. In the first twelve months after the law was passed, some 133,000 co-operatives were set up, providing goods and services to the value of 12.9 billion rubles, about 2 per cent of the national product. One can see them dotted around most towns: restaurants, hairdressers, fruit and vegetable stalls, shoe repair booths and so on, where the decor is a little more imaginative, the supplies somewhat more abundant, the quality a little higher – and the prices three or four times those prevailing in the state sector. There was initial public welcome for them, since they provided commodities previously only available on the black market. But pretty soon this welcome turned to hostility, as people began to feel that the co-operatives were not only profiting by scarcities, but actually aggravating them by diverting goods from the state sector and reselling them, without improvement, at much higher prices.[20]

The co-operatives have found it difficult to rebut this charge. It may be partly justified. After all, they are foreign bodies in an economy still 98 per cent run by the state. They have to rely for premises and credit on the soviets and the state banks. They have few sources of supplies other than official state agencies, who do not usually include them in their output and trading plans. So they are more or less obliged to adopt irregular practices to get started at all and then to keep themselves in business. Add to this the fact that some cooperatives started life in the old 'black' economy: they have since become legal, but have not necessarily abandoned all their old practices. Some of them are the victims of protection rackets run either by criminals or by corrupt officials: a recent survey suggested that about a fifth of the cooperatives in Moscow have 'protectors', for whom they have to pay heavily. There have even been shoot-outs on the street between rival gangs of racketeers.[21]

To sever their ties with the underworld and operate normally, the co-operatives need access to credit through banks, and to supplies and premises through the market. They also require a proper framework of commercial and contract law within which to operate, so that they can be confident of their own future. One of the reasons they charge high prices is that they are insecure: they can at any time be shut down or have their operations arbitrarily curtailed without any redress. Far from offering them security, however, the government has taken the opposite course, restricting the fields in which they may trade, and giving local authorities considerable freedom to tax them highly or restrict the prices at which they may sell.[22]

The high prices in the co-operatives fuelled ordinary people's fears of what a full-scale market reform would mean for them. If the 'dependence economy' was finally abolished and the huge state subsidies for housing, food and transport withdrawn, then the ruble incomes of most Soviet citizens would be revealed for what they were: modest even by third world standards. Besides, the spectre of hyper-inflation loomed even without wholesale marketisation. Since 1985, the state budget deficit had risen steeply for a number of reasons: the fall in the price of the Soviet Union's principal export, oil, the loss of vodka revenue, the failure to cut back over-ambitious projects or to stop subsidising firms which had got into difficulties through producing unsaleable commodities in the way described by Latsis. By 1989 the budget deficit had reached 120 billion rubles, six times what it had been in the late Brezhnev years, and in relation to GNP about three times the very serious US deficit. The government filled it by printing money. In this way the indiscipline of the planned economy conspired with the pressures of the market to generate a 56 per cent rise in the money supply in 1989, and 70 per cent in the first nine months of 1990.[23] The ruble came to seem more and more like 'toytown money', not to be used for serious transactions, a fact which the government tacitly acknowledged when it legalised the holding of foreign currency in July 1990.

Loss of confidence in the currency is a social cancer which affects every individual every day, disrupting both markets and centralised distribution systems by causing hoarding and bartering. It also reinforces ethnic centrifugalism. Union republics, autonomous republics and sometimes individual regions and towns have been forced to espouse economic autarky and to assert control over their own resources. As shortages got worse during 1990, local or regional soviets would pass by-laws requiring shoppers to produce documents showing they lived locally before they could buy sugar or soap powder (or whatever currently happened to be in short supply). This measure hit hard those accustomed to travel into big cities from the smaller towns and villages to secure 'deficit' goods: as a result some regional soviets round Moscow threatened to retaliate by stopping deliveries of food to the city.[24] Similarly, annoyed by the failure of Moscow construction firms to complete much needed housing, Tyumen' oil workers threatened to reduce the supply of oil to the capital.[25] The country seemed on the verge of disintegrating into tiny economic fiefs trading with each other, if at all, by primitive barter deals. Gorbachev's economic blockade of Lithuania only compounded the problem.

By the spring of 1990 it was becoming obvious that the government would have to abandon half measures and move decisively towards the full-scale marketisation of the economy. There was much interest in the recent reforms introduced by the Mazowiecki government in Poland, accompanied by a lively debate in the press about the advisability of 'shock therapy'. The trouble was that, as even a convinced proponent of the market like Gorbachev's adviser Nikolai Petrakov conceded, the Soviet government did not enjoy the almost universal legitimacy which enabled the Polish reformers to demand considerable sacrifices of their population.[26] There were also good objective reasons for clinging to the remnants of a centralised distribution system, however outmoded. When Leonid Abalkin, also a market reformer, became Deputy Prime Minister, he began to see the advantages of Gosplan. As he explained to a journalist, 'In order to ensure that the towns didn't freeze this winter, we had to create a fuel reserve in the country. For that purpose someone had to control the flow of coal and direct it to the right places.'[27]

So the question remained: how to proceed towards the market? To do it all at once would cause tremendous social dislocation and resentment. To do it piecemeal would create distortions and contradictions between one sector of the economy and another. Such dilemmas underlay the confusion which ensued. In May

1990 Prime Minister Ryzhkov unveiled a marketisation programme which tried to compensate for the government's lack of
legitimacy by offering a referendum. But, before it even got that
far, the Supreme Soviet rejected his whole package as inadequate,
and told him to go away and reconsider it.[28] Meanwhile, a
member of the President's Council, Academician Shatalin,
brought out an alternative programme, much more radical.

The differences between the Ryzhkov and Shatalin plans were
crucial. Ryzhkov's reflected the fears expressed by Abalkin (his
deputy): it kept control over procurement and distribution mainly
in the hands of the all-Union government throughout the early
phases of the transition, first raising prices by administrative
decree and only then moving towards anti-monopoly legislation
and an incomplete privatisation of the means of production. Shatalin's differed in three respects. Firstly, he accepted the notion of
private property in the means of production (including land);
secondly, he acknowledged the sovereignty of the republics and
did not attempt to keep control in all-Union hands; thirdly, he
began his reform with anti-monopoly measures and the selling-
off of enterprises together with huge cuts in government spending
(by axing most foreign aid, much military expenditure and prun-
ing large industrial projects), and only then moved to free prices.
The Ryzhkov programme was less risky, but would allow the
nomenklatura officials to arrange the transfer to the market on
their own terms and to their own advantage; the Shatalin programme offered the danger of greater upheavals, but undermined
the nomenklatura empire and gave real clout to the republics at
the outset.

The union republics naturally preferred Shatalin's plan. Boris
El'tsin sponsored a version of it as his own '500 Days' blueprint
for transition to the market, which was duly passed by the Russian Supreme Soviet. Gorbachev, alarmed at the prospect of
having the largest republic implement a reform incompatible with
that of the Union as a whole, overcame his personal antipathy
and consulted with El'tsin. Together they set up a commission to

study the possibility of reconciling the two projects. But it proved impossible to paper over the cracks. Deadlines came and went, but still no compromise could be achieved. The crunch point of perestroika had been reached, where the nomenklatura, faced with real loss of control, was fighting desperately to keep its grip on the economy. The conflict over marketisation became part of the general constitutional crisis of autumn 1990.

How is one to evaluate perestroika in terms of the Marxist-Leninist ideology Gorbachev professes? At times one is tempted to conclude that he has abandoned ideology altogether. During a visit to Siberia in September 1988, he was confronted by an earnest young man who asked him, 'What stage of socialism have we reached now?' Gorbachev replied disarmingly: 'You've all got used to thinking like this: you're a young fellow, and all you're interested in is stages! [Laughter] I believe we are at the stage of restructuring that which we have so far created. That's the stage we're at.'[29]

This cheerful renunciation of any tangible goal, even of any sense of the forward march of history, must be for old-timers one of the most disconcerting aspects of the world view now being projected in the Soviet media. As Yurii Bondarev (secretary of the RSFSR Writers' Union) has complained: 'We do not need to destroy our past in order to build our future . . . Could our restructuring be compared to an aircraft which has taken off without knowing whether there is a landing strip at its destination?'[30] It is true that the 'landing strip' has been located in very general terms. The political commentator Fyodor Burlatskii, for example, has suggested that 'socialism has one simple and obvious goal: the welfare and culture of the working man. Everything else – industry and socialisation – is a means to that end.'[31] Nor did Lenin himself ever produce a detailed blueprint of socialist society beyond the vague and non-committal observations contained in State and Revolution about a self-administering society in which the exploitation of man by man will have ceased.

So Gorbachev has good authority for the unspecific nature of his vision. One sometimes suspects, indeed, that the invocation of Lenin has become a substitute for clear thinking. The more Gorbachev criticises all the intervening leaders – and with them nine-tenths of Soviet history – the more he needs to cling to the one name which remains inviolate. But his Lenin is selective. The Lenin he quotes is from the period of the transition from War Communism to the New Economic Policy in 1921, when extremes of centralisation and coercion had been shown to lead to social breakdown, when the economy was being freed, culture diversified, and society allowed once more to reveal its tensions and conflicts, simply in order to restore some kind of normality: the first perestroika of Soviet history, in other words. The fact that that same Lenin was simultaneously banning factions and platforms within the party – and thus suppressing serious discussion – is not mentioned.

One notable aspect of Gorbachev's 'socialism' is that it is no longer defined in implacable opposition to 'capitalism'. 'Class struggle' has been sharply downgraded. 'With the emergence of weapons of mass . . . destruction, there appeared an objective limit to class confrontation in the international arena: the threat of universal destruction . . . The backbone of the new way of thinking is the recognition of the priority of human values, or, to be more precise, of humankind's survival.'[32]

Of course, the Khrushchev and Brezhnev leaderships had in their own ways also recognised this priority, but they always maintained that the class struggle nevertheless continued. Gorbachev has gone much further than arrangements for mutual survival. He has explicitly declared that in a world of rapid travel and instant mass communications it is hardly possible – or only at ruinous cost – to preserve a closed society. Glaring economic inequality and the threat of a global ecological catastrophe make more concerted international co-operation imperative.[33] As he told a meeting of representatives of culture and the media in January 1989: 'The vital imperative which faces mankind is the priority of all-human values, a world without violence and wars, diversity [*mnogovariantnost'*] of social progress, dialogue and co-operation for the sake of development and the preservation of civilisation, and movement towards a new world order.'[34]

These are not just words: they have led to a palpable reassessment of the Soviet Union's strategic needs, as a result of which it has decided that a less confrontational stance towards the outside world would provide greater security than endless rearming. Hence the withdrawal from a costly and demoralising war in Afghanistan. Hence also the agreement to scrap intermediate range nuclear missiles, with proper provision for mutual inspection, to reduce strategic arms, and to begin a unilateral reduction in conventional forces both in Europe and on the Chinese frontier.

In further pursuit of closer interdependence, the Soviet Union during 1987–8 released most (though not all) of its political prisoners, established its own Human Rights Commission under Fyodor Burlatskii, and took a more open and constructive part in the European Security and Co-operation process, to the extent of offering to host the next major review conference, in 1991. It has simplified travel procedures for its own citizens, so that both personal visits and professional consultations with the outside world have become easier and more frequent. The Soviet Union has in a real sense rejoined the international community.

The culmination of these steps was the momentous decision to authorise the dismantling of the Berlin Wall and to refrain from intervening to prevent the revolutions of Eastern Europe in the autumn of 1989. No other act of Gorbachev has demonstrated so fully how far a western liberal and humanist culture had penetrated his way of thinking, whether from his days studying law, from his visits with Raisa to France and Italy, or from the urbane and cosmopolitan advisers with whom he had surrounded himself. His decision was the decisive contribution towards ending the Cold War, in the sense that it eliminated what had been its principal cause.

Both internally and externally, then, 'socialism' has become a much more open and fluid concept. The terms in which it is discussed – decentralisation, pluralism, popular representation, freedom of information and discussion – are more reminiscent of John Stuart Mill than of Karl Marx, and remind one that Marxism is a bastard child of bourgeois liberalism. And indeed a Soviet philosopher has recently argued that when Marxism is expounded rigidly and in rejection of the past, then it naturally engenders Stalinism: it needs to return to its origins. 'We shall create nothing meaningful if we stick to our old conviction that it is only by means of destruction that man will attain happiness. The rule of law is a legacy of bourgeois culture. Freedom of conscience was also born there.'[35]

Vadim Medvedev, head of the Central Committee ideological commission, confirms this openness to the experience of others: 'We cannot indiscriminately brush aside the experience accumulated by capitalism merely on the grounds that it is a different social system . . . This is not just a matter of scientific and technological achievements, but of a whole variety of forms of social organisation, and of solutions to social problems. I believe we shall have to undertake a serious reassessment of the practice of present-day social democracy in defending the social and democratic attainments of working people.'

By the spring of 1990, Gorbachev's political aide, Georgii Shakhnazarov, was arguing that systems of ownership of the means of production were not the determinant of the nature of a society. The Stalinist experience showed that a socialist society could 'trample on the foundations of humanity' just as much as a capitalist one. What was crucial was not whether a society was socialist or capitalist, but whether it was democratic or tyrannical.[36]

The heritage of liberalism and social democracy were thus unambiguously on the agenda in developing the new version of socialism. In fact, they became so dominant that the border dividing them from 'socialism' became more and more blurred. If there was anything distinctive about Soviet socialism, it became progressively more difficult to discern what it was. For a long time, it is true, Gorbachev stuck to the idea of the 'leading role' of the Communist Party and rejected any notion of a multi-party system. When he established new legislative assemblies in 1989, he guaranteed the Communist Party a hegemonic position within them by reserving seats for it and also for social organisations which it dominated. At that stage he was endeavouring to mobilise the mass membership of the party against its apparatchiks; he was certainly not trying to weaken the position of the party itself.

Progressively, however, the party's monopoly came to seem more and more incongruous both with Gorbachev's magnanimity in Eastern Europe, and with the reality of politics in the Soviet Union, where not only were other political movements becoming active, but the Communist Party itself was falling apart into its national components.

In February 1990, therefore, Gorbachev recommended abolishing Article 6 of the Soviet constitution, which guaranteed the party its 'leading role', in effect its right to supervise and monitor all political life. 'In a society which is renewing itself,' he argued, 'the party can exist and fulfil its vanguard role only as a democratically acknowledged force. This means that its position ought not to be enforced through being constitutionally legitimised.' Even if he was prepared to renounce the party's monopoly, though, he was not envisaging a completely parliamentary party, alternating with others in government, as the word 'vanguard' signalled. 'We say frankly that the CPSU is capable of fulfilling a consolidating, integrating role and of ensuring the progress of perestroika for the benefit of all the people.' Consequently, 'the CPSU naturally intends to fight for the position of being the leading party, but it intends to do this strictly within the framework of the democratic process, renouncing any legal and political advantages.'[37]

It is difficult to know whether he had any specific models in mind. The Christian Democrats in Italy perhaps, or the Liberal Democrats in Japan: permanent parties of government by virtue of winning election after election over a divided opposition.

Whatever he intended, he was in any case now preparing to shift the political centre of gravity out of the party into his own post of President and into the revivified soviets.

Previously the Presidency had been largely an honorific post, as was suggested by its full title: Chairman of the Presidium of the Supreme Soviet. He might be said to have combined the positions of monarch and speaker of the House of Commons in the British system. Under changes proposed by Gorbachev in March 1990, all that changed sharply. Henceforth, the President would (subject to confirmation in the Supreme Soviet) appoint and dismiss the Prime Minister and other leading government officials; he would have the right to dissolve the Supreme Soviet, to veto legislation (to be overturned only by a two-thirds majority in the Supreme Soviet), to issue decrees, to declare martial law, a state of emergency or 'temporary presidential rule' in any area of the Soviet Union (without the consent of the relevant republican Supreme Soviet, provided the USSR Supreme Soviet approved by a two-thirds majority). This was a full-scale executive presidency – even an 'imperial presidency', as the Moscow People's Deputy Sergei Stankevich called it.[38] The powers were similar to those enjoyed by the French President. But France had a long tradition of democratic politics, while in the Soviet Union a free press, an independent judiciary and opposition parties were still mere springtime shoots among the ruins of one-party rule. Moreover, though future Presidents were to be elected by popular ballot, Gorbachev had reached the post by a show of hands in the undemocratic Congress of People's Deputies.

If the new presidency was not to fill the vacuum in an altogether overbearing way, then the key extra ingredient needed was the rule of law. This was the cornerstone of the logic of perestroika Mark 2, and also its sharpest break with the past. Traditionally the attitude of the Soviet state towards the law has been ambivalent. On the one hand Marxist theory views the state as the governing committee of the ruling class and law as an instrument by means of which it maintains itself in power; this implies that with the overthrow of all ruling classes and the withering away of the state the law itself is no longer needed. On the other hand, the Soviet state, having conspicuously not withered away under Stalin, has required a normative framework for the regulation of society, and especially to direct the complicated channels of economic planning.

After Stalin's death the law was called in to perform further functions. The party leaders actually had an interest in strengthening legality as a guarantee against the resumption of arbitrary one-man terror, under which all their heads had been at risk. They also regarded law as a means of educating people in their social responsibility and involving them in the process of 'self-administration', which theoretically would eventually become universal and render the state superfluous. At the same time, they did not want to deprive themselves of the judicial weapons on which they were accustomed to rely for the maintenance of their power. So they formalised and propagandised what they called 'socialist legality', while reserving to themselves the right to bend its procedures to their own ends. They made no secret of what they were doing: indeed, in case anyone was in doubt, they specifically rejected the notion of the primacy of the rule of law, and reasserted the party's right to take ultimate decisions.[39]

All the same the concern to preserve juridical decorum created opportunities which, as we have seen, the dissenters used to project their own concept of legality. When the authorities arrested them, they at least had to genuinely try them, however much they distorted court procedures in order to obtain an acceptable verdict. As for the dissenters, their behaviour, in calling on the state to observe its own constitution, meant they had emancipated themselves from the outlook of most Soviet citizens, who helplessly regard law as something to be manipulated by the authorities for their own purposes. They asserted Vladimir Bukovskii's 'small core of freedom in each individual'.

Whether as a result of Soviet legal education, or through western broadcasting of information about the dissenters, I would say that the legal consciousness of many Soviet citizens today — especially educated ones — is higher than we commonly realise, and certainly as high as among my own colleagues in Britain. I find that Soviet friends talking among themselves, even casually, take for granted a knowledge of the constitution, of judicial institutions and of the more frequently applied articles of the Criminal Code. Of course some acquaintance with pass book and residence regulations, or with labour law, is essential just to get by in life, but in my experience nowadays many Soviet citizens are quite searching in their analysis of these enactments: they feel it is worthwhile making a fuss if their rights are infringed, and they know how to go about it. The Soviet people are gradually becoming a nation of barrack-room lawyers, which is a decided advance on their past juridical ignorance and apathy. Indeed, this must be one of the most significant social changes to have taken place in the last generation or so.

Altogether, then, legal awareness is another field in which the political authorities had been lagging behind social consciousness, and had some catching up to do if they were to counteract mounting public cynicism. It was partly a matter of removing vaguely worded laws which could be brought to bear against people inconvenient to local grandees: the parasite law, for instance, which made it a criminal offence not to be in paid employment, and, like the vagrancy laws of Elizabethan England, could be used to get rid of troublemakers. But partly it was a matter of ensuring that the procuracy and the courts observed their own procedures and were independent of political pressure. Many recent articles by the new breed of Soviet investigative journalist focused on the phenomenon of 'telephone law', that is, the practice by which party or soviet officials rang up the judge and advised him what the outcome of a particular case should be. Jurists have pondered how judges could be effectively shielded from this kind of pressure, perhaps by lengthening their terms of office, perhaps through having them appointed by superior bodies rather than by the local soviet. Defence counsels have asked for access to their clients at an earlier stage of criminal proceedings, at the beginning of the investigation rather than only at the end of it, to affirm the principle that the accused is presumed innocent until proved guilty and is therefore entitled to competent advice from the outset on how best to present his case.

Already in 1987 Gorbachev had linked the rule of law to his vision of the politics of the future. 'Democracy,' he wrote, 'cannot exist and develop without the rule of law, because law is designed to protect society from abuses of power and to guarantee citizens and their organisations and work collectives their rights and freedoms.'[40] The 19th Party Conference in July 1988 took up this concern and talked of 'forming a socialist legal state' (*sotsialisticheskoe pravovoe gosudarstvo*). 'The law,' it declared, 'is paramount in all spheres of society's life.' The conference resolution added as a gloss: 'It is necessary to give paramount attention to the legal protection of the individual and to consolidate guarantees of the Soviet people's political, economic and social rights and freedoms.'[41]

These were historic words, for they implied that the ultimate goal of the socialist state was no longer the building of communism, and that the final authority in all questions no longer rested with the party. Furthermore, they focused on the individual, no longer the collective or society, as the repository of the rights guaranteed by law.

Here the visions of jurists merged with those of writers, scientists, economists, even religious believers, to generate an image of man very different from the 'new Soviet man' projected in the hitherto prevailing ideology. This is where perestroika Mark 2 broke totally with perestroika Mark 1. The new outlook has since been consolidated in legislation, and further draft laws are in preparation.

'New Soviet man Mark 2' enjoys in principle a whole range of rights and immunities, some of which are completely new, while others were previously guaranteed in theory but ignored or repeatedly violated in practice. He has the right to be a free economic agent within the framework of a family or co-operative business. If he is employed in the state sector, he can elect his superiors and has the right to be consulted about their major decisions. He enjoys the protection of a criminal law whose penalties have been moderated, and where the accused is explicitly presumed innocent till proved guilty. He is guaranteed freedom of belief and worship, the right to undertake charitable activity and to give religious instruction to his children. He is free from arbitrary arrest, his telephone conversations and personal correspondence are confidential, his home in inviolable. He can participate in political life by choosing between different candidates put forward for soviets at local, republican and all-Union level; to exercise this right responsibly, he is entitled to obtain information and discuss it openly with others. He can join with like-minded fellow citizens in voluntary associations of all kinds, including political ones designed to oppose the Communist Party.

Much of this is already enshrined in law. Some of it has still to be embodied in legislation being drafted in the ministries and in the committees of the Supreme Soviet. As a whole, though, it testifies to a legal consciousness in the authorities and among the educated public not very different from that prevailing in western Europe.

Unfortunately, however, the political underpinning is still lacking, and without it the law on its own is a fragile and uncertain instrument. The Communist Party's monopoly may in theory have been abolished and a multi-party system sanctioned, but the party is still the closest thing to a Union-wide political organisation, and it still has its own departments in the KGB and the armed forces. Furthermore, as we shall see in the next chapter, the 'informal' political associations have not yet become full-scale parties, nor have they found a way of interacting effectively with state institutions at central or local level.

The political system has not, then, yet been brought into line with the new legal spirit, but it has all the same come a long way since 1988. It received its first real test in the Congress of People's

Deputies which met in May–June 1989. The Congress was constituted in such a way as to ensure the dominance of the apparatus. One-third of the seats were reserved for 'public organisations' – which meant not the informal associations which I have described at length, but rather the established institutions and corporations of Soviet society, such as the Communist Party, the Komsomol, the Council of Soviet Women, and the Council of War and Labour Veterans, all of which are thoroughly penetrated by the *nomenklatura* and its appointees. In many of these institutions, including the Communist party itself, the election of delegates proceeded in time-honoured fashion through the authoritative nomination of just enough candidates to fill the seats available. Only in a few cases – like, as might be expected, the Academy of Sciences and the creative unions – were there serious and vigorously contested electoral meetings which produced a few oppositional delegates. One of them was Andrei Sakharov, who, however, was finally elected only after a virtual *coup d'état* in the Presidium of the Academy of Sciences.[42]

In the other two-thirds of seats, elected in normal territorial constituencies, electoral commissions could and did arrange procedures in such a way as to discourage unofficial candidates. Denied any access to the curia for 'public organisations', the informal associations had to put forward their candidates for these constituency seats. As we have seen (Chapter 5), they did remarkably well in a few cases, especially in the Baltic. But overall the domination of the apparatus remained overwhelming: 85 per cent of deputies to the Congress were members of the CPSU – more than was usual in the old unreformed Supreme Soviet. Not that party membership is a fair measure of loyalism, since some elected party members were oppositional in outlook, while some non-party delegates were unswervingly deferential. However one measures it, though, not more than 15 to 20 per cent of deputies could be considered oppositional.[43]

Even this modest admixture made a startling difference from the insipid unanimity of previous Soviet legislative assemblies. As it turned out, the Congress of People's Deputies faithfully reflected the ambiguities of the new political system. Convening without its procedures or even its functions fully worked out, it could be saved from chaos during its first days only by the adroit and authoritarian chairmanship of Gorbachev himself. He handled the procedural wrangles skilfully and forthrightly, intervening in good-humoured manner to put speakers right and even on occasions prompting or correcting the deputy chairmen who stood in for him. More substantial controversies he diverted into 'special commissions' for prolonged examination. It was a virtuoso display of what might be called 'presidential democracy'. In keeping with the new spirit, it did not go unchallenged: several speakers rebuked him for his constant interruptions.[44]

According to the political reform agreed at the 19th Party Conference, the Congress was to meet for only a few days, and its principal duty was to elect the head of state and the 540 delegates to the new-style Supreme Soviet, which was to meet for several months each year and carry out the substantive work of law-making. Even those fundamental parameters were not accepted without question by all deputies. There were a few who felt that, like the Estates General of 1789, the Congress should assume the powers of a sovereign popular assembly. Andrei Sakharov argued at the outset that the Congress should itself take on the supreme law-making function, and not delegate that responsibility to a haphazardly elected one-quarter of its members.[45] He was supported by A. Obolenskii, who proposed that the leading role of the party should be expunged from the constitution, and the slogan 'All power to the Soviets' made into a reality. The Congress should moreover act immediately, he exhorted, for who could be certain that it would not suffer the fate of the Constituent Assembly in 1918 (which was forcibly dissolved by Lenin before it could hold its second meeting because its elected majority was opposed to Bolshevik rule).[46]

Constitutional controversies of this kind were constantly being inflamed by ethnic tensions. When Gorbachev proposed that a new constitutional control commission should adjudicate on issues of disputed sovereignty between Moscow and the union republics, the Lithuanians walked out in support of their claim that all powers belonged to the republics unless specifically entrusted by agreement to Moscow. To mollify them, a decision had to be delayed, while a special commission was mandated to study the issue, with radical and non-Russian representatives sitting on it. Yet another commission was set up on the insistence of the Balts, to examine the Nazi-Soviet Pact of 1939, and therefore the basis on which rested the Baltic republics' membership of the USSR.[47]

There were sharp disagreements on the crucial matter of the procedure to be adopted in electing the members of the Supreme Soviet. The Lithuanian delegation spoke for many of the non-Russians in urging that those elections should be held in republican and regional caucuses. Otherwise, argued Vytautas Landsbergis, chairman of Sajudis, the Lithuanian delegates would be elected by a vast body of deputies who could not possibly know them individually. 'We are entitled not to vote in the dark,' he proclaimed, and threatened that the Lithuanians would boycott the ballot. This proposal to regionalise the elections was opposed both by the rank-and-file deputies, and by the Russian radicals, who did not want to see the reform drive fragmented and dissipated by ethnic animosities. 'We are not electing the Lithuanian Supreme Soviet, but the USSR Supreme Soviet,' declared the historian Roy Medvedev.[48]

The Moscow radicals were, however, also concerned about the crude majority voting power held by the rump of the deputies, which seemed set to bolster and perpetuate the power of the apparatus under the new system. 'The apparatus has been in power for decades,' stormed economist Gavriil Popov, 'and the leadership has got nowhere as a result of that, except into a blind alley.' He warned that Moscow's scientific and cultural delegates might break away from the rest of the capital city's delegation and vote separately.[49]

The results of the voting were exactly as Popov and his colleagues had feared. The radical Moscow delegates, being conspicuous targets, received a particularly high number of negative votes, and El'tsin failed to be returned. He eventually secured a place in the Supreme Soviet only because another delegate altruistically yielded his seat.[50] The might of the usually silent majority was occasionally made noisily manifest, as when they acclaimed General Rodionov, commander of the troops involved in the Tbilisi massacre, or when they shouted down Sakharov for attacking atrocities committed by the Soviet Army in Afghanistan.

If the Congress of People's Deputies carried out its constitutional functions unevenly, it fulfilled its informal ones with sensational success. John Stuart Mill taught that one of the crucial roles of any legislative assembly is to inform the public and stimulate political debate. This the Congress achieved with a vengeance. Operating with greater glasnost than the British House of Commons, it allowed its proceedings to be televised live. From Vil'nyus to Vladivostok, from Arkhangel'sk to Astrakhan', the Soviet peoples were transfixed in front of their television sets, watching the spectacle of their lives, the last and greatest 'return of the repressed'. They saw Egor Ligachev, the party's agricultural chief, ridiculed as a man who had 'failed in ideology' and knew not the first thing about agriculture. They saw the weightlifter Yurii Vlasov denounce the KGB as 'an underground empire stained with blood'. They saw the Minister of the Interior summoned to the rostrum without warning to explain why the police had forcibly broken up a peaceful political meeting in Moscow the previous evening. They saw General Rodionov, commander of the Caucasian Military District, squirming in the face of hostile questions about why his troops had used spades and poison gas to massacre peaceful demonstrators in Tbilisi. And in the evenings Muscovites would leave their televisions and go off to public meetings, at Luzhniki Stadium or elsewhere, to hear their deputies report on the day's speeches and to ask probing questions.[51]

Another achievement of the Congress of People's Deputies,

though it remained incomplete, was to begin the process of crys-
tallising a formal parliamentary opposition, known as the Inter-
regional Group of Deputies, with its nucleus among the Moscow
radicals and the Baltic representatives. They were not numerous,
but they were vociferous, and they addressed the chambers with
the confidence that they spoke for millions of concerned and
informed fellow-citizens. As the political scientist L. Batkin commented, 'A constructive opposition, resting on a mass movement
of voters' clubs and Popular Fronts, is already on the agenda.'[52]
The appearance of the Inter-regional Group, and their support
for the national liberation movements, eventually provoked the
creation of a countervailing 'legitimist' caucus, under the name
Soyuz, directed against 'separatism, chauvinism and nationalism',
and dedicated to the conservation of the Union.[53]

At this stage Andrei Sakharov called Gorbachev's political
reform 'a campaign to achieve democratic change by undemocratic means'.[54] That aptly sums up the institutional paradox
which was on display at the first Congress of People's Deputies,
and which was rooted in the Soviet Union's whole political culture. A Communist Party proclaiming on its banners the rule of
law and respect for individual human rights was still insisting on
its right to a dominant rule in politics. Great advances were being
made, but over roadblocks which were not being removed, and
which were to prove obstructive as the conflicts engendered by
political reform intensified.

8

From 'informals' to political parties

The elections of spring 1989 were only the first stage in the mobilisation of public opinion against the regime which had so long disdained it. The second stage was strongly influenced by events in Eastern Europe in the autumn. The spectacle (daily watched on television by millions of Soviet viewers) of crowds surging through the streets of Leipzig and Prague, peacefully toppling regimes previously considered impregnable, proved to be highly infectious.

In the first days of the new year (on the Orthodox Christmas Eve, as it happened) there was a minor road accident in the Ukrainian town of Chernigov. One of the cars involved belonged to a senior local Communist Party official, and it was his misfortune that the impact caused his boot lid to spring open. Inside inquisitive passers-by spotted tins of best-quality ham, smoked salmon, French wine and cognac – luxuries undreamed of in the daily struggle to buy bread and sausage meat in empty shops. An indignant crowd gathered and manhandled the car, towing it to party headquarters, where they demanded the resignation of its occupant and then, getting into the spirit of the occasion, that of the regional first secretary as well. Within a few days they had secured both.[1]

The hapless Chernigov apparatchik had only been acquiring what for decades had been considered an undisputed perquisite of his official position. Yet now, all of a sudden, a public which had always shrugged its shoulders helplessly at these routine abuses was deciding to put up with them no longer. The Chernigov incident proved to be only the first of a whole series which over the next few months brought large crowds out on the squares of provincial Russia and Ukraine, calling for (and often winning) the resignation of local party bosses.

Perhaps the best-publicised was the drama in Volgograd, where an article by an investigative journalist from *Ogonyok* revealed that the first secretary, Vladimir Kalashnikov, had been allocating apartments to friends and relatives, jumping the queue ahead of war veterans, some of whom had been on the waiting list for decades. At two dramatic plenums of the regional party committee, both broadcast live, Kalashnikov was questioned closely about this and other suspected abuses. Between the two plenums there were large street demonstrations, organised by informal political groups, representatives of which were allowed to attend the second plenum. In the end Kalashnikov and most of the party bureau were forced to resign. Thereafter surviving party officials met with the informals at a special conference to begin the work of remoulding local government on a new basis in time for the approaching local elections.[2]

In a sense, of course, these upheavals were what Gorbachev had been aiming at with his policy of glasnost: the public was mobilising to drive corrupt officials from office. But their new-found initiative could be turned against him too: on the first of May, demonstrators on Red Square confronted Gorbachev himself with slogans like 'Seventy years on the road to nowhere!' and 'An unelected president is a dictator!' He turned his back on them and stalked off the podium.[3]

These oppositional demonstrations brought to a head a split which had long been maturing within the party. A new kind of alliance, adumbrated already a couple of years earlier, was being cemented and preparing itself to offer a real political alternative, not just locally but even at the centre: that of radical Communists with the leaders of the 'informals'. 'Party clubs' had long existed in many areas, consisting of members anxious to work with the 'informals' rather than condemn them as 'extremists'. Now radical minorities in the local party leaderships were getting together with initiative groups and Popular Fronts to consider how best to reform the system, at first locally and ultimately at a national level. The Polish 'round table' of 1989 offered an example of what might be achieved by such methods.

At the centre the Inter-Regional Group of Deputies was the obvious focus for such negotiations. Set up at the first Congress of People's Deputies under the leadership of Boris El'tsin, and with the support of Andrei Sakharov, it included deputies from several parts of the USSR, especially the big cities and the Baltic, and it was calling for human rights, a substantial private sector in the economy, and a federation based on a new treaty between the Union republics. It started publishing a regular broadsheet and opened a centre for the collection and storing of socio-political information and the drafting of alternative versions of laws – rather along the lines suggested by Boris Kurashvili.[4]

In the summer and autumn of 1989, Associations of Voters were set up in Moscow and a number of provincial towns to co-ordinate the nomination of candidates supporting the Inter-Regional Group, and then to organise their campaigns, in preparation for the local elections of spring 1990. The object was to ensure that some oppositional candidates, but not too many, were registered in each constituency, and to help them circumnavigate the legal and practical obstacles put up by electoral officials who were often in the pockets of the party apparatus. In Moscow the Voters' Association co-operated closely with a bloc called 'Elections-90', which included a broad span of liberals and socialists such as the Moscow Popular Front, Memorial, the Social Democratic Association, the party club 'Communists for Perestroika', the Club of Anarcho-Syndicalists and the writers' club April. On the democratic wing of politics only the Democratic Union, set up in May 1988 as the first opposition party in the

Soviet Union, declined to participate: it boycotted all Soviet elections on principle.[5]

Out of this co-operation grew a loose political alliance, called 'Democratic Russia', designed to outlast the elections and offer a coherent opposition to the Communist Party apparatus in the soviets of the RSFSR. Its electoral programme invoked the memory of Andrei Sakharov, who had recently died, and commended his proposals for a new Soviet constitution and a new government. 'The first Congress of People's Deputies of the RSFSR should do what has not yet been achieved at all-Union level, assume *the full power of the state in the RSFSR*.' The new bloc identified as its principal enemy 'the conservative elements in the apparatus who preach the egalitarianism of poverty and stir up zoological chauvinism'. Against them 'Democratic Russia' asserted the patriotism of a democratic Russian state no longer claiming imperial power over its neighbours, but bound by treaty relations with its equal and sovereign Soviet partners.[6]

The formation of this bloc was a historic turning point in Russian political theory and practice. In the past it had always been thought that a patriotic movement in Russia must be authoritarian and imperialist. This was the first time a patriotic organisation had explicitly recognised that a democratic Russian nation state could only be created by renouncing the Russian empire. The age-old confusion of 'nation' and 'empire' was on the way to being resolved. As the political philosopher Alexander Tsipko put it, 'there are two distinct processes taking place in Russia: democratisation and reawakening of national self-consciousness. If these two processes are separated, it will be very dangerous.'[7]

The elections of March-April 1990 in the RSFSR produced *apparat* majorities in most local soviets, but 'Democratic Russia' did well enough to secure, by a narrow margin, the election of Boris El'tsin as Chairman of the RSFSR Congress of People's Deputies and the declaration of sovereignty of the RSFSR. In addition, radicals took control of some of the major cities, electing mayors like the economist Gavriil Popov in Moscow and the lawyer Anatolii Sobchak in Leningrad.

The march of the radicals into the town halls was observed with mixed feelings inside the CPSU. The Communist Party is not a political party in the normal sense, but essentially a kind of 'closed shop' for the Soviet establishment. It was natural therefore that in turbulent times it should generate from within its own counter-establishment, ready to make common cause with the 'informals' in an attempt to reform the Soviet political system.

For the mavericks of the CPSU to set up a radical movement *within* the party was, however, a further step of momentous import. Ever since 1921 'fractions' and 'platforms' inside the party had been strictly prohibited on the authority of Lenin himself. Nevertheless, contemplating the increasingly radical and impatient public mood, some Communists began to feel it was time for this taboo to be infringed, if the party was not to be left stranded by the political tide.

In January 1990 some 450 Communist radicals convened for a weekend conference in Moscow, at which they created the 'Democratic Platform', whose declared aim was to prepare the CPSU for the transition to a new, pluralist politics. Its policy statement anticipated the abolition of the party's political monopoly and recommended 'the creation of a multi-party system, the transformation of the CPSU into a political party of the parliamentary type and the abandonment of the principle of democratic centralism'. As Vladimir Lysenko, one of its leaders, commented: 'From a commanding structure which directs everything, the CPSU should become a purely political party which bases its right to leadership exclusively on its own authority, and which acquires that right only by means of parliamentary general elections.'[8]

At the February Central Committee plenum, when Gorbachev proposed the abolition of Article 6 of the Soviet constitution (which had guaranteed the party's 'leading role'), he used language reminiscent of the Democratic Platform, talking of 'breaking with the authoritarian-bureaucratic system', encouraging pluralism and 'opening up dialogue with the new political organisations'. There was, however, a subtle but important difference of emphasis in his approach: he still regarded the CPSU as a 'vanguard', embodying the spirit of the Soviet state, only now required regularly to prove its right to this role by winning elections rather than relying complacently on a constitutional guarantee. The Central Committee's response to the Democratic Platform reflected this ambivalence: it conceded most of the points the Platform was making, and called for a full and frank discussion, yet still condemned the Platform's creators for weakening party unity and thus undermining the drive for perestroika.[9]

In any case Gorbachev was preparing by this time to transfer the centre of gravity of his authority away from the party into the state Presidency (see previous chapter). He seems at this stage to have envisaged using the next party congress (the 28th, brought forward to June 1990) to carry through corresponding changes in the party, democratising its elections at all levels, cutting down the size of the Central Committee and abolishing the executive post of General Secretary, replacing it with the more honorary position of Party Chairman.[10]

Before he could get that far, however, the adversaries of the Democratic Platform had also swung into action, determined to preserve the party's existing structure and as far as possible its dominance, and to hold the Soviet Union together under the tutelage of Russia.

Already since the autumn of 1988, Russian nationalists, faced with the vociferous and organised anti-Russianism they encountered in most of the non-Russian republics, had set about creating their own organisations, beginning with the Interfronts mentioned in Chapter 5. By the autumn of 1989, they, like the radicals, were trying to consolidate in anticipation of the approaching elections. However, unlike the radicals, who created open organisations to which people could belong as individuals, the nationalists tended to establish separate organisations for distinct social collectives:

for soldiers and officers Fatherland (*Otechestvo*), for Orthodox clergy and lay believers the Union for Spiritual Rebirth of the Fatherland, for artists and creative intellectuals the Association of Russian Artists and the 'Unity' Association of Lovers of Russian Literature (intended to ally Ukrainians and Belorussians with Russians). For Russians living in non-Russian republics, there were the International Fronts and Unity movements. Most important of all, the United Workers' Front was set up in September 1989 to mobilise the 'leading class' to defend socialism, the Communist Party and the integrity of the Union. An important element in its platform was the registration of the population for elections on the 'production principle', that is to say at the workplace rather than at their place of residence. It was natural for the Communist Party to prefer this system, since it had its cell at every workplace and could most conveniently organise and agitate there, while the 'informals' had to use the streets and squares.[11]

The conservatives formed their own equivalent of Democratic Russia, a 'bloc of social-patriotic movements of Russia', whose election manifesto proclaimed 'the Fatherland is in danger! . . . The deepening political crisis has cast in doubt the existence of a thousand-year-old power as a socio-economic and moral-cultural whole.' It warned that the party was capitulating to 'left-wing radicals' and was about to sell out the people's wealth to western business interests. The only hope was to rally round the 'Great Russian Federation'.[12]

The 'social-patriotic bloc' did poorly in the elections, however. In the big cities, where it had hoped for working-class support, nearly all its candidates were defeated in the first round, including such well-known personalities as Stanislav Kunyaev, editor of the literary journal *Nash sovremennik*, and Il'ya Glazunov, the painter.[13]

Rejected by voters, the conservatives adopted an alternative plan instead. They decided to utilise the Communist Party as a vehicle for their aims. Their strategy was to revive the Communist

Party of Russia. Since 1922 Russia had been unique among the republics in not having its own Communist Party. That had never mattered in the past. But now that the non-Russian Communist parties were becoming overtly nationalist, it did matter that no republican party organisation was specifically representing Russia's interests. Conservatives wanted to set it up in order to use it as a counterweight both to the non-Russian Communists and to the Democratic Platform. This device had a cunning but double-edged twist to it. A Russian Communist Party would not have to be a 'fraction': once formed, it would automatically absorb as its birthright all the party organisations on the territory of the RSFSR. That was both its strength and its weakness. On the one hand, no organisational efforts would be required to make it a formidable voting bloc at the forthcoming 28th Party Congress. On the other hand, it would never be 'pure': it would always contain an infuriating and perhaps growing minority of radicals who would water down its resolutions and blunt its cutting edge.

This drawback was evident at the Russian Communist Party's founding congress in June 1990. Most of the delegates came by unreconstructed nomenklatura nomination from the provincial apparatus, and they elected the colourless and highly conservative Ivan Polozkov from Krasnodar as their first secretary. They heaped reproaches on Gorbachev for having no strategic plan and leaving Communists defenceless in the face of their enemies – 'crouching unarmed in trenches under massive shelling from anti-socialist forces,' as one speaker put it.[14] General Makashov, from the Urals Military District, warned that radicals recommending the abolition of the army's political departments were deliberately 'undermining the fighting capacity of their own armed forces.' If the state refrained from taking action against such agitators, he added, then 'the people should stone the traitors.'[15] All the same, the resolutions passed cannot have satisfied those who wanted urgent action to stop the rot: they were unexciting, even evasive, and did not differ markedly from Gorbachev's own outlook.

Besides, the very strategy of using the Soviet Communist Party as a means of mobilising public opinion was by now outmoded. Executive power had shifted sideways to the Presidency and downwards to the Supreme Soviets, national Communist parties and even Popular Fronts in the republics. Delegates from the Russian Communist Party did succeed in setting the tone of the 28th Party Congress, but it did not do them much good: they had no alternative strategy to propose and no prospective leader to carry it out. They therefore voted for Gorbachev and his programme. In any case they were operating within a power vacuum. At the end of the Congress, the Politburo was doubled in size to admit representatives of each of the fifteen Union republics, rendering it too large to be an effective executive body: besides, it no longer contained the party's principal ideologist, the Prime Minister, Foreign Minister, Defence Minister, the chairman of the KGB or the head of Gosplan, all of whom had resigned or been displaced from it. The post of Deputy General Secretary was created, and Vladimir Ivashko was brought from Ukraine to fill it, so that Gorbachev could devote more attention to the patently more important job of state President.[16]

In the end, neither the Democratic Platform nor the Russian Communists got their way. The Soviet Communist Party was shown by its congress to be divided, irresolute and increasingly less relevant. Adherents of the Democratic Platform, having failed to turn it into a party of parliamentary type, duly announced their separate existence. However, they seemed reluctant actually to quit the party, claiming to oppose not it, but the 'conservatives from the nomenklatura camp' who had usurped power within it. The truth seems to be that, whatever the political weight of the CPSU, it still owned an immense amount of property, means of communication, and so on, which could be very useful to an inheritor: the Democratic Platform was anxious to claim its share of these assets.[17]

By the autumn of 1990, then, the CPSU was no longer quite a ruling party, but it could certainly not be said that a multi-party system had come into existence. It is true, there was by now in the RSFSR an abundance of so-called 'political parties', formed from splintering Popular Fronts and electoral blocs. Though there were many of them, their political programmes had a lot in common. Whether Anarcho-Syndicalists, New Socialists, Greens, Constitutional Monarchists, Liberal Democrats, Constitutional Democrats, Social Democrats, Christian Democrats, or just plain Democrats, they all agreed on the necessity to dismantle totalitarian structures, to establish a market economy, to guarantee civil rights, to create a pluralist political system and a federal state, from which any republic would have the right to withdraw. Thereafter emphases differed somewhat. New Socialists wanted economic enterprises to be run by their workers; the Confederation of Anarcho-Syndicalists agreed about that, and also aimed at maximum decentralisation of government, so that power would be concentrated in self-governing local soviets. Social Democrats envisaged an extensive system of social security, to protect the disadvantaged against the vagaries of the market. The Russian patriotic movements, which I have described on p 176, really did differ from most of the parties in their aims, though even they agreed about dismantling totalitarianism.[18]

Some of these 'parties' seem to consist of little more than a handful of enthusiasts, a telephone number, a news sheet and (sometimes) a word processor. None of them has a clearly identifiable source of mass support. Since there are so many of them, and they have so much in common, one is bound to ask why they do not try harder to amalgamate into fewer and larger associations. Organisational inexperience, lack of information, personal ambitions and antipathies all help to explain their reluctance or inability to do so. Some observers maintain that the Communist Party is deliberately encouraging the creation of numerous splinter groups, in order to divide and defeat the opposition.[19] There may be something in this, but I suspect that the habits of the *kruzhok* are still strong in the world of embryonic multi-party politics.

The group which has perhaps the greatest potential for uniting something like a coherent opposition round itself is 'Democratic Russia'. This loose association of deputies from the anti-apparatus majority in the RSFSR Supreme Soviet grew out of the electoral pacts of spring 1990, and has tried to perpetuate them into the parliament. Its members represent all the political views I have outlined, and more besides. At its congress in Moscow on 20 September – 1 October 1990 nine political parties and eighteen associations were represented, including Memorial and the writers' club April. To judge by a Moscow Radio report, the congress was highly charged and inconclusive.[20] The attempt to create a nationwide party to back up the efforts of their deputies has also foundered on a split, over the eternal vexed question of how far to co-operate with the party-state apparatus.[21]

In short, then, none of the Russian parties possesses the resources, finances, organisational strength or popular support which would enable them to throw their weight around the political battlefield. Only a loose coalition like Democratic Russia, which does not even have any voting discipline, can exercise continuing influence, and that in a wavering and amorphous manner, and only within the soviets of the RSFSR. To present a coherent opposition – even perhaps to serve in a coalition government of 'public confidence' – the parties need to work together much more closely than they have found possible so far.

In the summer of 1989 a whole new social class made its dramatic appearance as an organised force on the political scene – perhaps the most significant and certainly the most numerous of all: the working class. First in the Kuzbass, then in the Donbass and Vorkuta, miners refused to go down the pit, filed into the main squares of their towns and sat there round the clock – shift replacing shift like those at the coal face – discussing, formulating and declaring their demands. These varied from one town to another, but can be divided into two main categories. First, there were the purely economic demands: for higher pay, holiday entitlements and social welfare benefits, for more satisfactory safety precautions, for better housing, medical care and supplies (particular indignation was caused by the shortage of soap, peculiarly demeaning to a worker who emerges from his shift covered in grime). Then there were demands for reforms in the structure of their industry: for the legal and economic autonomy of their mines, for the right of work brigades to lease shafts and conclude contracts, selling their coal at market prices. (The Kuzbass miners were especially interested in this, since their coal is more economical to produce than that of the Donbass, and they hoped to sell some of it to the Japanese – and perhaps buy Hondas in return!) Yet their devotion to private enterprise was selective: many of the strike committees complained of the high prices for food and consumer goods charged by the recently established co-operatives, and the Donetsk oblast soviet actually passed a decree banning further registration of them.

Not the least remarkable aspect of the strikes was the degree of organisation and peacefulness displayed by the miners. At each pithead, initiative groups, without the authorisation of the party authorities or the official trade unions, convened meetings to elect strike committees, which in turn organised the strikes, negotiated with the authorities, and made contact with other pits which had come out. They were determined the strikes should be orderly, and set up a *druzhina*, or patrol, to keep drunks and troublemakers away from the squares and help the militia keep order in the towns. They arranged for maintenance work to be kept up in the mines, and insisted that some enterprises in their towns should stay at work, to provide services, like transport, for ordinary people. At this stage they also kept away intellectuals and representatives of the informal political movements, regarding them with suspicion as alien to the miners' movement.

Revealingly, the strike committees soon found that members of the public came to them with all kinds of requests and complaints, about housing, medical care and other matters, which had not received satisfaction through normal channels. They were, in short, accepted with amazing rapidity as legitimate authorities by most of the population. In all these respects, they were strongly reminiscent of the soviets of 1905 and 1917, which had also arisen almost overnight to replace corrupt and unresponsive local authorities. Soviet history seemed to have come full circle! Like their predecessors, these committees remained in being after the strike was over, and established working relations with their neighbours to form regional miners' associations.

The position of local party secretaries was tricky. On the one hand, they could utilise the miners' demands to beef up their own lobbying on behalf of their regions; on the other, the miners regarded them with suspicion and resentment, and Moscow was likely to blame them for allowing matters to get out of hand. It is not surprising that between these dual pressures, a number of regional party secretaries resigned or were dismissed. The official trade unions were in an even less enviable situation: they belatedly hastened to espouse many of the miners' demands, and even appeared on the scene with hot meals for their meetings. But the miners had decided by now that they were quite capable of presenting their own case without mediation, so that the official unions took no part in their negotiations with the government.

These negotiations went not just to the coal minister, Shchadov, but right up to prime minister Ryzhkov, before they produced a settlement. The government signed an agreement promising concessions on most of the points at issue, with a precise timetable for implementation. The initial purpose of the strike committee's remaining in being was to monitor the fulfilment of this agreement.[22]

Only as it became apparent that the government either could not or would not carry out its side of the bargain did the strike committees gradually begin to espouse political demands, to take up links with other workers outside the coalmining industry, and eventually to create nationwide workers' unions independent of the official structures. This was far from easy to accomplish, though. The interests of one group of workers did not necessarily coincide with those of others: even among miners, for example, the Kuzbass had a greater interest in a market economy, since their coal was more economical to mine. The elaboration of political goals required greater input from intellectuals and from existing political movements, yet many workers remained mistrustful of all outsiders.

The first organisation to combine miners with workers from other industries was the Kuzbass Workers' Union, set up in autumn 1989 on the initiative of the Kuzbass strike committees. It took the lead in trying to establish a Union-wide alternative trade union structure to replace the official All-Union Council of Trade Unions which had by now proved its impotence. This was a slow and frustrating process, because of the variety of viewpoints involved and the reluctance of many workers to be drawn into an explicit political stance. In autumn 1989, for example, when the Vorkuta miners struck demanding the abolition of Article 6 of the Soviet constitution (i.e. of the party's political monopoly) and the removal of party cells from all state institutions, they found little support from workers elsewhere. Similarly Sakharov's call in December 1989 for a two-hour 'warning strike' in support of the Inter-regional Group's political programme fell more or less on deaf ears.[23]

All the same, the first congress of the newly created Confederation of Labour finally took place at the beginning of May 1990, bringing together some 34 regional workers' committees, and it did adopt a political declaration, calling for abolition of the exclusive status of Communist Party cells in enterprises and in official institutions such as the armed forces, KGB, courts and procuracy. The new Confederation demanded the resignation of the government, because of its economic incompetence and its close links with the 'party-state bureaucracy', and its replacement by a government enjoying the confidence of the workers and including participants from 'democratic social movements' (*demokraticheskaya obshchestvennost'*).[24]

In June 1990 an independent Miners' Union was formed with its headquarters in Donetsk. It heralded a new principle in Soviet labour organisation, in that it accepted for membership only genuine miners: managers and administrators were excluded. The demands formulated at its founding congress were similar to those of the Confederation of Labour.[25] Its declaration sparked off 24-hour strikes and other forms of action in pits over much of the country on 11 July, the anniversary of the original strikes. In addition, some collectives started voting to expel the Communist Party from their pits. The strikes were not, however, supported everywhere even within the coal industry, and received very little support from outside. Indeed, some leading democratic politicians, including Boris El'tsin and Nikolai Travkin, requested the miners to postpone the strike in order not to aggravate the already very serious economic troubles.[26]

The official trade unions (the All-Union Central Council of Trade Unions) have responded only sluggishly to the opportunities and hazards of the new era. Only in April 1990 did they kick out their Brezhnevite leaders and draw up a new charter proclaiming their independence from the Communist Party. Since then they have taken up more boldly the defence of workers' material interests, understood as the fight against co-operatives, price rises and lay-offs. Unlike the independent unions, then, they are pitching their tent in the camp of those who want to hedge the market economy round with restrictions. On the other hand, in direct imitation of their rivals, they are now preparing to decentralise and establish regional federations to respond more rapidly to workers' grievances. What will come of this remains to be seen: many workers, especially the more skilled, continue to be suspicious of them.[27]

An independent labour movement is now a fact of Soviet life – there is even a trade union for servicemen in the armed forces, called *Shchit*, or 'shield'. There is also a remarkable degree of agreement about the political programme which that movement should espouse: decisive transition to a market economy, removal of the Communist Party from enterprises and from official institutions, return of property to the people, and creation of a multi-party democracy with a coalition government of popular confidence to handle the tricky transition period. Yet the workers have had great difficulty in agreeing on the best strategy for achieving that programme, and in attracting consistent support from the democratic politicians and movements. In one sense, they are *too* powerful: any serious strike is a grave setback for the already weak economy, and threatens to backfire on the workers themselves. Even a threat from a single group of workers can have consequences very destructive to some sector of the community. When the Tyumen' oil workers, discontented at poor deliveries of household supplies and building materials, threaten to reduce the flow of heating fuel, then the authorities in Moscow and Leningrad have to react, if necessary by concluding some kind of barter agreement.[28] All this aggravates the disintegration of the economy, its breakdown into regionalised units cobbling together bilateral deals.

The labour movement, then, displays the traditional strengths and weaknesses of popular movements in Russia. It has shown a remarkable capacity for improvisation and local self-organisation (many of its most successful campaigns having been ethnic ones – see Chapters 5 and 9), while finding it much harder to create structures above the regional level and to make the crucial linkage with political movements active in central politics. Since economic reform is (at best) so much slower than political reform, there is a danger that the labour movement will not only weaken the economy but deepen the fragmentation of politics. As against that, the workers' unanimous hatred of the apparatus has helped them to disdain the allures of the United Workers' Front and to achieve a measure of unity on a political programme which includes the transfer to a market whose blessings for them are not unmixed.

9

Towards the dissolution of the Soviet Union

Up to the autumn of 1989, it did not seem that the burgeoning national liberation movements described in Chapter 5 posed a threat to the integrity of the Soviet Union. At that stage most or all Soviet nations would probably have welcomed a proposal to set up a new Soviet federation by renegotiating the treaty between constituent republics which had originally formed the Soviet Union in 1922. The long-awaited Communist Party Central Committee plenum of September 1989, however, missed its opportunity: it talked vaguely of a federation, but clearly envisaged one whose main features would be laid down by Moscow, not hammered out in negotiations between sovereign partners. The plenum insisted, moreover, that the Communist Party should remain centralised, not break up into national self-governing units, and that Russian should continue to be an official language throughout the USSR.[1]

During the next few months, the situation was transformed, not least as a result of the demonstration effect from Eastern Europe. The sight of the nations there freeing themselves from the Communist Party and the Warsaw Pact, especially the sensational street revolutions in the GDR, Czechoslovakia and Romania, had an intoxicating effect on the nations of the Soviet Union. The self-emancipation of Eastern Europe was perceived immediately as one of those major historical turning points when huge power structures undergo tectonic upheavals, and great new opportunities are open to those who act decisively. National independence began to seem a practical possibility, even though there were great differences within and between nations about whether and how it might be achieved. Those differences were concealed in many cases under the word 'sovereignty', which could be used to mean anything from limited self-government to complete independence outside the USSR. A declaration of 'sovereignty' was a palpable challenge to Moscow, but did not yet constitute a threat of divorce, nor did it predetermine the future of the nation which made it.

The Balts were in the vanguard. The Estonians had issued a declaration of 'sovereignty' as early as November 1988, defining it as the right to veto any law which came from Moscow.[2] But it took a further year of political debate and of symbolic assertions of nationhood before all three nations decided that 'sovereignty' could only be definitely secured by secession from the USSR. The question remained how it should be done.

One tactic was to work through existing Soviet institutions. The elections of March 1990 offered the hope that in all three Baltic republics the Popular Fronts would win majorities in their Supreme Soviets, which would then declare that independence was the goal and open negotiations with Moscow in order to achieve it. In Estonia and Latvia, however, many people were nervous that the sizeable non-indigenous population (35 per cent in Estonia and very nearly half in Latvia), with their 'Interfronts', would be able, with the help of the Communist Party, to block the way. Some therefore espoused an alternative non-Soviet procedure, one which excluded from politics all post-1940 immigrants. Starting from the premise that incorporation in the USSR under the Nazi-Soviet Pact had been acknowledged as an illegal act and was therefore null and void, they registered everyone who had been citizens of Estonia and Latvia in June 1940, together with their direct descendants. On the basis of these lists they then held elections to a national congress whose function would be to restore the constitutional status quo of pre-1940. The movement received overwhelming support: in Estonia an estimated 93 per cent of those entitled to register actually did so, and 98 per cent of those turned out to vote in the elections.[3]

In the event, however, the Lithuanians were the first actually to declare independence from the USSR, and they did so through existing Soviet institutions, on 11 March 1990. Lithuanians constitute 80 per cent of their republic's population, so that they did not share the worries of the Estonians and Latvians, and were able to use their Supreme Soviet for the purpose. The way was prepared by the Lithuanian Communist Party which in December 1989 broke away from the CPSU and reconstituted itself as a self-governing national party. This meant that both Sajudis and the Communist Party were agreed in seeking secession from the USSR. Despite differences of nuance, they could and did work together, and so there was no need for an alternative Lithuanian Congress.[4]

The Lithuanian declaration was precipitated by the constitutional rearrangements going on in Moscow in February-March 1990 after the CPSU's renunciation of its monopoly: Gorbachev was seeking new powers as Soviet President which, in the opinion of many, would enable him to prevent a republic seceding from the USSR.

Gorbachev refused to accept the Lithuanian declaration, and countered it by putting forward a law stipulating the procedure to be followed by any republic wishing to leave the USSR. This was a considerable step forward from the Communist Party's unyielding stance of the previous September, and it was the first time in Soviet history that the right to secede, always theoretically acknowledged, had been defined in practical terms. Yet the steps envisaged on the way to independence were cumbersome, and they were to be under the control of Moscow. First, there would have to be a two-thirds majority in a referendum; then there was to be a transition period of up to five years for the details of secession to be negotiated, during which time Soviet law would remain in force; then finally, the USSR Congress of People's

Deputies would meet to confirm that the process had been duly completed.[5]

One has the sense here, not for the first time, of Gorbachev making belated and inadequate concessions. Even a few months earlier, such a law on secession might well have been acceptable to most republics. Now the Lithuanians rejected it out of hand. For his part, Gorbachev refused to negotiate with them unless they withdrew their declaration of independence and accepted the new procedures. He backed up his words by imposing an economic blockade on the rebel republic. This did not dissuade the other two Baltic republics from announcing their determination to follow Lithuania's example, albeit by somewhat different routes. On 30 March the Estonian Supreme Soviet announced that it was entering a 'transition period' towards the restoration of the pre-1940 constitution, and called on Moscow to enter negotiations as between two equal sovereign partners.[6] This avoided a Lithuanian-style *fait accompli*, but all the same was equally forthright in declining to recognise Moscow's right to determine procedures. On 4 May the Latvians did the same, having just managed to achieve the necessary two-thirds majority in their Supreme Soviet.[7]

These three declarations of independence, though differing from one another in detail, transformed the national-constitutional situation in the Soviet Union. True, the juridical position of the Baltic republics, annexed under the Nazi-Soviet Pact, was distinct from that of most others (though not from Moldavia or western Ukraine and western Belorussia). But the other nations could also point to violent occupations of their territory, even if twenty years earlier and under other legal pretexts. Besides, the temerity of the Baltic republics was not punished by any effective retribution. When it came to decisive confrontation, the position of the Soviet authorities turned out to be surprisingly weak. Anxious for economic help from the west, and for arms reduction agreements, Gorbachev was reluctant to authorise any kind of coercion against the Balts.

Besides, the armed forces on which he would have had to rely in order to do so were in disarray, especially after the bungled intervention in Azerbaijan (see below). In the non-Russian republics more and more young men were refusing to obey their call-up orders, and often enjoyed the protection, tacit or open, of local authorities who considered the Soviet army an 'occupying force'. Even in Russia the primacy of military discipline no longer went unchallenged: a trade union, known as *Shchit* (the Shield) was defending servicemen's interests, while a Committee of Soldier's Mothers had been formed, calling for the investigation of unexplained deaths of conscripts, and protesting against the despatch of their sons to risk their lives in places like Baku in 'other people's conflicts'.[8] Many officers were also said to feel that the army's duty was to defend the Soviet Union's frontiers, not to sort out its internal disputes, especially since many conscripts had themselves a stake in ethnic conflicts.[9] So poor was morale, and so low the army's reputation among the population that Marshals Akhromeyev and Ogarkov, with 45 generals, complained in an open letter to *Komsomol'skaya pravda* of an 'anti-army psychosis' abroad in society.[10]

If military action was hazardous, economic blockade was also difficult to sustain. For one thing, it ran against the grain of the centralised planned economy. Dotted across the Soviet Union were factories dependent on this or that spare part made only in Lithuania: so quite a number of enterprises, cities and regions had an interest in breaking embargoes. Thus, at the end of June Gorbachev abandoned the blockade: the Lithuanians in return agreed to suspend their declaration of independence while negotiations were conducted in Moscow.[11]

Even here, however, the two sides did not see eye to eye about the significance of such negotiations. Gorbachev was at last – as usual, belatedly and forced by events – taking an interest in the idea of a new Union treaty, to define relationships within a 'Union of Sovereign Soviet Republics'. The Balts had themselves proposed such a new treaty back in 1988: now they were no longer interested. The Lithuanians wanted negotiations as equal partners with Moscow, not as members of a Union whose main features were still defined in Moscow. 'Neither Finland nor Poland is represented in Moscow, so why should Lithuania be there?' asked the Lithuanian President, Vytautas Landsbergis. If Gorbachev held up the European Community as an example of how modern nation states were tending to create common institutions and were even moving towards a common currency, the Lithuanians replied that the European states had started from a position of independence.[12]

So in the end all three Baltic republics found themselves conducting a delicate and indeterminate minuet with Moscow, talking about talks, but not really getting started because they could not agree on the status of the negotiations. This playing for time suited the Balts, as more and more republics lined up with declarations of sovereignty and Moscow's economic difficulties got worse.

The dour cunning of the Balts contrasted strongly with the audacious panache of the Caucasian peoples. The first to make a definite move towards independence were the Azerbaijanis, even though this was not in accordance with the stated policy of their leading protagonist, the Azerbaijani Popular Front. This movement had emerged during the early months of 1989 with a liberal programme similar in most respects to those of the Baltic Popular Fronts. The regional conflict produced a sting in the tail, however. The Azerbaijani Popular Front programme offered guarantees of national rights to Armenians living in the republic, but insisted that Nagornyi Karabakh was an integral part of Azerbaijan, whose forcible severance would undermine the nation's self-determination.[13]

The Azerbaijani Popular Front has been slower to develop than its Armenian counterpart, and, although its leaders were similar in social background to those of the Armenian Karabakh Committee, its rank and file membership was different, increasingly so as it grew in size. Azerbaijan is a much more industrialised republic, and accordingly the Popular Front attracted a considerable working class membership. A more radical and populist wing grew in strength, headed by the metal worker Nemet Panakhov, a brilliant speaker described by a British journalist as the 'Azerbaijani Lech Walesa'.[14]

In September 1989 the Popular Front called a general strike in protest against Moscow's continuing direct rule in Karabakh; this action included a blockade of both Karabakh and the Armenian Republic, much of whose food, fuel and construction materials passed through Azerbaijani territory. From then on the relations between the two nations deteriorated sharply, with both sides forming armed self-defence units to protect their villages against attack. The Soviet Army proved unable or unwilling to stop the fighting. Thousands of refugees fled from areas dominated by the rival nation and streamed into Baku and Erevan, overcrowding already strained urban environments. Baku became 'home' to 150,000 or so Azerbaijani refugees, mostly rural dwellers who lacked urban skills, became unemployed and often homeless, and swelled the ranks of the irreconcilables in the Popular Front.[15] Arkadii Vol'skii, head of the Special Committee administering Karabakh, spoke of an armed stalemate which could burst out into civil war at any time, and warned of the example of Ulster.[16]

Moscow reacted to the situation in an irresolute and inconsistent manner. On 29 November 1989 it abolished the special status of Nagornyi Karabakh and returned it to Azerbaijani administration. The Armenian Supreme Soviet reacted by announcing the creation of a 'United Republic of Armenia', including the disputed region. The Azerbaijani Supreme Soviet in its turn declared sovereignty on the model of the Baltic republics, over a territory which included Karabakh. Radicals from the Popular Front seized power in the Caspian coastal town of Lenkoran and, no doubt inspired by the recent television pictures from Berlin, cut through barbed wire and stormed frontier checkpoints in order to celebrate national unity with their fellow countrymen across the border in Iran. The tiny region of Nakhichevan' (an Azerbaijani enclave on the far side of Armenia) even declared itself an independent Republic.[17]

On 13 January 1990, thousands attended a Popular Front rally in Baku, at which speakers demanded the resignation of the Azerbaijan Communist Party first secretary, Abdul-Rakhman Vezirov, for his servility to Moscow, and a referendum on Azerbaijan's secession from the USSR. Afterwards crowds of people, many of them refugees, set out to hunt down the few thousand Armenians still living in the city. A radio Moscow commentator remarked, 'It was as if a modern city had reverted to the middle ages.'[18] A few days later, just as the pogrom seemed to be subsiding (most of its potential victims having fled), the Soviet authorities declared martial law and sent the army into Baku to restore order, which they did with indiscriminate violence, adding to the casualty lists. Altogether, according to official figures, at least 150 people were killed in the days of violence, 83 of them in Baku itself.[19]

Subsequent explanations of what had happened differed sharply. Official Soviet spokesmen maintained that martial law had been declared in order to stop inter-ethnic violence and to prevent the Popular Front seizing power in Baku. Azerbaijanis claimed that the real aim of the army had been to suppress the Popular Front and arrest its leaders, and that the pogroms had been artificially provoked to provide a pretext for the intervention. The Azerbaijani Writers' Union, for example, condemned the pogroms unreservedly, but maintained that the Soviet Army was not seeking out and bringing to justice the criminals responsible for them, but was 'taking vengeance on an entire people'.[20]

Whatever the original intention of the intervention, there is not much doubt that it had the effect of destroying the power of the Popular Front. Its leaders were imprisoned, and many of its more moderate members, horrified by the pogroms, left it to form a Social Democratic Party. Vezirov was dismissed, and a new Communist Party first secretary was elected, Ayaz Mutalibov, who yielded nothing to the Popular Front in his determination to assert Azerbaijan's national interests. He stuck severely to the practical, however: dropping all talk of secession or union with the Azerbaijanis in Iran, he concentrated instead on securing Karabakh and on developing Azerbaijan's economic assets for the benefit of its own people. In September 1990, using all the advantages of an incumbent government under a state of emergency, the Communist Party won the local elections convincingly, amidst widespread allegations of electoral malpractice.[21]

The Azerbaijani example shows how a national Communist party can exploit turbulent situations to take over part of the programme of the local nationalist opposition, along with much of its popular support, to stand up to Moscow and to consolidate its own power. In Armenia, by contrast, the Karabakh Committee was able to profit from the popular support it had enjoyed in the early stages of the struggle, to convert itself into a fully fledged Popular Front and to crowd out a divided and demoralised Communist Party. Its leaders, released from custody in May 1989, worked to create the Pan-Armenian National Movement, which held its first congress in November. The title signified that it claimed members not only in the Armenian Republic, but also from the diaspora elsewhere in the Soviet Union, and indeed all over the world. The Movement did envisage economic self-rule, a market economy, a national army and the right to join international organisations independently. It was behind the declaration of a United Republic of Armenia which sparked off the crisis of January 1990.[22]

The following year saw the Movement establish itself as the leading spokesman for the people of an exhausted and embattled republic. It gained about a third of the seats in the Armenian Supreme Soviet election of May. This relative success was, however, marred by a less than 50 per cent turnout, much of the population having evidently decided that there was little point in giving Soviet institutions legitimacy by voting for them. This irreconcilable attitude to Soviet power was reflected in the armed vigilante bands who continued to patrol the Armenian settlements in and around Nagornyi Karabakh, arguing that Armenia could no longer trust the Soviet Union and must in future fend for itself.

When Gorbachev issued a decree in July banning armed bands and ordering them to surrender their weapons, the new President of the Armenian Republic, Levon Ter-Petrosian (formerly one of the jailed leaders of the Karabakh Committee) flew to Moscow and returned with plenipotentiary powers to carry out the disarming of the Armenian National Army on his own authority. After an incident in which the ANA killed an Armenian parliamentarian, he outlawed it and was able to persuade its leader, Ramzik Vasilyan, to televise an appeal to its members to hand in their arms. At the same time, he started setting up volunteer defence units attached to the Armenian Ministry of the Interior, as part of an Armenian declaration of independence, which took place on 23 August.[23]

Armenia remained a vulnerable and insecure nation, in an exposed region of the world, where the assumption of independence seemed especially foolhardy. All the same, by late 1990, signs were beginning to emerge that it had a government enjoying the support of the people and able to negotiate both with Azerbaijan and Moscow.

Compared with Azerbaijan and Armenia, Georgia constituted a third variant, where neither the Communist Party nor the Popular Front has been able to mobilise and sponsor national feeling. The Georgian Communist Party proved too inflexible, and the Popular Front too moderate to give voice to the intense desire for independence which gripped the Georgian people after the Tbilisi massacre of April 1989. Nor was either movement able to offer a charismatic leader, vital for serious influence in the highly personalised politics of the country. Instead, there was a plethora of small organisations, each clustering around a personality, and differing very little from one another in outlook or tactics.

After the emotional revulsion caused by the Tbilisi massacre, the greatest success went to those movements which exhorted the population to ignore all Soviet institutions, and to create in their place new and independent Georgian national ones, preparatory to seceding from the USSR. Apart from hatred for the Soviet army, another motive for this attitude was the desire to keep a tight grip over all the ethnic groups living in the Georgian Republic. Separatism is infectious: if Georgians could declare their sovereignty, then smaller nations inside their republic might be tempted to do likewise.

Two minority peoples in particular, the Abkhaz in the northwest, and the Ossetians in the north, were resisting the Georgianisation of their territories – as symbolised, for example, by the exclusive official status of the Georgian language – and looked to Moscow for support in asserting their own national sovereignty. When in the summer of 1989 the Georgians opened a branch of Tbilisi University in Sukhumi, capital of the Abkhaz Autonomous Republic, the Abkhaz protested and fighting broke out between the two communities, both of whom proved to possess an unexpected quantity of firearms. Shortly afterwards the Ossetian Popular Shrine movement (*Ademon Nykhas*), began a campaign to ensure that their region would not be torn away from the USSR, but that on the contrary they could be reunified with their fellow countrymen just over the border in the RSFSR. Any such move would have carved out a chunk of traditionally Georgian territory, and in November 1989, Zviad Gamsakhurdia set out from Tbilisi with a column of several thousand Georgians to march to Tskhinvali, capital of the South Ossetian Autonomous Region. The marchers were turned back by armed Ossetians and troops of the Georgian Ministry of the Interior, but a series of bloody clashes followed during the winter, until Gorbachev sent troop reinforcements from Moscow to keep the peace.[24]

The cumulative effect of these violent incidents, on top of the Tbilisi massacre, was to keep the initiative in the hands of the most radical and determined movements. Principal among them was the National Democratic Party, under Georgi Chanturia, a student leader from the late seventies, and, like most other radicals, a founder member of the Il'ya Chavchavadze Society. His greatest rival was his former colleague, Zviad Gamsakhurdia, and the Society of Saint Il'ya the Righteous, with a political programme which differed only in nuances. In uneasy co-operation the two radical movements managed to gather a whole variety of radical splinter groups around themselves in the National Forum, which organised a successful boycott of the local and republican soviet elections of March 1990, and thus humiliated both the Communist Party and the Popular Front. Their aim, like the Estonian and Latvian Congress movements, was to register Georgian citizens as voters eligible to elect a Georgian Congress untainted by any association with the Soviet authorities, and empowered to declare independence.[25]

However, the rules of the game changed abruptly after the electoral boycott. The ending of the Communist Party's political monopoly throughout the USSR gave Gamsakhurdia the opportunity to reverse the humiliation he had suffered in the abortive Ossetian 'long march'. He saw that, with some changes in the electoral law, the new multi-party system could become a reality in Georgia even with the Supreme Soviet as its base. He walked out of the National Forum and founded a new radical bloc, the Round Table, which campaigned for proportional representation and a Supreme Soviet made up of full-time paid parliamentarians. When negotiations with the Communist Party proved sticky, he called a railway strike to lend emphasis to his demands. The elections held at the end of October vindicated his volte-face and his peculiar combination of civil disobedience and parliamentarism: the Round Table gained 165 seats out of 250, its nearest rivals, the Communist Party, only 64.[26]

On this basis, Gamsakhurdia became President of Georgia. He declared his intention of refusing to sign Gorbachev's Union treaty and of steering Georgia towards full secession from the USSR. Ironically, he had thus taken over the aims of the National Forum, and was moving to achieve them through the established Soviet institutions which the National Forum disdained.

The situation in Moldavia resembled that in the Baltic, not least in the sense that Moldavia had been annexed to the Soviet Union as a result of the Nazi-Soviet Pact. Public opinion there was mobilised in similar ways, if somewhat more gradually. In May 1988 the Moldavian Writers' Union addressed an appeal to the 19th Party Conference very like the one from the Estonian cultural unions and it was followed up in a meeting of representatives from all Moldavia's creative unions a few days later. This announced an initiative group to set up a Moldavian Democratic Movement in support of Perestroika (as Popular Fronts were often known in their infancy). It was immediately attacked by the local party press, but its first rally, held in Kishinyov on 27 June, attracted some five thousand people.[27] Rallies like this became frequent the following year: their main demands were that Moldavian — in the Latin rather than the Cyrillic alphabet — should be made the official language of the republic, and that the Nazi-Soviet Pact should be fully published and disavowed.

Feeling threatened, like their counterparts in the Baltic, the Russians and other non-Moldavians banded together in their own Inter-Front, and began to hold protest strikes and demonstrations. In September 1989, the Moldavian Supreme Soviet attempted a compromise by making Moldavian the official language, but designating Russian a legitimate means of inter-ethnic communication. The Russians were not mollified and continued to demand that their language have full official status.[28] A climax was reached in November: the revolution day parade was blocked by a counter-demonstration of Moldavian protesters, some of whom lay down in front of Soviet tanks, while others hustled the party leadership ignominiously from the reviewing stand. A few days later, angered by the use of force against these demonstrators, a crowd carrying tricolour flags with an auroch's head — the historical Moldavian coat of arms — set fire to the Ministry of Internal Affairs. A 'state of emergency' was declared in Kishinyov, and troops were sent in from outside the republic to restore order. A few days later, however, the Popular Front was able to celebrate a partial victory: Grossu, the Communist Party leader they execrated, was replaced by a more acceptable figure, Petru Luchinskii.[29]

The Romanian revolution of December 1989 opened up new dimensions in the Moldavian situation. While Moldavians declared the sovereignty of their republic (renamed Moldova) and opened border crossings to promote closer relationships with their fellow-nationals on the other side, Russians prepared to set up their own breakaway 'Dniester Republic', a sort of Moldavian Ulster. In the south 150,000 Gagauz, Turkish-speaking Christians who had sought refuge from the Ottoman Empire in the nineteenth century, announced a referendum in the regions where they lived to determine the degree of public support for the formation of their own republic. When the Moldavian government bussed volunteers down to prevent the referendum, Gagauz vigilantes stopped them on the road and erected frontier posts with placards reading 'Welcome to Gagauzia!'[30]

Before long, there was fighting too in the 'Dniester Republic', with each side mustering armed volunteers to defend its own dwelling areas.[31] The Moldavian government had already suspended the Soviet military draft on its territory and announced plans to create 'national military forces of the Moldavian SSR', backed up by 'Carabinieri', or armed police, under the control of the Interior Ministry, to maintain public order. Another ethnic flashpoint had ignited.[32]

In Central Asia, the same kinds of problems have motivated political activity as in other republics: the environment, the economy, language, culture and history. Yet they have not penetrated so deeply into the population, and the issues which have aroused popular passions seem to come from an earlier age, as if from a semi-feudal society with very localised consciousness.

We have already seen how mass violence in Uzbekistan was set off by market competition and access to official patronage. Later conflict has taken the same general form. Kazakhs have attacked Chechens and other North Caucasians who they believed were taking their jobs in the petroleum centre of Novyi Uzen'. In February 1990 a crowd of Tadjiks went on the rampage in their capital city, Dushanbe, assaulting people of non-local appearance and destroying public buildings: 37 people were officially said to have been killed. The precipitant of the disorder was a rumour that Armenian refugees were to be rehoused in Dushanbe, occupying recently completed flats which should have been assigned to local nationals who had been on waiting lists for years.[33] Similarly, in June 1990, the city of Osh in Kirgizia was torn apart by ethnic strife which arose when a group of Kirgiz inhabitants was given a plot of land for building homes on an area which had traditionally been used by Uzbeks for farming. In both cases, MVD troops had to be ferried in from outside to restore order, despite the authorities' reluctance, after the Baku massacre, to involve central forces in local conflicts.[34]

These outbursts were no more than the flashpoints of a very tense situation which persists in Central Asia, and which has moved one commentator to ask whether a classical revolutionary situation does not exist there.[35] The combination of ecological disaster with shortage of housing, land, water and jobs, has heightened the resentment local people feel at being dominated from outside by forces which do not have their interests at heart. Local leaders, shaken up by repeated corruption investigations from Moscow and unsettled by events in other parts of the Soviet Union, can no longer apply self-assured repression when faced with opposition.

So far, however, the emerging social and political movements do not seem either to have found a convincing basis on which they can work together. A priori one might have expected Islam to have played this role, especially in view of the fundamentalist revolutions going on across the border in Iran and Afghanistan. Actually, however, the Sunni Islam of Central Asia seems in practice to be very different in outlook from the Shiism further south. Besides, as was pointed out in Chapter 6, it has been extensively secularised during the Soviet period, so that it has become a tradition and way of life rather than a burning faith overriding all other loyalties. This can be seen in the way most of the ethnic conflict in the region has been directed by one Muslim nation against another (rather than against non-Muslims), on the basis of localised grievances arising from problems of everyday life.[36] That is not to say that Islam will never become a major political force in Central Asia: indeed, with the growing reaction against Soviet-style secularism, it may well do so. In August 1990 the establishment of an Islamic Democratic Party was announced, aiming to found a sovereign Islamic state in the traditionally Muslim regions and to make the Shariat the law of the land there.[37] There is no evidence, though, that this movement has mass appeal: Islam has not yet moved into the forefront of politics.

At the same time, the development of secular civic associations has been much slower and more hesitant than elsewhere in the Soviet Union. It is true that a Popular Front has emerged in Uzbekistan, known as *Birlik* (Unity), or, to give it its full name 'The Unity Movement for the Preservation of Uzbekistan's Natural, Material and Spiritual Riches.' Founded in Tashkent in May 1989, it adopted a programme rather like that of the Baltic Popular Fronts: that is, it was westernised, liberal and secular in outlook.[38] It has agitated over matters such as the cotton monoculture, environmental pollution, the status of the Uzbek language, and the treatment of Uzbek soldiers serving in the Red Army. It appears to have undergone the same kind of evolution as the Azerbaijani Popular Front, with radicals gaining greater influence as its membership grew and pulling it towards more populist and Islamic policies, so that it gradually became a kind of rainbow coalition of environmentalists, Uzbek nationalists, pan-Turks and Islamic fundamentalists.[39]

At first the authorities reacted in a very unbending manner to the appearance of Birlik. Later, in response perhaps to its growing popularity and following examples elsewhere in the Soviet Union, they began to seek co-operation with it, taking over part of its programme, in the hope of giving themselves a broader basis of popular support locally in face of the increasingly confusing signals emanating from Moscow. Such motives doubtless underlay the Uzbek declaration of sovereignty on 20 June.[40]

Elsewhere in Central Asia, political movements have remained largely at the stage of single issue pressure groups such as characterised an earlier stage of development in the European part of the Soviet Unon. Perhaps the most successful of them is the Kazakh 'Nevada-Semipalatinsk' movement, set up in February 1989 as the result of an appeal by the best known Kazakh writer, Olzhas Suleimenov, at a well-attended meeting organised by the Writers' Union. They established a link at the outset with a similar anti-nuclear movement in the American state of Nevada: hence their name. They called for the closure of the nuclear testing site at Semipalatinsk, claiming that nomads and their flocks on the steppes round it had absorbed massive doses of radiation. Within eighteen months both the Kazakh Communist Party and the Supreme Soviet of Kazakhstan had backed their demands for closure. If Moscow accedes to this pressure, it will disrupt the Union's whole military nuclear programme.[41]

Another tendency which may worry the authorities in Moscow is the growing popularity of the notion of a united Turkestan, which would bring together the republics of Kazakhstan, Uzbekistan, Turkmeniya, Kirgiziya and Tadjikistan. In June 1990 there were meetings at both official and unofficial levels to put some flesh on this idea. In Alma-Ata the leaders of the republics signed an agreement on economic, scientific and cultural co-operation, decided to consult among themselves at least annually and set up a co-ordinating council to conduct their mutual business between sessions. They also appealed to the President of the USSR to declare the Aral region a 'national disaster area', and they announced a jointly funded programme to save the Aral Sea; they also demanded that the diversion of Siberian rivers to Central Asia be put back on the agenda.[42] The unofficial meeting brought together Birlik, Nevada-Semipalatinsk and a dozen or so other movements. They were trying to assuage the troubled relations between the region's peoples and to forge closer ties, for which they urged the creation of a common parliamentary forum.[43]

Overall, since civic associations have been slower to develop in Central Asia than elsewhere in the Soviet Union, grievances have tended to be articulated in more primitive and localised ways. For the same reason, the republican Communist parties have been able without too much difficulty to sponsor and act as the spokesmen for local ethnic feeling. For this purpose they have concluded a cautious tacit alliance with official Islam and begun to co-operate among themselves in ways which may prefigure a future federal Turkestan.[44]

Though it has been peaceful so far, the most threatening situation of all to the Soviet leadership is that in Ukraine. As was pointed out in Chapter 5, the formation of a national movement there was much slower than in most European republics of the USSR, because of the Communist Party's resistance, but at last, in September 1989, the 'Popular Movement for the Support of Perestroika', or 'Rukh', held its first congress in Kiev. Nearly 1,200 delegates passed a programme which called for full sovereignty for Ukraine and disavowed the 'leading role' of the Communist Party. By later standards it was relatively timid, since it envisaged a federal Soviet Union, but, as we have seen, this was well beyond what the Soviet Communist Party was prepared to concede at the time. The very existence of Rukh was enough to bring down at last Shcherbitskii, the last survivor of Brezhnev's Politburo (apart from Gorbachev himself): he handed over leadership of the Ukrainian Communist Party to Vladimir Ivashko.

The weakness of Rukh at this stage was that its support was unevenly distributed over the republic. Its great stronghold was the west, the areas which had been in Austria-Hungary in the nineteenth century, and in Poland till 1939, and where the Ukrainian Catholic Church was especially strong. In the east, on the other hand, in Khar'kov and the Donbass, where much of the population was Russian, it had relatively few members: with 25 per cent of the population, this region accounted for only 6 per cent of the delegates.[45] The Donbass miners were actively discontented, but were not at this stage seeking a specifically Ukrainian solution to their grievances. An indication of this was the celebration of Ukrainian Independence Day on 21 January 1990: hundreds of thousands of citizens, many of them with blue and yellow national flags, formed a human chain which stretched 300 miles from Kiev to L'viv.[46] But the chain did not continue east of Kiev.

The eleven million Russians living in Ukraine did not, however, form any kind of Interfront on the Baltic model. Perhaps they never felt really threatened by the idea of Ukrainian sovereignty, since they were closely related by language and culture. In fact, the opposite gradually took place: contemplating the mounting economic chaos in the Russian republic, many Ukrainian Russians, including the Donbass miners, gradually came round to the view that sovereignty, and even perhaps independence, could not be worse and might have something to offer them.

Rukh's support grew correspondingly, but at first it had a difficult ride. The Communist Party managed to prevent its official registration until it was too late to nominate candidates for the local elections of March 1990. It was able to participate only as part of a Democratic Bloc of opposition groups, whose programme included the political and economic sovereignty of Ukraine, the abolition of the Communist Party monopoly (conceded but not yet made effective by the time the elections took place), the creation of a market economy, and full religious freedom, including the re-legalisation of the Ukrainian Catholic and Ukrainian Autocephalous Orthodox Churches. Even the Democratic Bloc was able to put forward candidates in only about 130 out of 450 seats in the Ukrainian Supreme Soviet, mostly in the larger towns. It performed weakly in Odessa and eastern Ukraine, but elsewhere won almost all the seats it contested, and was able to gain control of the municipal councils of Kiev and L'viv (where the veteran dissenter Vyacheslav Chornovil became mayor).[47] On

2 April 1990, in a Baltic-style assertion of national dignity, the Ukrainian flag was raised over the L'viv Town Hall, having been blessed by bishops of the Ukrainian Catholic Church, while the choir of the Lion Society (called after the city's name) sang the national anthem.[48]

Nominees of the party-state apparatus had a considerable majority in the Supreme Soviet, but over the following months many of those deputies, like Communists in the Baltic, began to move towards political positions close to Rukh. A number of prominent figures left the Communist Party, including Ivan Drach, chairman of Rukh. Inside the party itself, a split was opening up between Ivashko's wing, which remained loyal to Moscow, and a nationalist wing, which wished to see Ukraine governing itself. Apart from national pride, there were a number of powerful factors stimulating this change of mood. The slow-down in the economy was generating ever more serious shortages, both of food and fuel, in a land with abundant mineral resources which used to be known as the 'granary of Europe'. Furthermore, it was becoming evident that the full truth about radiation from the Chernobyl' explosion had been withheld from those most affected, and only now were many people, thoroughly alarmed and resentful about their fate, being belatedly resettled.[49]

The upshot was that on 16 July 1990 the Ukrainian Supreme Soviet passed a declaration of sovereignty which was in some respects the strongest yet issued by any republic. It did so, more-over, with virtual unanimity, by 355 votes to 4. The declaration envisaged Ukraine not merely passing its own laws and taking command of its own economic resources, but having its own army, conducting its own international relations and becoming a 'permanently neutral state not belonging to any military bloc'. Were it not for the continual use of the term 'Ukrainian Soviet Socialist Republic' and a reference to 'concluding a Union treaty', one would have called this a declaration of secession: the ties envisaged with the rest of the Union seemed no closer than those obtaining between members of the British Commonwealth.[50] In a sense, it was even a little suspicious that such a radical declaration should be passed so overwhelmingly by such a conservative assembly. It may turn out that the clause on the Union treaty is the overriding one. Certainly at the moment, Ukraine lacks the means to make a reality of its declared intentions: no Ukrainian frontier posts are being established, and no Ukrainian visas are being issued.

Such suspicions were evidently held at least by part of the Ukrainian public. In October students went on hunger strike on Kiev's main square, demanding that a new Ukrainian constitution should be worked out before the signing of the Union treaty, and that the Ukrainian government, which still consisted of nomenklatura nominees, should resign. In the latter they were successful. The Supreme Soviet also acceded to the students' demands to start bringing Ukrainian law into line with the declaration of sovereignty, to nationalise all property belonging to the Communist Party, and to prevent Ukrainian recruits being compelled to do their military service outside the republic's frontiers.[51] At its second congress Rukh reaffirmed that independence, not the signing of a Union treaty, was the aim of their movement.[52] With Rukh's popularity growing even in eastern Ukraine, and with economic collapse and constitutional chaos spreading throughout the Union, the pressure for Ukraine actually to secede seemed to gain momentum, in spite of the reluctance of the Supreme Soviet to follow up its bold words with action.

Events in Belorussia followed a similar pattern. Here public indignation about Chernobyl' was if anything even stronger, especially after an official commission reported in April 1990 that some two million inhabitants of the republic were living in the area of radioactive contamination.[53] Towards the end of July a Supreme Soviet of similar political complexion to the Ukrainian one unanimously passed a sovereignty declaration which yielded little to Ukraine's, including provisions for a separate army and neutrality in international affairs, but with the same crucial reservation about a Union treaty. When this clause was accepted, members of the Belorussian Popular Front walked out of the chamber.[54]

Whatever the background manoeuvres, the fact remained that two of the hitherto most submissive republics – and critical ones for the future of the Union – had announced their intention of going their own way, in language which would be difficult simply to countermand.

Most important of all, though, of course, was Russia. In May 1990 Boris El'tsin was elected President of the RSFSR (or, strictly speaking, Chairman of the Presidium of the RSFSR Supreme Soviet), with the support of Democratic Russia, by the comparatively narrow margin of 535 votes to 467.[55] This was the culmination of the latest stage of his political evolution, from loyal apparatchik through maverick Communist and then hero of the Popular Fronts to become the first authoritative proponent of a new-style Russian national consciousness: liberal and democratic rather than authoritarian and imperial. After centuries during which Russia's national interests had been automatically identified with its empire, El'tsin now stood for a political structure in which Russians would cease to oppress other nations and would therefore cease to be oppressed themselves.

Not that this necessarily implied dissolving the Soviet Union. As El'tsin affirmed at his final nomination speech, 'I have never advocated Russia's secession . . . I am in favour of . . . equal rights and independence for all republics.'[56] In spite of his use of the word 'independence', he also favoured a 'strong Union', but, as he explained in a later interview, one which 'rests on firm horizontal links between republics.' As an example of what he had in mind, he suggested that the current dispute with Lithuania should be solved, not by pressure from Moscow, as Gorbachev was doing, but by an agreement between Russia and Lithuania as equal partners.[57] He wanted to end the situation in which 'years of imperial policy of the centre have led to uncertainty about the status of the Union republics and the vagueness of their rights, obligations and responsibilities'.[58]

This was always going to be a difficult balancing act to sustain, both because of Russia's predominant weight within the Union, and also because of the numerous national territories *within* the Russian Federation, each with their own claim. Russia is not just a patchwork quilt, but one with enormous moth-holes in it.

These difficulties were vividly demonstrated when on 14 June a rally in Kazan' organised by the Tatar Public Centre (in effect the Tatar Popular Front) addressed a resolution to Gorbachev and El'tsin claiming that for Russia to declare sovereignty without consulting its own autonomous republics and regions about what status they wished to attain was a 'usurpation of the sovereign rights of the peoples living on the territory of Russia'.[59]

The Russian declaration of sovereignty was in some respects weaker than those subsequently adopted in Ukraine and Belorussia, though the difference is scarcely important: the dominant nation in the Union does not need to make a fetish of having its own army or its own currency. What really mattered was that Russia was to become a 'democratic, law-governed state', whose laws would take precedence over those of the Union, except in those areas where Russia explicitly and voluntarily vested its powers in the Union through a freely negotiated treaty. Autonomous territories within the RSFSR were to have equivalent rights in relation to it.[60] Some of them, such as the Tatars, the Chuvash, the Komi and the Yakuts, accordingly declared their own sovereignty, and El'tsin undertook a summer journey round the republic to hear at first hand of their wishes. He also put into practice his conception of 'horizontal links' by negotiating treaties with other Union republics regulating their relationships and providing through bilateral commercial clauses a makeshift substitute for the crumbling system of central economic planning.

The sovereignty of Russia, nominal though it was for the time being, transformed the constitutional situation throughout the Soviet Union, especially since, as an opinion poll showed, the majority of the population of the RSFSR identified their interests with Russia rather than with the Union.[61] Russia now had its own voice, and such was its weight that no Union government could in practice pursue a policy or implement a law which was decisively rejected by Russia. This new correlation of forces soon produced a deadlock on the question of economic reform, and before long El'tsin was demanding the resignation of the Soviet government headed by Nikolai Ryzhkov. Without a resolution of this conflict between the father and the over-mighty eldest son, it began to seem that no serious political questions could be decided any more.

Gorbachev was hoping to resolve this and other conflicts by means of his new Union treaty, details of which were at last published in November 1990. It does not seem likely to achieve its end. Although it rests on the principles of a 'voluntary association of republics, of 'civil society' and the 'law-governed state', in several respects it contradicts the sovereignty declarations of most republics, including that of Russia. It states for example that 'laws of the USSR adopted on questions falling within its competence take precedence and are mandatory for execution on the territory of all republics'. Among those questions were to be defence, foreign policy, the currency, economic strategy, energy and transport systems and the basic principles of social policy – all of them spheres which several of the republics had by now appropriated for themselves.[62] In any case, four republics – Estonia, Latvia, Lithuania and Georgia – stated that they were not even interested in negotiating on the document, let alone in signing it.

Gorbachev warned that if such 'separatism' was not ended, if some soviets at all levels continued to 'adopt anti-constitutional decisions which are paralysing the activities of the government', then there was a real danger of the 'Lebanisation' of the Soviet Union.[63]

At present the republics of the USSR find themselves in a kind of limbo. They have made declarations which imply that they are self-governing, even independent states, yet they lack the means – secure frontiers, armed forces, a customs service, a separate and stable currency – to make a reality of that independence, and in any case Moscow has not acknowledged it. That is an extremely unsatisfactory, even dangerous situation, especially in conditions of impending economic collapse, which even now require them to conclude bilateral trade treaties with each other. It is more than doubtful now whether a new Union treaty could resolve the situation. The only role which the Union government has at the moment is to devise means of ensuring a peaceful transition while the republics wishing to do so negotiate their peaceful departure from the Soviet Union. Even this role it can only fulfil if it contains representatives of the public movements from the non-Russian republics.

Conclusion

A recent letter-writer in *Izvestiya* put it in a nutshell. 'Is there any problem that we can agree about nowadays?' he asked. 'We overthrow all authorities, from Lenin monuments (the dead feel no pain?) to the government and presidential decrees. Perhaps we're taking vengeance for our long years of unanimity. But is freedom only the freedom to destroy?'[1]

There is a deep mood of dissatisfation abroad, and a questioning of the most fundamental traditions and beliefs. Desperately serious problems, smothered for decades by totalitarian make-believe, are out in the open. In a sense the dissenters have been vindicated: their convictions about the 'old regime' have been shown to be substantially correct. Yet they too were part of that old society, and are no less drawn into the painful self-reassessment which follows its collapse.

Underlying it all is the transition from a traditional society, based on local, tightly-knit communities, to a modern one, where individuals stand much more on their own in the political, economic and religious marketplace, thrown onto their own resources both for physical survival and for the elaboration of a set of beliefs and moral principles. The totalitarian regime may have destroyed the institutions of traditional society, but it preserved much of its mentality, in increasingly degenerate form, by prolonging the shared poverty, the limited mental horizons and the personal dependencies inherited from the past.

Now real changes are taking place, and they are coming all at once, superimposing themselves on one another. The British sociologist Theodor Shanin has characterised the resultant social mood as 'anomie' – a 'vacuum of values', the term originally used by Durkheim to describe the sense of rootlessness which afflicts members of a society undergoing rapid change. One result has been a sharp increase in crime, violence and suicide, as well as a proliferation of bizarre beliefs and aberrant behaviour.[2] Another, as we have seen, has been the ethnicisation of all political issues, as people redirect their dislocated loyalties from the local community to the nation. As a result of the enmities which have ensued, there are now more than half a million refugees, people without the most elementary rights, who squat in temporary quarters or impose on overburdened relatives.[3]

One upshot of all this is that 'civil society' still seems a long way away. In the far off tranquil days when I was writing the Reith lectures, out of which the first edition of this book grew, the term 'civil society' was being increasingly used, though mainly as a gleam in the eye of oppositional intellectuals who were beginning to come out of their shells and involve themselves in political life. It designated not much more than 'what we currently lack', namely political, social and economic institutions independent of the state and the ruling party apparatus, able to play their own autonomous role within the framework of the rule of law and to make their own input into the political process.

Now, two and a half years later, there is a surfeit of such institutions: in their riotous profusion they get in each other's way, and, if anything, impede rather than advance the cause of freedom and prosperity. This is where another desideratum of 'civil society' comes into focus: 'civil peace'. The rule of law cannot be sustained unless there is sufficient consensus about the basic rules which all must observe, and that means there must be substantial agreement about the shape of the polity, its 'constitution', and there must be generally accepted instruments of coercion which in the last resort can protect that constitution against violence.

The events of 1990 have shown that there is no such consensus. On the contrary, there is fundamental disagreement about the constitution, and even the very existence, of the Soviet Union. Each nation, in some cases each city and province, has its own version of its relationship to the Union and to each other. For that reason no instrument of coercion commands general acceptance, no one knows whose laws to obey, the economy fragments and loses its Union-wide scope. Primitive barter deals, a thriving mafioso black market, and para-military bands are beginning to take a grip. Unless this process is halted, and indeed reversed, there is little prospect of the benefits of civil society being available to the citizens of the Soviet Union, or even of the successor states which may succeed in carving out an existence for themselves among its ruins. What we are witnessing could turn into the 'Lebanisation' of the Soviet Union, as Gorbachev himself has warned.[4] A superpower which ruptures in this way is a danger not only to its own citizens, but to the whole world, especially if, as in this case, it possesses nuclear weapons. So we all have an interest in 'civil society' in the Soviet Union.

To achieve it, two contradictory processes have to be managed at the same time. On the one hand, the Soviet Union must reconstitute itself in a manner acceptable to most of its citizens, allowing those nations which wish to do so to depart peacefully, and guaranteeing the remainder sovereign status within a confederation or whatever they may agree jointly to institute. On the other, the authorities who guide this delicate transition must enjoy – and presumably sometimes genuinely exercise – real power, which means they must rest that power on the consent of the governed.

Gorbachev's greatest problem is that he enjoys no legitimacy with the majority of the population. He reached the top via the now discredited Communist Party apparatus. He was elected President by the Congress of People's Deputies, which, though an improvement on its predecessors, is far from being democratic. To the non-Russians, he is simply the chieftain of an occupying power which is reluctant to let go, while most Russians regard him as the last survivor of an old regime which has deceived and exploited them far too long.[5]

Yet someone is needed to stand for the unity of the state, even – perhaps especially – one which is falling apart. Gorbachev, as I have argued, has often been overtaken by processes which he unleashed, but which he could not control; yet so far he has, on the whole, displayed the skill and flexibility to adapt to the resultant changes and even to turn them to his advantage. Those qualities are not negligible, and are sorely needed in today's mounting chaos.

The basic question now is whether the Soviet Union dissolves violently or peacefully. The latter can best be guaranteed if there are still political institutions which can hold the ring, sustain a minimal consensus and enforce it if need be, during the period of transition. To achieve this, Gorbachev needs to bolster his presidential powers by appointing a government of 'public confidence', whose declared purpose would be to manage the process by which the Soviet Union transforms itself into a new kind of union, from which those republics which wish to do so will depart in orderly fashion. Such a government would need to contain distinguished members of the opposition, both from within Russia and from the non-Russian republics. It would need to supervise the complete renegotiation of the Union treaty which Gorbachev has already proposed, and to ensure as smooth a resolution as possible of the human problems which must arise when some republics leave the Soviet Union. It would certainly have to take extraordinary powers to deal with the dangers of economic breakdown and communal violence. It would need to be complemented by co-ordinating committees or 'round tables' in the regions and towns, bringing together elected representatives enjoying public trust with members of the *apparat*, who still have the administrative experience. Only an emergency could make such an alliance work, but an emergency is what the Soviet Union faces right now.

So great is the fear of famine and civil war among the Soviet peoples that I believe a government of this kind would enjoy some genuine public support for trying to keep the peace and ensure the movement of basic supplies. Even those nations who are determined to leave the Soviet Union are apprehensive about the conflict which may accompany the process, and may be prepared to compromise in the short term for guarantees of the long term.

Alas, at the time of writing (December 1990), it does not appear that Gorbachev has any such scheme in mind. He is taking extraordinary powers, but seeks to justify them by his existing threadbare authority. He will not face up to the implications of the pluralist political system he has launched, declaring unambiguously that he still puts his faith in the vanguard party: 'I shall never agree to the other concept, that we should be a parliamentary party, a party of political clubs, with cosy meetings and symposia'.[6] He wants to keep the Union together in a form which most of the nations constituting it have already rejected. That way lies only a further breakdown of civil peace and fragmentation of political power; or alternatively, an authoritarian coup with the support of the army, KGB and Ministry of the Interior, which, though seriously weakened (especially the army), are still the only serious forces of coercion in the country. Such a coup, whether it happened with or without Gorbachev in charge, would probably fail and lead directly to civil war.

Yet this is the direction in which Gorbachev is moving. With his customary skill at turning misfortunes to his own advantage, he is manipulating the current food crisis – real enough, but exaggerated for effect – to make use of his extraordinary powers, supported by the *Soyuz* faction in the USSR Supreme Soviet. He has dismissed Vadim Bakatin, a Minister of the Interior who was trying to find a way to restore order by working *with* the republics, replacing him with Boris Pugo, former chairman of the Latvian KGB, who has no such reputation, backed by General Boris Gromov, former Soviet commander in Afghanistan. At the lowest level he is sending in workers' committees to examine the food distribution and sale network, specially empowered to close establishments and make arrests. This innovation has a somewhat Stalinist ring.[7]

At the top, he is giving executive powers to the Federation Council, which brings together the Presidents of the Union Republics. If tactfully handled, this could prove to be a sensible move, for it will give him a direct line of communication to the largest nations – but then several of them, at least initially, will not be taking part. A State Inspectorate will see that the President's decrees are implemented – instead of being widely flouted, as at present. A new Security Council is promised, which looks like the crisis management centre, but it is too early yet to say what its powers will be.[8]

Gorbachev's reorganisations at the top have an increasingly frenzied air, reminiscent of Khrushchev in his later years. They are all vitiated by his failure to take in the implications of what he himself has created. In the end, he may go down to history after all as the 'last survivor from Brezhnev's Politburo', the leader who tried to save the party-state apparatus from the forces he himself had unleashed against them. That would be a tragedy, but it would have a certain historical logic. A totalitarian system, unlike an authoritarian one, does not bear within itself the seeds of its own supercession: these have to be planted afterwards, in soil which is ill-prepared.

Perestroika is over, overwhelmed by its own contradictions. What is needed now is first of all crisis management and then *novostroika*, a process of patient building from below which rests on the consent of the governed. If Gorbachev can display once more the qualities of flexibility and imagination which he has manifested in the past, he may yet succeed in doing it. One regards the future with both hope and foreboding, but at the moment foreboding is much stronger.

*   *   *

As this book was going to press, the dangers of the radicals' disorganisation and of Gorbachev's renewed authoritarianism were dramatised by the sudden resignation of Foreign Minister Edvard Shevardnadze. He reproached democrats with 'scattering' and 'backing away into the wilderness' and warned of 'advancing dictatorship', which might lead to a military adventure of the kind that had already produced so much blood and bitterness in Tbilisi and Baku.

As if to take him at his word, Gorbachev sent paratroopers and Ministry of the Interior Black Berets (riot troops) into the Baltic republics in January, with the declared purpose of rounding up draft-dodgers. This step threw the spotlight on to the clash of jurisdictions between Union and republics, since all three Baltic states had legalised alternatives to military service, and they now advised young men practising them to go into hiding for the time being. It is significant that the troops were sent not to Moldavia or Georgia, where ethnic self-assertion had created a genuine threat to social peace, but to the Baltic, where law and order still reigned, but where verbal and symbolic defiance of Moscow had gone further than anywhere else.

In the event, the intruders proved to be more interested in systems of communication than in draft-dodgers. They occupied newspaper buildings and radio stations in Vil'nyus, causing at least fourteen deaths, and four more in Riga, where they occupied a police headquarters. Meanwhile anonymous 'National Salvation Committees' in both republics issued statements claiming to be ready to assume power in order to avert economic collapse and the establishment of a 'bourgeois dictatorship'. El'tsin immediately joined with the three Baltic presidents in condemning 'armed acts damaging each other's state sovereignty'. In Moscow at least 200,000 people took to the streets in a demonstration organised by Democratic Russia to protest against the use of violence in the Baltic.

Faced also with (not very tough) criticism from western governments, Gorbachev decided not to proceed immediately with further repression, but withdrew the special units from the Baltic for the time being. This retreat reportedly prompted from Colonel Viktor Alksnis, one of the leaders of *Soyuz*, the reproach that 'Gorbachev has betrayed us!'

It was not certain whether the retreat was more than temporary. In other areas of policy, Gorbachev was also endeavouring to make his presidential authority more effective, without, however, doing anything to strengthen its legitimacy. He objected to the frankness of some of the mass media, and proposed that the press law be suspended; the Supreme Soviet of the USSR denied him this, but did promise to investigate ways of ensuring the 'objectivity of news'. A number of popular television programmes were censored and the outspoken Radio Russia was moved to a waveband not available to many listeners. The KGB were given new powers to investigate economic enterprises where criminal activity was suspected. Army detachments joined the police in patrolling the streets of the large cities, in a move denounced by a number of republican Supreme Soviets as unconstitutional.

Everything pointed to a counter-offensive by the party-state apparatus, using their entrenched position in the armed forces and KGB to try and recover positions lost through disarray the previous year. Gorbachev, without a robust and well-organised radical political force on which to rely, seemed inclined to revert to the alliances familiar to him as an *apparatchik* himself, away from the hazards of perestroika Mark 2 towards the more familiar haven of perestroika Mark 1: that is to say, change controlled by the centre.

The apparent security of this haven is, however, illusory. The armed forces and the conservative sections of the apparatus, in their present jumpy mood, are unlikely to prove more reliable allies than the radicals. Besides, the forces Gorbachev's reforms have released cannot simply be stuffed back into the bottle, for they are the product of long-term changes in society.

Perhaps one may leave the last word with Academician Shatalin, since the tacit abandonment of his economic reform plan marked a decisive turn in Gorbachev's policies. In a bitter open letter of 22 January 1991, he called upon the President to return to the '500 Days' programme, basing a union of 'absolutely sovereign republics' upon it and dropping the planned Union Treaty. He exhorted Gorbachev to resign his party post, leaving the Communist Party to split, and himself to form an 'inter-ethnic, inter-party, inter-class government enjoying the confidence of the people'. Only a strategy of that kind has any hope of bringing peaceful change to the Soviet Union. It seems unlikely to be adopted.

Notes

NB   *RL* = Radio Liberty Research Report
     SWB = Summary of World Broadcasts (BBC monitoring service)

1 A great power in crisis

1   *Pravda*, 26 August 1988, p. 1
2   L. Karpinskii, 'Pochemu stalinizm ne skhodit so stseny?' in Yu.
    N. Afanas'ev (ed.), *Inogo de dano* (Moscow, Progress, 1988), p.
    655
3   Paul Kennedy, *The Rise and Fall of the Great Powers* (London,
    Unwin Hyman, 1988), p. 515
4   'Appeal of Soviet scientists to the party-government leaders of the
    USSR', *Survey*, 70 (1970), pp. 160–70
5   Figures extrapolated from: B. Kerblay, *Modern Soviet Society*
    (London, Methuen, 1983), p. 55; F. Starr, 'The Soviet Union: a
    civil society' in *Foreign Policy*, 70 (spring 1988), p. 27
6   L. A. Anokhina & M. N. Shmelyova, *Byt gorodskogo naseleniya
    srednei polosy RSFSR v proshlom i nastoyashchem* (Moscow,
    Nauka, 1977), pp. 58–9
7   *Narodnoe khozyaistvo SSSR v 1985g: statisticheskii ezhegodnik*
    (Moscow, Finansy i Statistika, 1986), pp. 27–30
8   Kerblay, p. 213
9   Starr, p. 30
10 *Ibid.*, p. 27
11 For the theory of totalitarianism, see especially: Carl Friedrich &
    Zbigniew Brzezinski, *Totalitarian Dictatorship and Autocracy*
    (Cambridge, Massachusetts, Harvard University Press, 1956); and
    Leonard Schapiro, *Totalitarianism* (London, Pall Mall, 1972)

12 See the discussion in Susan Solomon (ed.), *Pluralism in the Soviet Union: essays in honour of Gordon Skilling* (London, Macmillan, 1983)

13 See the excellent analysis by Abbott Gleason, ' "Totalitarianism" in 1984', *Russian Review*, 43 (1984), pp. 145–59

14 Richard Pipes, 'Can the Soviet Union reform?' in *Foreign Affairs*, 63:1 (Fall 1984), p. 49

15 Julia Wishnevsky, 'Soviet television discusses Stalin's legacy', *RL*, 205:88, 17 May 1988

16 Robert Conquest, *The Great Terror* (London, Macmillan, 1968), p. 533. Roy Medvedev, who has spent much of his life gathering material about Stalin (though he was not till recently permitted to publish any of it in the Soviet Union), estimates the number of those 'illegally repressed' throughout his leadership at 40 million. It is clear that a very substantial proportion of those died. *Argumenty i fakty*, 4 February 1989

17 Boris Pasternak, *An Essay in Autobiography* (London, Collins Harvill, 1959), pp. 119–20

18 Varlam Shalamov, *Kolymskie rasskasy* (London, Overseas Publications Interchange, 1978), p. 220

19 Some of them have been published in English in two selections: *Kolyma Tales*, 1980; and *Graphite*, 1981, both published by W. W. Norton of New York.

20 A. Zinoviev, *Zheltyi dom* (Lausanne, L'Age d'Homme, 1980), 1, p. 48

21 Vladimir Voinovich, *The Life and Extraordinary Adventures of Private Ivan Chonkin* (London, Jonathan Cape, 1977), p. 145

22 R. H. McNeal (ed.), *Resolutions and Decisions of the Communist Party of the Soviet Union 1898–1964* (Toronto University Press, 1974), 2, pp. 97–8

23 M. Voslensky, *Nomenklatura: anatomy of the Soviet ruling class* (London, Bodley Head, 1984)

24 Marshall I. Goldman, *USSR in Crisis: the failure of an economic system* (New York, W. W. Norton, 1983), p. 86

2 Communities and ideals in Russian society

1 For a view of the origins of this spirit in Muscovy, see Edward Kennan, 'Muscovite political folkways', *Russian Review*, 45:2 (April 1986), pp.115–82

2 S. G. Pushkarev, *Krest'yanskaya pozemel'no-peredel'naya obshchina v Rossii* (Newtonville, Massachusetts, Oriental

Research Partners, 1976); B. Mironov, 'The Russian peasant commune after the reforms of the 1860s', *Slavic Review*, 44 (1985), pp. 438–67

3 M. M. Gromyko, *Traditsionnye normy povedeniya i formy obshcheniya russkikh krest'yan XIX veka* (Moscow, Nauka, 1986)

4 Stepniak, *The Russian Peasantry*, 2nd edn (London, 1905), p. 636

5 R. E. Zelnik (ed.), *A Radical Worker in Tsarist Russia: the autobiography of Semyon Ivanovich Kanatchikov* (Stanford University Press, 1986), p. 9

6 Solomon Schwarz, *The Russian Revolution of 1905; the workers' movement and the formation of Bolshevism and Menshevism* (University of Chicago Press, 1967), pp. 135–8, 335–8; Abraham Ascher, *The Revolution of 1905: Russia in disarray* (Stanford University Press, 1988), pp. 145–50

7 Teodor Shanin, *Russia 1905–7: revolution as a moment of truth* (London, Macmillan, 1986), ch. 3, especially pp. 89–90; Graeme Gill, *Peasants and Government in the Russian Revolution* (London, Macmillan, 1979), pp. 154–7

8 Alexander Rabinowitch, *The Bolsheviks Come to Power* (London, New Left Books, 1979)

9 Sheila Fitzpatrick, *The Russian Revolution* (London, Oxford University Press, 1982); Robert Service, *The Bolshevik Party in Revolution: a study in organisational change, 1917–23* (London, Macmillan Press, 1979)

10 For a statistical analysis of the urbanisation process and its effects on mentality, see Part One of Moshe Lewin, *The Gorbachev Phenomenon: a historical interpretation* (London, Radius, 1988)

11 Merle Fainsod, *How Russia is Ruled*, revised edn (Cambridge, Massachusetts, Harvard University Press, 1965), pp. 236–7

12 J. S. Berliner, *Factory and Manager in the USSR* (Cambridge, Massachusetts, Harvard University Press, 1957), pp. 243–7, 259–63

13 Alexander Zinoviev, *The Reality of Communism* (London, Victor Gollancz, 1984), p. 72

14 *Ibid.*, p. 92

15 *Ibid.*, p. 114

16 See his article of that title in *Survey*, 26:1 (spring 1982), pp. 28–48

17 Gregory Freeze, *The Russian Levites: parish clergy in the eighteenth century* (Cambridge, Massachusetts, Harvard University Press, 1977); and *The Parish Clergy in Nineteenth*

Century Russia: crisis, reform and counter-reform (Princeton
University Press, 1983)

18 Daniel Brower, *Training the Nihilists: education and radicalism
    in Tsarist Russia* (Ithaca, NY, Cornell University Press, 1975)

19 Richard F. Gustafson, *Leo Tolstoy – Resident and Stranger: a
    study in fiction and theology* (Princeton University Press, 1986),
    p. xii

20 V. G. Belinsky, 'Thoughts and notes on Russian literature', in his
    Selected Philosophical Works (Moscow, Foreign Languages
    Publishing House, 1948), p. 339

21 From 'Byloe i dumy', *Polnoe sobranie sochinenii* (Moscow, 1919),
    12, p. 106

22 N. Valentinov, *Encounters with Lenin* (London, Oxford
    University Press, 1968), p. 64

23 N. Bukharin & E. Preobrazhensky, *ABC of Communism*
    (Harmondsworth, Pelican Books, 1969), p. 300

24 Naum Jasny, *Soviet Industrialization, 1928–52* (Chicago
    University Press, 1961), p. 73

25 David Joravsky, *The Lysenko Affair* (Cambridge, Massachusetts,
    Harvard University Press, 1970); for the situation of the
    intelligentsia under Stalin, see Boris Kagarlitsky, *The Thinking
    Reed: intellectuals and the Soviet state, 1917 to the present* (London,
    Verso, 1988), Ch. 3

26 Geoffrey Hosking, 'The institutionalisation of Soviet literature', in
    G. A. Hosking & G. F. Cushing (eds), *Perspectives on Literature
    and Society in Eastern and Western Europe* (London, Macmillan,
    1989), pp. 55–75

27 Hans Günther, *Die Verstaatlichung der Literatur* (Stuttgart, J. B.
    Metzler Verlag, 1984)

3 The return of the repressed

1 Raisa Orlowa & Lew Kopelew, *Wir lebten in Moskau* (Munich,
   Albrecht Knaus Verlag, 1987), p. 28

2 Gerald Stanton Smith, *Songs to Seven Strings: Russian guitar
   poetry and Soviet 'mass song'* (Bloomington, Indiana University
   Press, 1984)

3 Lyudmila Alekseeva, *Istoriya inakomysliya v SSSR: noveishii
   period* (Benson, Vermont, Khronika Press, 1984), p. 247

4 Vladimir Bukovskii, *To Build a Castle: my life as a dissenter*
   (London, Andre Deutsch, 1978), pp. 191–2

5 Alekseeva, p. 251

6 Mark Hopkins, *Russia's Underground Press: the Chronicle of Current Events* (New York, Praeger, 1983), p. 6
7 *Ibid.*, p. 148
8 *Ibid.*, pp. xix-xx
9 V. Haynes & O. Semyonova, *Workers Against the Gulag* (London, Pluto Press, 1979)
10 Alekseeva, pp. 386–8
11 Peter Reddaway (ed.), *Uncensored Russia* (London, Jonathan Cape, 1972), p. 23
12 B. Shragin, 'Oppozitsionnye nastroeniya v nauchnykh gorodkakh', *SSSR: vnutrennie protivorechiya*, 1 (1981), pp. 100–19
13 Ann Shukman, *Literature and Semiotics: a study of the writings of Yu. M. Lotman* (Amsterdam, North Holland Publishing Company, 1977), Ch. 1
14 See Alec Nove's introduction to A. Aganbegyan, *The Challenge: economics of perestroika* (London, Hutchinson, 1988); for further discussion of such 'intra-structural dissent' see Alexander Shtromas, 'Dissent and political change in the USSR', Erik P. Hoffmann and Robbin F. Laird (eds), *The Soviet Polity in the Modern Era* (New York, Aldine Publishing Co., 1984), pp. 727–33
15 V. Lakshin, *Solzhenitsyn, Tvardovsky and Novy Mir* (Cambridge, Massachusetts, MIT Press, 1980), pp. 80–1
16 L. Labedz (ed.), *Solzhenitsyn: a documentary record* (London, Allen Lane, 1970), pp. 15–16; on the applicability of Freudian theory to the Soviet literary situation, see Sidney Monas, 'Censorship as a way of life', in G. A. Hosking & G. F. Cushing (eds), *Perspectives on Literature and Society in Eastern and Western Europe* (London, Macmillan, 1989), pp. 7–22

4 A civil society in embryo

1 *Pravda*, 10 May 1987, p. 3
2 Boris Komarov, *Unichtozhenie prirody* (Frankfurt am Main, Posev, 1978), p. 73
3 V. Chivilikhin, 'Svetloe oko Sibiri', *Oktyabr'*, 4/63, pp. 151–72
4 *Komsomol'skaya pravda*, 11 May 1966; A. Babyonyshev (ed.), *On Sakharov* (New York, Vintage Books, 1982), p. xxi
5 Conversation with V. Rasputin, 31 May 1988; Charles E. Ziegler, *Environmental Policy in the USSR* (London, Frances Pinter, 1987), pp. 53–7
6 V. Rasputin, 'Kak tam, na slavnom more?' *Literaturnaya gazeta*, 24 August 1988, pp. 1–2

7   Thane Gustafson, *Reform in Soviet Politics* (Cambridge University Press, 1981), p. 61
8   Komarov, Ch. 4
9   Gustafson, p. 46
10 Violet Connolly, 'Turning the rivers of Siberia in their courses', RL 189/78, 29 August 1978
11 *Russkaya mysl'*, 15 July 1982, pp. 10–11
12 *Literaturnaya gazeta*, 2 July 1986
13 Interview with Professor O. Kolbasov, expert on environmental law at the Institute of State and Law, 15 April 1988
14 Sergei Zalygin, 'Povorot: uroki odnoi diskussii', *Novyi Mir*, 1/87, pp. 3–18; Nicolai N. Petro, 'The project of the century', *Studies in Comparative Communism*, 20:3–4 (autumn/winter 1987), pp. 235–52
15 *Pravda*, 20 May 1988
16 Victor G. Snell, 'The cause of the Chernobyl accident', in David Marples, *The Social Impact of the Chernobyl Disaster* (London, Macmillan, 1988)
17 Victor Haynes & Marko Bojcun, *The Chernobyl Disaster* (London, Hogarth Press, 1988) Ch. 6
18 Marples, pp. 114–15; Haynes & Bojcun, Ch. 5
19 *Moscow News*, 7, 14 February 1988, p. 10
20 Ales' Adamovich, ' "Chestnoe slovo, ne vzorvyotsya", ili mnenie nespetsialista', *Novyi Mir*, 9/88, p. 169
21 *Ibid.*, p. 164
22 Bohdan Nahaylo, 'Non-Russian national democratic movements hold another meeting', *RL* 465/88, 10 October, 1988; David Marples, 'New protests against Soviet nuclear energy programme', *RL* 448/88, 28 September 1988
23 Marples, 'New Protests . . .', *RL*, 448/88, p. 4
24 Material on the Trust Group is drawn from Olga Medvedkov, 'The Moscow Trust Group: an uncontrolled grassroots movement in the Soviet Union', *Mershon Centre Quarterly Report* (Ohio State University), 12:4 (spring 1988)
25 *Izvestiya*, 20 May 1988, p. 3
26 *Literaturnaya gazeta*, 25 June 1986, p. 6
27 Bill Keller, *International Herald Tribune*, 8 February 1988, p. 2
28 According to an opinion poll conducted by its own research institute: ' "Neformaly" – synov'ya ili pasynki?', *Politicheskoe obrazovanie*, 7/88, p. 83
29 I. Yu. Sundiev, 'Neformal'nye molodyozhnye ob"edineniya: opyt

ekspozitsii', *Sotsiologicheskie issledovaniya*, 5/87, pp. 56–62; M.
Malyutin,'Neformaly v perestroike: opyt i perspektivy', in Yu.
Afanas'ev (ed.), *Inogo ne dano* (Moscow, Progress, 1988),
pp. 216–17

30   *Pravda*, 1 February 1988, p. 4; 10 February 1989, p. 1; A.
Maisenya, 'Kto oni, "neformaly"?', *Sovetskaya Belorussiya*, 1
October 1987, p. 4; *Argumenty i fakty*, 31/88, 30 July 1988,
pp. 6–7

31   *Politicheskoe samoobrazovanie*, 7/88, p. 85

32   *Russkaya mysl'*, 18 September 1987, p. 5; Alan Bookbinder *et al.*,
Comrades (London, BBC Publications, 1985), pp. 159–60

33   Vera Tolz, 'Informal groups in the USSR', *RL* 220/87, 11 June
1987; K. Sochnev, 'Nevostrebovannye lyudi', *Sel'skaya
molodyozh'*, 6/88, pp. 8–10

34   Malyutin, p. 218

35   Interviews with Grigorii Pel'man, 18 April and 5 May 1988; Nick
Lampert, 'Russia's new democrats: the club movement and
perestroika', *Detente*, 9–10 (1987), p. 10

36   Interview with Grigorii Pel'man, 5 May 1988; Lampert, pp. 10–11

37   *The Friend*, 13 May 1988, p. 595; 'Informatsionnyi byulleten'
SMOT', no. 7, June 1988, *Materialy samizdata*, AS 6300, p. 41

38   *Russkaya mysl'*, 19 February 1988; *Materialy samizdata*, AS 6015,
pp. 39–45; interview with Vyacheslav Igrunov of Perestroika-88,
22 April 1988

39   Interview with Aleksandr Podrabinek, 18 April 1988

40   *Glasnost'*, 2–4, p. 2, published as an appendix to *Russkaya mysl'*,
24 July 1987

41   *Zhurnal zhurnalov*, 1, in *Materialy samizdata* AS 6132

42   Boris Kagarlitskii, *The Thinking Reed: intellectuals and the Soviet
state, 1917 to the present* (London, Verso Books, 1988); Vera
Tolz, 'Informal groups hold first officially sanctioned conference',
RL 380/87, 23 September 1987; L. Alekseeva, 'Obshchestvennye
ob"edineniya v SSSR', *SSSR: vnutrennie protivorechiya*, 21
(1988), pp. 90–4

43   Conversation with Boris Kagarlitskii, 15 April 1988;
Komsomol'skaya pravda, 31 January 1988

44   Vera Tolz, 'Informal groups in the USSR in 1988', *RL* 487/88, 30
October 1988, pp. 6–7; B. Kurashvili, *Bor'ba s byurokratizmom*
(Moscow, Znanie, 1988), pp. 55–6

45   Boris Kagarlitsky, *Farewell Perestroika: a Soviet chronicle*,
London: Verso, 1990, p. 99

46   ibid, pp. 9–10
47   *Guardian*, 9 May 1988; Jonathan Aves, 'The Democratic Union
     – Soviet opposition party?', *Slovo*, vol. 1, no. 2 (November
     1988), pp. 92–8
48   Kagarlitsky, pp. 110–12
49   *Ogonyok*, no. 34, 20 August 1988, pp. 25–7
50   *Moskovskie norosti*, 23, 5 June 1988, p. 15; *SWB* SU/0172, 8 June
     1988, p. i.
51   *Posev*, 3/88, pp. 4–7
52   Kagarlitsky, p. 112
53   Vladimir Brovkin, 'Revolution from below; informal political
     associations in Russia, 1988–9', *Soviet Studies*, vol. 42, no. 2
     (April 1990), pp. 249–50
54   Kagarlitsky, pp. 117–20
55   *Independent*, 31 March 1989, p. 10; *Russkaya mysl'*, 7 April
     1989, p. 1; M. Malyutin, 'Nechto o vyborakh iti tret'ya volna',
     Otkrytaya zona, 9 (April 1989), pp. 147–50
56   *Independent*, 29 March 1989, p. 12

5 The flawed melting pot

1   Gail Lapidus, 'Ethnonationalism and stability: the Soviet case',
    World Politics, 36 (1983–4), pp. 555–80; Mary McAuley,
    'Nationalism and the Soviet multi-ethnic state', in Neil Harding
    (ed.), *The State in Socialist Society* (London, Macmillan, 1984),
    pp. 179–210; Roman Karklins, *Ethnic Relations in the USSR*
    (Boston, Massachusetts, Allen & Unwin, 1986); Alexander J.
    Motyl, *Will the non-Russians rebel? State, ethnicity and stability
    in the USSR* (Ithaca, NY, Cornell University Press, 1987)
2   Ernest Gellner, *Nations and Nationalism* (Oxford, Basil Blackwell,
    1983), pp. 43–50
3   V. I. Kozlov, *Natsional'nosti SSSR: etnodemografischeskii obzor*,
    (Moscow, Finansy i statistika, 1982), pp. 240–1
4   From the protest document of autumn 1987, quoted in *Radio Free
    Europe Research*, RAD Background Report, 39, 11 March 1988,
    p. 1
5   Tamara Dragadze, 'The Armenian-Azerbaijani conflict: structure
    and sentiment', *Third World Quarterly*, 11:1 (January 1989),
    pp. 63–5
6   Dragadze, p. 62; Lyudmila Alekseeva, *Istoriya inakomysliya v
    SSSR: noveishii period* (Benson, Vermont, Khronika Press, 1984),
    pp. 83–95

7 *Soviet Analyst*, vol. 17, no. 3, 10 February 1988, pp. 1–2
8 *Posev*, 4/88, p. 10; *Sunday Times*, 28 February 1988, pp. 1, 13.
9 *SWB* SU/0210, 22 July 1988, B/16–17
10 Dragadze, pp. 67–9; S. Enders Wimbush, 'Divided Azerbaijan: nation-building, assimilation and mobilisation between three states', in W. O. McCagg, Jr & Brian D. Silver (eds), *Soviet Asian Ethnic Frontiers* (New York, Pergamon Press, 1979), pp. 61–82
11 Ronald Grigor Suny, *The Making of the Georgian Nation* (London, Tauris, 1989), Chs. 1–3
12 Robert Parsons, 'Informal organisations in Georgia', paper presented to the Georgian Study Group at the School of Oriental & African Studies, University of London, 5 May 1989
13 Elizabeth Fuller, 'Independent political groupings in Georgia', *RL* 527/88, 25 November 1988
14 *The Times*, 10 April 1989, p. 1; *Sunday Times*, 16 April 1989, p. B1
15 *SWB*, SU/0436, 17 April 1989, B/3
16 Alexander Shtromas, 'The Baltic States', in R. Conquest (ed.), *The Last Empire: nationality and the Soviet future* (Stanford, California, Hoover Institution Press, 1986), pp. 183–217
17 N. R. Miuzneks, 'The Daugavpils hydro-station and glasnost in Latvia', *Journal of Baltic Studies*, 18:1 (spring 1987), pp. 63–70
18 *Radio Free Europe Research*, 13:26, 3 June 1988, pp. 3, 13–14
19 *RFER*, Baltic Area Situation Report 7, 15 July 1988, pp. 15–19
20 *RFER*, Baltic Area Situation Report 5, 20 May 1988, pp. 7–10; *SWB* SU/0251, 8 September 1988, B/3; *SWB* SU/0305, 10 November 1988, B/1–8
21 *Narodnyi Front Latvii: programma, ustav* (Riga, Arots, 1988)
22 *SWB* SU/0205, 16 July 1988 B/3–5
23 Alexander Rahr, 'Lithuanian party leadership demands more autonomy', *RL* 499/88, 8 November 1988
24 Rupert Cornwell, *Independent*, 24 October 1988, p. 1
25 Interview with Anatolii Belaichuk of the Latvian International Front, Novosti Press Agency report of 28 April 1989
26 Associated Press, 14 March 1989
27 Roman Szporluk, 'The Ukraine and Russia', in R. Conquest (ed.), *The Last Empire*; Bohdan Krawchenko, *Social Change and National Consciousness in Twentieth-Century Ukraine* (London, Macmillan, 1985)
28 Roman Solchanyk, 'Statistical *glasnost*': data on language and education in Ukraine', *RL*, 152/87, 15 April 1987, p. 2

29 Roman Solchanyk, 'Catastrophic language situation in major Ukrainian cities', *RL* 286/87, 15 July 1987

30 Bohdan Nahaylo, 'Mounting opposition in the Ukraine to nuclear energy programme', *Radio Liberty Supplement* 1/88, 16 February 1988

31 Bohdan Nahaylo, 'Informal Ukrainian Culturological Club helps to break new ground for *glasnost*", *RL* 57/88, 8 February 1988; interview with Vyacheslav Chornovil and Oles' Shevchenko, 25 April 1988

32 *Russkaya mysl'*, 29 July 1988, p. 2

33 Ukrainian Press Agency: Press Release no. 180, 19 November 1988; no. 183, 8 December 1988; David Marples, 'Mass demonstration in Kiev focuses on ecological issues and political situation in the Ukraine', *RL* 525/88, 5 December 1988

34 *Literaturna Ukraina*, 16 February 1989, quoted in *SWB* SU/0403, 8 March 1989, B/1–6

35 *Pravda Ukrainy*, 18 February 1989, quoted in *SWB* SU/0400, 4 March 1989, B/7–10

36 Kathleen Mihalisko, 'Police crack down on demonstration in Minsk', *RL* 510/88, 16 November 1988; 'Belorussian Popular Front off to a good start', *RL* 560/88, 12 December 1988; V. Bykov, 'Dubinki protiv glasnosti?' in *Ogonyok*, no. 47, 19 November 1988, p. 31

37 Bohdan Nahaylo, 'Representatives of non-Russian national movements establish co-ordinating Committee', *RL*, 22 June 1988; 'Non-Russian national-democratic movements hold another meeting', *RL* 645/88, 10 October 1988

38 Bohdan Nahaylo, 'Non-Russian democratic movements adopt charter and issue appeal to Russian intelligentsia', *Report on the USSR*, 1:8, 24 February 1989, pp. 15–17

39 *Current Digest of the Soviet Press*, 40:3, 17 February 1988, p. 4

40 James Critchlow, ' "Corruption", nationalism and the native elites in Soviet Central Asia', *Journal of Communist Studies*, 4:1 (March 1988), pp. 142–61

41 See Chapter 3; Nancy Lubin, *Labour and Nationality in Soviet Central Asia* (Princeton University Press, 1984); Alistair McAuley, 'Economic development and political nationalism in Uzbekistan', *Central Asian Survey*, 5:3–4 (1986), pp. 161–82; *Pravda*, 14 April 1988; James Critchlow, 'Desertification of the Aral region: economic and human damage', *RL* 392/87, 26 August 1987

42 *Literaturnaya gazeta*, 20 January 1988, p. 13

43 Bess Brown, 'Corruption reported flourishing again in Uzbekistan', *RL* 492/88, 3 November 1988

44 Ann Sheehy, 'The Alma Ata riots and their aftermath', *RL* 3/87, 23 December 1986; Alistair McAuley, *Civil Disturbances in Alma Ata: a Comment* (Russian & Soviet Studies Centre, University of Essex, Discussion Paper no. 8, December 1987)

45 *SWB* SU/0476, 7 June 1989, p. i; *Sunday Times*, 11 June 1989, p. A16; *Independent*, 15 June 1989, p. 11

46 Annette Bohr, 'Formation of a People's Front in Tadjikistan', *RL*, 498/88, 16 November 1988; *SWB* SU/0343, 24 December 1988, B/5–7; SU/0350, 5 January 1989 B/9–10

47 *SWB* SU/0405, 10 March 1989 B/1–6

48 'Soviet antisemitism unchained: the rise of the "Historical and Patriotic Association Pamyat" ', *Institute of Jewish Affairs Research Report*, no. 3 (July 1987), pp. 1–8; Ol'ga Dorenskaya, 'Besy nashego vremeni', *Daugava*, 2/89, pp. 82–91; *Materialy Samizdata*, AS 6079

49 One is reproduced by a recipient, Grigorii Baklanov, chief editor of *Znamya* in his journal, 10/88, p. 233

50 *Materialy samizdata*, AS 6079, p. 1

51 For an analysis which is very sensitive to the dangers presented by such an alliance, see Alexander Yanov, *The Russian Challenge* (Oxford, Basil Blackwell, 1987)

52 On the face of it, this is an implausible claim, in view of the fact that Vikulov in 1969 signed a letter which helped to bring about Tvardovskii's downfall. But in a conversation with me in December 1988, Vladimir Lakshin, Tvardovskii's deputy at that time, substantially confirmed it. Lakshin told me that Tvardovskii was not the man to bear a grudge, and was anxious above all to see good literature flourish.

53 This distinction is fully explored in John Dunlop, *The Faces of Contemporary Russian Nationalism* (Princeton University Press, 1983)

54 V. Soloukhin, 'Pochemu ya ne podpisalsya pod tem pis'mom', *Nash sovremennik*, 12/88, pp. 186–9

55 V. Kozhinov, 'Pravda i istina', *Nash sovremennik*, 4/88, pp. 160–75

56 V. Kozhinov, 'Samaya bol'shaya opasnost', *Nash sovremennik*, 1/89, pp. 141–75, especially p. 147

57 M. Antonov, 'Na perelome', *Moskva*, 3/88, pp. 3–26, especially 5–6

6 Religion and the atheist state

1 *Pravda*, 30 April 1988, p. 1
2 A. Krasnov-Levitin, *Ruk tvoikh zhar* (Tel-Aviv, Krug, 1979), p. 102
3 Jane Ellis, *The Russian Orthodox Church: a contemporary history* (London, Croom Helm, 1986), p. 14
4 V. Zelinskii, *Prikhodyashchie v tserkov'* (Paris, La Presse Libre, 1980), p. 46
5 Ellis, pp. 215–17
6 D. Pospielovsky, 'The survival of the Russian Orthodox Church in her millennial century; faith as *martyria* in an atheistic state', paper delivered at the conference on *Christianity in the Eastern Slav Lands*, School of Slavonic & East European Studies, University of London, July 1988
7 Moshe Lewin, 'Popular religion in twentieth-century Russia', in his *The Making of the Soviet System* (London, Methuen, 1985), pp. 57–71
8 V. Rasputin, *Farewell to Matyora* (New York, Macmillan, 1979)
9 Jane Ellis, 'USSR: the Christian seminar', *Religion in Communist Lands*, 8 (1980), pp. 92ff.
10 Ellis, *Russian Orthodox Church*, Ch. 13
11 Interview with Metropolitan Filaret of Minsk, 5 May 1988
12 Michael Bourdeaux, *Gorbachev, Glasnost and the Gospel*, London: Hodder & Stoughton, 1990, pp. 52–3
13 Jane Ellis, 'Hierarchs and dissidents: conflict over the future of the Russian Orthodox Church', *Religion in Communist Lands*, vol. 18, no. 4 (winter 1990), pp. 307–18; John B. Dunlop, 'The Russian Orthodox Church and nationalism after 1988' ibid. pp. 292–306
14 Oxana Antic, 'Draft law on freedom of conscience criticised', *Report on USSR*, 28 September 1990, pp. 13–14
15 *Izvestiya*, 9 October 1990, p. 3
16 *Keston News Service* (henceforth *KNS*), no. 343, 8 February 1990, p. 22; no. 353, 28 June 1990, p. 3; no. 359, 27 September 1990, p. 2
17 Bourdeaux, p. 99
18 Bourdeaux, p. 88
19 *KNS*, no. 360, 11 October 1990, p. 2

20 Vasyl Markus, 'Religion and nationalism in Ukraine', in Pedro Ramet (ed.), *Religion and Nationalism in Soviet and East European Politics*, 2nd edn, Durham, North Carolina: Duke University Press, 1989, pp. 138–70

21 *Observer*, 30 October 1988, p. 29; Ivan Hvat, 'The Ukrainian Catholic Church, the Vatican and the Soviet Union during the pontificate of Pope John Paul II', *Religion in Communist Lands*, vol. 11, no. 3 (winter 1983), pp. 264–80

22 Bourdeaux, pp. 166–7, 171

23 G. Rozhnov, 'Eto my, gospodi', *Ogonyok*, 16 September 1989, pp. 6–7

24 *KNS*, no. 342, 25 January 1990, pp. 14, 17; no. 345, 8 March 1990, pp. 10–11

25 *KNS*, no. 346, 22 March 1990, pp. 5–6

26 *KNS*, no. 357, 30 August 1990, pp. 2–3

27 *Russkaya mysl'*, 28 April 1989, p. 8

28 *Ibid.*, pp. 107, 177–9

29 Rev. Michael Bourdeaux, *Religious Ferment in Russia: Protestant opposition to Soviet religious policy* (London, Macmillan, 1968), pp. 117–19

30 On Baptist numbers, see Christel Lane, *Christian Religion in the Soviet Union: a sociological study* (London, Allen & Unwin, 1978), pp. 140–1

31 For general studies of Islam in the Soviet Union, see especially A. Bennigsen & C. Lemercier-Quelquejay, *Islam in the Soviet Union* (London, Pall Mall, 1967); M. Rywkin, *Moscow's Muslim Challenge: Soviet Central Asia* (London, M. E. Sharpe, 1982)

32 A. Bennigsen & S. Enders Wimbush, *Mystics and Commissars: Sufism in the Soviet Union* (London, C. Hurst & Co, 1985)

33 Taras Kuzio, 'Opposition in the USSR to the occupation of Afghanistan', *Central Asian Review*, 6 (1987), pp. 99–117

34 Yaacov Ro'i, 'The Islamic influence on nationalism in Central Asia', *Problems of Communism*, vol. 39, no. 4 (July-August 1990), pp. 49–64; James Critchlow, 'Islam in public life: can this be "Soviet" Uzbekistan?' *Report on USSR*, 16 March, 1990, pp. 23–5; Bess Brown, 'Religion and nationalism in Central Asia', *Report on USSR*, 20 July 1990, pp. 25–7

7 The paradox of Gorbachev's reforms

1 Dev Murarka, *Gorbachev: the limits of power* (London, Hutchinson, 1988), pp. 54–6; V. P. Gagnon, Jr., 'Gorbachev and the collective contract brigade', *Soviet Studies*, 39:1 (January 1987). pp. 1–23; for the frustration of earlier experiments of this kind, see A. Yanov, *The Drama of the Soviet 1960s: a lost reform* (Berkeley, California, Institute of International Studies, 1984)

2 Murarka, p. 241

3 *Ibid.*, p. 239

4 *Materialy samizdata*, AS 5785, pp. 1–3

5 *Oktyabr'*, 6/89, pp. 30–108

6 *Moskovskie novosti*, 24 June 1990, p. 11

7 David Marples, 'A retrospective of a nuclear accident', *Report on USSR*, 20 April 1990, pp. 9–14

8 *SWB* SU/0806, 3 July 1990, C2/1–6; Peter J. Duncan, 'From glasnost to freedom', *Index on Censorship*, vol. 19, no. 10 (December 1990), p. 23

9 *Literaturnaya gazeta*, 18 September 1990, p. 1

10 Walter Laqueur, 'Glasnost', *Commentary*, 86:1 (July 1988), pp. 13–24

11 *Pravda International*, 12 (1988): 7, p. 36

12 Philip Hanson, 'The Economy', in Martin McCauley (ed.), *The Soviet Union under Gorbachev* (London, Macmillan, 1987), pp. 97–117

13 V. Selyunin, 'Revansh byurokratii', in Yu. Afanas'ev, *Inogo ne dano* (Moscow, Progress, 1988), p. 199

14 At a meeting of the Presidium of the Council of Ministers, 29 July 1988, *SWB* SU/0217, 30 July 1988, C/3

15 Otto Latsis, 'Ugroza perestroike', *Znamya*, 7/88, p. 178

16 *Pravda*, 6 March 1989, p. 3

17 Karl-Eugen Wädekin, 'Agriculture', in Martin McCauley (ed.), *The Soviet Union under Gorbachev*, pp. 118–34

18 See Gorbachev's speech at the 19th Party Conference, *SWB* SU/0191, 30 June 1988, C/4–5

19 *SWB* SU/0411, 17 March 1989, C/3–20

20 See for example A. Kazarina, 'Vina?', *Literaturnaya gazeta*, 11 January 1989, p. 11

21 V. M. Rutgaizer, S. P. Shpil'ko, V. L. Koshmarskii, 'Kooperatory i reketiry: kto kogo?' *Eko*, 11/89, pp. 9–16; Anthony Jones and William Moscoff, 'New cooperatives in the USSR', *Problems of*

Communism, vol. 38, no. 6 (November, December, 1989), pp. 27–39
22   *SWB* SU/0351, 6 January 1989; SU/0784, 7 June 1990, p. i
23   'A survey of the Soviet Union', *Economist*, 20 October 1990, p. 14; *SWB* SU/0916, 8 November 1990, B/2
24   *SWB* SU/0781, 4 June 1990, p. i; SU/0783, 6 June 1990, p. i
25   *SWB* SU/W0132, 15 June 1990, p. i
26   *SWB* SU/0750, 28 April 1990, C1/1–2
27   *Literaturnaya gazeta*, 21 February 1990, p. 10
28   *SWB* SU/0796, 21 June 1990, C2/1–2
29   Soviet television, 15 September 1988, *SWB* SU/0261, 20 September 1988, C/11
30   At the 19th Party Conference: *SWB* SU/0195, 5 July 1988, C/9
31   *Sovetskaya kul'tura*, 2 April 1987, p. 2
32   Mikhail Gorbachev, *Perestroika: new thinking for our country and the world* (London, Collins, 1987), pp. 146–7
33   Address to the UN General Assembly, New York, 7 December 1988: SWB SU/0330, 9 December 1988, C1/1–4
34   *Pravda*, 8 January 1989, p.2
35   A. Tsipko, 'Istoki stalinizma', *Nauka i zhizn'*, 11/88, p.55
36   G. Shakhnazarov, 'Obnovlenie ideologii i ideologiya obnovleniya', *Kommunist*, 4/90, pp. 46–59
37   *SWB* SU/0682, 7 February 1990, C/2–3
38   TASS, 15 March 1990; Elizabeth Teague, 'Executive Presidency approved', *Report on USSR*, 9 March 1990, pp. 14–16
39   R. Conquest (ed.), *Justice and the Legal System in the USSR* (London, Bodley Head, 1968), pp. 13–21
40   Mikhail Gorbachev, *Perestroika: new thinking for our country and the world* (London: Collins, 1987), p. 105
41   *Pravda*, 5 July 1988, p. 1
42   *Independent*, 3 February 1989; 11 April 1989; 22 April 1989
43   Dawn Mann, 'Elections to the Congress of People's Deputies nearly over', *Report in the USSR*, 14 April 1989
44   E.g. Tolpezhnikov from Riga, *SWB*, SU/0470, 31 May 1989, C/11
45   *SWB*, SU/0468, 29 May 1989, C/1, 3–4
46   *SWB*, SU/0475, 6 June 1989, C/2
47   *Observer*, 4 June 1989, p.25
48   *SWB*, SU/0470, 31 May 1989, C/2–3
49   *Ibid.*, C/9–10
50   *Independent*, 30 May 1989, p.12
51   *Independent*, 1 June 1989, p.10; *Sunday Times*, 4 June 1989, p.B9

52 L. Batkin, 'Vstrecha dvukh mirov na s"ezde deputatov',
    Moskovskie novosti, 11 June 1989, p.9
53 *Independent,* 17 February 1990, p. 13
54 *New York Times Review of Books,* 35:20, 22 December 1988,
    pp.28–29

8 From 'informals' to political parties

1   *SWB* SU/0663, 16 January 1990, p. i; *Economist,* 3 February
    1990, p. 51; *Literaturnaya gazeta,* 28 March 1990, p. 12
2   Dawn Mann, 'Authority of regional party leaders crumbling',
    Report on USSR, 23 February 1990, pp. 1–5
3   *Independent,* 2 May 1990, p. 1
4   *Narodnyi deputat* (broadsheet of Inter-regional Group of
    Deputies), no.1, 28 July 1989, pp. 1–2
5   V.P., 'Po zamyslu neformalov', *Russkaya mysl',* 2 February 1990,
    pp. 8–9; Vera Tolz, 'Informal groups prepare for elections in
    RSFSR', *Report on USSR,* 23 February 1990, pp. 23–7
6   *Ogonyok,* 3 February 1990, pp. 17–18
7   Vera Tolz, 'Democrats start their own discussion of Russian
    national problems', *Report on USSR,* 30 March 1990, pp. 1–3
8   *Argumenty i fakty,* no.484, 20 January 1990, pp. 6–7; Julia
    Wishnewsky and Elizabeth Teague, ' "Democratic Platform"
    created in CPSU', *Report on USSR,* 2 February 1990, pp. 7–9
9   *SWB* SU/0682, 7 February 1990, C/1–8; SU/0688, 14 February
    1990, C/1–11
10 *Independent,* 6 February 1990, p. 1
11 Vera Tolz, 'The United Front of Workers of Russia: further
    consolidation of antireform forces', *Report on USSR,* 29
    September 1989, pp. 11–13; John Dunlop, 'Russian nationalists
    reach out to the masses', paper delivered at the colloquium on
    'Russian national consciousness', University of Cologne,
    November 1989
12 *Literaturnaya Rossiya,* 30 December 1989, p. 2
13 *Russkaya mysl',* 9 March 1990, pp. 1–3; John Dunlop, 'Moscow
    voters reject conservative coalition', *Report on USSR,* 20 April
    1990, pp. 15–17
14 *SWB* SU/0797, 22 June 1990, C/1–2
15 ibid, C1/6
16 *SWB* SU/0821, 20 July 1990, C2/1–8; Peter Frank, 'The 28th
    Congress of the CPSU: a personal assessment', *Government and
    Opposition,* vol.25, no.4 (Autumn 1990), pp. 472–83

17 *Independent*, 7 July 1990, p. 11

18 I am grateful to Alexander Suetnov for assembling for me the programmes of most of the Russian parties, and helping me to obtain interviews with many of their activists in September 1990.

19 See for example Julia Wishnewsky, 'Multiparty system, Soviet style', *Report on USSR*, 23 November 1990, pp. 3–6

20 Wishnevsky, p. 3; *SWB* SU/0903, 24 October 1990, B/8–9

21 Interview with Lev Ponomaryov, deputy chairman of the organisational committee of Democratic Russia, 21 September 1990

22 The best account of the strike is in Theodore Friedgut and Lewis Siegelbaum, 'Perestroika from below: the Soviet miners' strike and its aftermath', *New Left Review*, no. 181 (May/June 1990), pp. 5–32; see also Boris Kagarlitsky, *Farewell Perestroika: a Soviet chronicle*, London: Verso, 1990, pp. 178–89

23 Uwe Krieger, 'Die Auferstehung der sowjetischen Arbeiterbewegung', *Osteuropa*, 9/90, pp. 824–6

24 *Russkaya mysl'*, 11 May 1990, p. 7

25 *Moskovskie novosti*, 24 June 1990, p. 4; *SWB* SU/0792, 16 June 1990, B/3

26 *SWB* SU/0815, 13 July 1990, B/1–2; *Independent*, 12 July 1990, p. 10; David Marples, 'The background of the coal strike of July 11', *Report on USSR*, 27 July 1990, pp. 13–14

27 Elizabeth Teague, 'Soviet workers find a voice', *Report on USSR*, 13 July 1990, pp. 13–17; *Independent*, 24 October 1990, p. 11

28 *Moskovskie novosti*, 21 October 1990, p. 6

9 Towards the dissolution of the Soviet Union

1 *Pravda*, 22 September 1989, p. 1

2 Bohdan Nahaylo & Viktor Swoboda, *The Soviet Disunion: a history of the nationalities problem in the USSR*, London: Hamish Hamilton, p. 315

3 Toomas Ilves, 'The Congress of Estonia', and Riina Kionka, 'The Congress convenes', *Report on USSR*, 23 March 1990, pp. 31–5

4 Saulius Girnius, 'The Lithuanian Communist Party versus Moscow', *Report on USSR*, 5 January 1990, pp. 6–8

5 *Pravda*, 7 April 1990, p. 2

6 *Keesing's Record of World Events*, March 1990, p. 37322

7 *SWB* SU/0757, 7 May 1990, B/1–2

8 *Yunost'*, 9/90, pp. 68–74

9 *SWB* SU/0729, 3 April 1990, B/4–5; Stephen Foye, 'Deputy Chief

of General Staff discusses manpower problems', *Report on USSR*, 18 May 1990, pp. 22–3

10 *SWB* SU/0844, 16 August 1990, B/1–3

11 *Independent*, 30 June 1990, p. 10

12 *Independent*, 21 July 1990, p. 10; 25 July 1990, p. 10

13 *Central Asia and Caucasus Chronicle*, vol. 8, no. 4 (August 1989), pp. 7–10

14 Jonathan Steele, in *Guardian*, 9 May 1989, p. 23

15 Elizabeth Fuller, 'Gorbachev's dilemma in Azerbaijan', *Report on USSR*, 2 February 1990, p. 14

16 *Literaturnaya gazeta*, 10 January 1990, p. 10

17 *Independent*, 4 January 1990, p. 1; 22 January 1990, p. 8; *Kommersant*, no.2, 1990, p. 6

18 Fuller, loc. cit., p. 14

19 *Independent*, 22 January 1990, p. 1

20 *Central Asia and Caucasus Chronicle*, vol.9, no.4 (August 1990), pp. 8–9

21 *SWB* SU/0885, 3 October 1990, B/1–3; SU/0889, 8 October 1990, B/4–5; SU/0896, 16 October 1990, B/9; interview with Mutalibov in *Literaturnaya gazeta*, 29 August 1990, p. 2

22 *Keesing's Record of World Events*, November 1989, p. 37044.

23 *Literaturnaya gazeta*, 5 September 1990, p. 2; *SWB* SU/0846, 21 August 1990, B/3; SU/0852, 25 August 1990, B/7–8; SU/0854, 28 August 1990, B/1–2

24 Elizabeth Fuller, 'The South Ossetian campaign for unification', *Report on USSR*, 8 December 1989, pp. 17–20; *The Times*, 8 January 1990, p. 1; Jonathan Aves, 'Opposition political organisations in Georgia', *Slovo*, vol.3, no.1 (May 1990), pp. 18–36

25 Aves, pp. 20–6

26 Jonathan Aves, paper delivered at the seminar on 'independent political movements in the USSR'. School of Slavonic & East European Studies, University of London, 19 November 1990

27 Vladimir Socor, 'The Moldavian democratic movement: structure, programme and initial impact', *Report on USSR*, 24 February 1989, p. 30

28 Vladimir Socor, 'Moldavian proclaimed official language of the Moldavian SSR', *Report on USSR*, 22 September 1989, pp. 13–15

29 Vladimir Socor, 'Mass protests and exceptional measures in Kishinyov', *Report on USSR*, 17 November 1989, pp. 21–4

30 *SWB* SU/0808, 5 July 1990, B/2–3; SU/0835, 6 August 1990, B/13–14; *Literaturnaya gazeta*, 29 August 1990, p. 9; *Guardian*, 26 October 1990, p. 9; *Independent*, 2 November 1990, p. 12; Vladimir Socor, 'Gagauz in Moldavia demand separate republic', *Report on USSR*, 7 September 1990, pp. 8–13

31 *Independent*, 3 November 1990, p. 11; 5 November 1990, p. 12

32 Vladimir Socor, 'Moldavia resists Soviet draft and seeks own "national" forces', *Report on USSR*, 26 October 1990, pp. 19–23

33 *Independent*, 13 February 1990, p. 1; 14 February 1990, p. 2; Bess Brown, 'Unrest in Tadjikistan', *Report on USSR*, 23 February 1990, pp. 28–31

34 Bess Brown, 'Ethnic unrest claims more lives in Fergana valley', *Report on USSR*, 15 June 1990, pp. 16–18

35 James Critchlow, 'Uzbekistan: the next nationality crisis?' *Report on USSR*, 18 May 1990, pp. 6–13

36 Bess Brown, 'Religion and nationalism in Soviet Central Asia', *Report on USSR*, 20 July 1990, pp. 25–7

37 *Independent*, 4 June 1990, p. 10; 6 June 1990, p. 11; 'This week in the USSR', *Report on USSR*, 17 August 1990, p. 27

38 *Central Asia & Caucasus Chronicle*, vol.9, no.1 (March 1990), pp. 10–12

39 Bess Brown, 'The role of public groups in perestroika in Central Asia', *Report on USSR*, 26 January 1990, pp. 20–25; *Independent*, 28 May 1990, p. 6; 21 June 1990, p. 10

40 James Critchlow, 'Party leaders in Fergana Oblast soften attitude towards Birlik', *Report on USSR*, 23 March 1990, pp. 19–20; *Independent*, 21 June 1990, p. 10

41 Bess Brown, 'The role of public groups', pp. 22–3; *Independent*, 25 May 1990, p. 11; *European*, 1–3 June 1990, p. 3

42 *Central Asia and Cacasus Chronicle*, vol.8, no.3, pp. 13–14; *SWB* SU/0801, 27 June 1990, B/5–6;

43 Paul Goble, 'Central Asians form political bloc', *Report on USSR*, 13 July 1990, pp. 18–20

44 James Critchlow, 'Islam in public life: can this be "Soviet" Uzbekistan?' *Report on USSR*, 16 March 1990, pp. 23–5

45 David Marples, 'A sociological survey of Rukh', *Report on USSR*, 12 January 1990, p. 18

46 *Ukrainian Review*, vol.38 (spring 1990), pp. 41–9

47 *Ukrainian Review*, vol.38 (spring 1990), pp. 57–61 and vol.39 (summer 1990), pp. 36–46

48 ibid, pp. 69–71
49 *Independent*, 26 April 1990, p. 10; David Marples, 'A retrospective of a nuclear accident', *Report on USSR*, 20 April 1990, pp. 9–14
50 *SWB* SU/0823, 22 July 1990, B/8–9; Kathleen Mihalisko, 'Ukraine's declaration of sovereignty', *Report on USSR*, 27 July 1990, pp. 17–19
51 *SWB* SU/0899, 19 October 1990, B/5; *Independent*, 19 October 1990, p. 14
52 *SWB* SU/0910, 1 November 1990, B/8–9
53 *SWB* SU/0751, 30 April 1990, B/4
54 *SWB* SU/0838, 9 August 1990, B/3–4; Kathleen Mihalisko, 'Belorussia as a sovereign state: an interview with Henadz Hrushavy', *Report on USSR*, 31 August 1990, pp. 11–16
55 *SWB* SU/0777, 30 May 1990, p. 1
56 *SWB* SU/0778, 31 May 1990, B/1
57 *Moskovskie novosti*, 10 June 1990, p. 7
58 *SWB* SU/0772, 24 May 1990, B/11
59 *SWB* SU/0794, 19 June 1990, B/1
60 *SWB* SU/0789, 13 June 1990, B/1–2
61 *Moskovskie novosti*, 7 October 1990, pp. 8–9
62 *SWB* SU/0931, 26 November 1990, C3/1–3
63 *SWB* SU/0891, 10 October 1990, B/3

Conclusion

1 *Izvestiya*, 29 September 1990, p. 3
2 Elizabeth Teague, 'The Soviet "disunion": anomie and suicide', *Report on USSR*, 23 November 1990, pp. 1–6
3 Margot Jacobs, 'USSR faces mounting refugee problem', *Report on USSR*, 21 September 1990, pp. 14–18
4 See his speech at the October Central Committee Plenum: *SWB* SU/0891, 10 October 1990, B/3
5 See Aurel Braun & Richard B. Day, 'Gorbachevian contradictions', *Problems of Communism*, vol. 39, no. 3 (May-June 1990), pp. 36–50
6 *SWB* SU/0936, 1 December 1990, B/6
7 *Independent*, 3 December 1990, p. 1
8 *Independent*, 5 December 1990, p. 8; *SWB* SU/0940, 6 December 1990, C1/1–4

Index

Abkhazia 93, 196
Academy of Sciences 49, 61–2, 165
Adamovich, Ales' 65–6
Adylov 108–9
Afghanistan, People's Republic 135, 157, 168, 200
Aganbegyan, Avel' 49, 76, 112, 116
agriculture
  brigade system 138, 150
  collectivisation of 9, 30, 51, 119, 138, 142, 149
  see also reform
Agroprom (agricultural authority) 65
Akhromeyev, Marshal 190
Albakin, Leonid 153, 154
alcohol, restrictions on 140, 148
Alekseeva, Lyudmila 43, 46
Alexander II, reforms 36
Alexii, Patriarch 125
All-Union Central Council of Trade Unions 183, 184
Andropov, Yuri 108, 138, 147
anecdote, political 14, 42
anti-Semitism 88, 111, 112, 116, 128
Antonov, Mikhail 116
apparatchiki 19, 79, 81, 82, 111, 138, 141, 159, 173
April (writers' club) 172, 180
Aral, Lake 56
Aral Sea 108, 202
armed forces 164, 190, 192, 215
  in Afghanistan 168
  in Armenia 195
  in Azerbaijan 193
  in Latvia 97, 98
  in Moldavia 198, 199
  and Tbilisi massacre (1989) 93–4, 168–9
Armenia 1, 95, 106, 136, 194–5, 200
  and Azerbaijan 191–4
  Communist Party 90
  earthquake (1988) 91
  and Nagornyi Karabakh 88–91, 191, 194
arms race 2, 67
arms reduction 157; see also peace movement

arteli (workmen's cooperatives) 25–6, 37, 116
Association of Russian Artists 176
associations,
  informal 37–8, 43–5, 76–81, 82, 102–5, 104–7, 110, 150–2, 164, 170–85, 171–2, 174
  and nationalism 111–12
Associations of Voters 172
authoritarianism ix, 10
Autonomous Republics 86–7
Azerbaijan 89–91, 190, 191–4, 195
  Communist Party 193
  Popular Front 191–4, 201
  Writers' Union 193

Baikal, Lake 55, 57–8, 112
Bakatin, Vadim 215
Balayan, Zorii 90
Baltic states 81, 84, 87, 94–100, 106, 111, 167, 172, 187–91, 209
  Estonia 95, 97–9, 111, 187–8, 189, 191, 197, 198
  Latvia 95, 96–8, 99, 187–8, 191, 197
  Lithuania 95, 98–9, 106, 188–91, 207
Baptists 131–3
Belinskii, Vissarion 36
Belorussia 56, 65, 84, 86, 87, 97, 119–20, 144, 176, 189, 206–7
  Communist Party 100, 105–6
Belov, Vasili 61, 113
Berg, Academician 57
Berlin Wall 157
Berliner, Joseph 32
Birlik (Uzbekistan Popular Front) 201–2, 203
black economy 5, 18, 107–8, 148, 151, 170–1, 213
Bolsheviks 29–30, 83–4
  and religion 122
Bondarev, Yurii 155
Brazauskas, Algirdas 98
Brezhnev, Leonid,
  and 'class struggle' 156
  and religion 132–3

Index

results of policies 2, 3, 8, 17, 49, 57, 72, 107, 109
Bukharin, Nikolai Ivanovich 37, 115, 149
Bukovskii, Vladimir 44, 162
Burke, Edmund 72
Burlatskii, Fyodor 155, 157
Bykau, Vasyl' 105–6

capitalism 146–8, 153–7
Catholic Church 85, 95, 119
  in Lithuania 95, 99
  Ukrainian 129–31, 203, 204, 205
censorship 35–6, 49–51, 57, 140–1; *see also* freedom of speech; glasnost
Central Asian republics 59–62, 107–10; *see also under individual republics*
Central Committee 15, 17, 80, 85, 89, 149, 158, 175, 186
centralisation 10–11, 153–5, 174
change, under totalitarian regime 5–7, 8, 31, 72
Chanturia, Georgi 196–7
Chernenko 68
Chernobyl explosion 55, 62–7, 68, 103–4, 140, 144, 205, 206
Chernovil, Vyacheslav 204
Chernyshevskii, Nikolai 36–7; *Chto Delat'?* 37
Chivilikhin, V. 57, 112
Chronicle of Current Events, The 46–7, 74–5
Churbanov, Yurii 109
church, *see* Baptists; Catholic Church; religion; Russian Orthodox Church
church–state relations 34–5, 117–21, 124–30, 132, 133–6
Chuvash people 208
Civil Dignity 78
civil society x, 12, 19–20, 41–3, 137, 211–13
civil war 29–30, 84
  danger of 215–16
class struggle 156–7
clergy, loss of autonomy 34–5; *see also* Catholic Church; religion; Russian Orthodox Church
Club of Anarcho-Socialists 172
Club for Social Initiatives (Moscow) 72–3, 76
Cold War 6, 157–8
collectivisation of agriculture 9, 30, 51, 119, 138, 142, 149
Committee of Soldiers' Mothers 190
communes 32–4
Communist Party,
  Armenian 90
  and Baptists 132–3
  Belorussia 100
Communist party, in Central Asia 60, 61, 203
Communist Party,
  Conference (1988) 77, 79, 96, 98, 161, 166
  control by 5–6, 7–10, 15–16, 19, 34, 83–7, 177, 182
  earlier policies attacked 114–15
  in Estonia 97, 98
  in Georgia 91–4, 195, 197
  Gorbachev's reforms of 19, 159–62, 213

in Latvia 97, 98
in Lithuania 188
and Orthodox Church 121–2
and rule of law 164–5
in Russia 110–11, 113, 178
Communist party, in Ukraine 64–5, 66, 100, 105, 203, 204–5
'Communists for Perestroika' 172
community spirit (sobornost) 22–40, 54, 118, 120–1, 123–4, 128
Confederation of Labour 183, 184
Congress of People's Deputies x, 80–1, 160, 165–9, 172, 173, 213–14
conscription 190, 199
conservatives, and Russian nationalism 176–8
conversation 13–14, 41–2
cooperatives 146, 150–2
corruption 18, 107–9, 139, 140, 151, 171, 213
Cosmos Club, Moscow 73
Council of Prisoners' Relatives 132
Council for Religious Affairs 121, 125, 126, 127
Council of Soviet Women 165
Council of War and Labour Veterans 165
Crimean Tartars 88, 106, 133
culture 13–14, 22, 24
  alternative 41–5, 70–3
  decentralisation of 85–6
  Georgian 91–2
  stifling of 38–9
  Ukrainian 101, 104
currency weakness 152–3
Czechoslovakia 186

Daniel, Yudi 44–5
decentralisation 49–50, 85–6, 146–55, 179
Democratic Perestroika 78
Democratic Platform 174–5, 177, 178
'Democratic Russia' alliance 173, 175–6, 180, 207
Democratic Union 78, 113, 172–3
democratisation,
  and nationalism 82–3, 186–210
  and Party 164–5, 170–85
  readiness for ix–x, 3, 4–5, 71, 76
demonstrations 44, 66, 71, 103–4, 105–6, 130–1, 168–9, 193
  and nationalism 88, 93–4, 96, 98–9, 104–6, 109, 168–9, 186, 192, 195, 196
dissent 14, 44–8, 95
Dneproges 56
Dniester Republic (Moldavia) 199
Dostoevskii, F., *The Brothers Karamazov* 122
Drach, Ivan 205
Duma (pre-Revolutionary parliament) 21–2
Durkheim, Emile 212

Eastern Europe 157–8, 159, 170, 186–7
economy,
  black 5, 18, 107–8, 148, 151, 170–1, 213
  centralised 5, 8, 15–18, 49–50, 107, 115–16, 152, 190

Index

see also centralisation; decentralisation; reform as stagnant 2–3, 53–4
education,
  expansion of 3–4, 41, 85–6
  and ideology 11
  religious 118, 121, 126, 128
Ekspress-Khronika 74–5
elections,
  in Baltic States 187–8
  boycotting in Georgia 197
  see also reform, electoral
'Elections-89' 80
'Elections-90' group 172
El'tsin, Boris 79, 80–1, 154–5, 168, 172, 173, 184, 207–9
emigration 88
enterprise law 73, 148
environment 55–67, 95–6, 103–5, 111–12
  and nationalism 66, 89–90, 104–5
Epicentre (Cultural Democratic Movement) 71–2
Estonia 1, 83, 95, 97–8, 99, 111, 187–8, 189, 191, 197, 198, 209
European Community 191
European Security Agreement (Helsinki, 1975) 47, 106

Fainsod, Merle 31–2, 41
Fatherland (*Otechestvo*) 176
federalism 85, 179, 186, 190–1, 197, 205–7, 209–10, 214
Federation Council 216
Filaret, Metropolitan 124–5
Filippov, P. S. 71–2
Finland 84, 191
Five Year Plans 38, 56
food production 150
France 160
Franco, General 8, 10
Free Inter-Professional Association of Workers (SMOT) 48
freedom of speech 144–5
  see also glasnost
FSOK (Federation of Socialist Clubs) 76–7

Gagauz people 199
Gamsakhurdia, Konstantin, *David the Builder* 92
Gamsakhurdia, Zviad 92–3, 196, 197
Georgia 83, 91–4, 106, 136, 195–7, 209
Germany (GDR) 186
Gidroproekt 59
Ginsburg, Alexander 45
glasnost 14, 61, 64, 70–1, 111, 113, 114, 140
  and nationalism 83, 89, 96
  proposed 3, 142–5, 171
Glasnost (journal) 75
Glazunov, Il'ya 176
Gorbachev, Mikhail 72, 171, 174–5, 178, 203
  background 138–40
  and intellectuals 142–3
  and nationalism 77, 89–91, 101–2, 109, 188–91, 195–6, 207, 209, 213
  public attitude to 19, 177, 213–14

reforms 2–3, 7, 18–19, 61, 63, 76, 89, 137–8, 146–55, 156–7, 160, 188, 203
  and religion 117, 120
  role in change 2, 5–7, 214–16
  and social problems 117–18
Gorbachev, Raisa 157
Gorbanevskaya, Natalya 46
Gor'kii Institute of Literature 52
Gosagroprom (ministry for agriculture and food-processing) 149
Gosplan (State Planning Committee) 59, 62, 92, 96, 153, 178
Gospriyomka (quality control inspectorate) 139–40, 148
Grigor'yants, Sergei 75
Gromov, Boris, Captain 216
Grossman, Vasilii, *Forever Flowing* 143
Grossu 199
Guchkov 22
Gustafson, Thane 58, 59, 62

Hanson, Philip 34
Helsinki Agreement 47, 106
Herald of the Urals (Ural'skii vestnik) 79
Herzen, Alexander 36
history 143
  attitudes to 39, 42, 53, 96
  repression of 9–10, 42, 51–3, 143
  Russian-centred 87
Hromada (Community) Society 104
Hrushevo apparition 129, 136
human rights 44–8, 54, 67, 68, 71, 75, 76, 93, 98, 105, 157, 172, 179
hydroelectric power 56, 59, 95–6

ideas, respect for 11–14
ideology, role of 5–6, 8, 11–12, 53
Il'insky, I, 69
Il'ya Chavchavadze Society 92, 197
immigration, and nationalism 85, 96–7, 98, 99, 109–10
Initiative Group in Support of Perestroika 66
Initsiativniki (reform) Baptists 132–3
Institute of Economics and Industrial Organization, Novosibirsk 49–50
institutions, popular 24, 32–4
intelligentsia 12–14, 34–40
  and nationalism 82, 86–7, 90, 97, 102–7
  and peace movement 67–9
  and religion 33, 120, 123–4
  and Russian domination 82
Inter-Regional Group of Deputies 172, 183
Interior, Ministry of 215
International Fronts ('Interfronts') 99, 111, 175, 176, 187, 198, 204
Iran 135, 192, 194, 200
irrigation schemes 55, 56, 108
Islam 90, 106, 107, 119, 133–5, 200–1, 203
  Sufi brotherhoods 134–5
Islamic Democratic Party 201
Ivashko, Vladimir 178, 203, 205
Izvestiya 211

Jasny, Naum 38

Index

Jews 88, 119
anti-Semitism 88, 111, 112, 116, 128
John Paul II, Pope 129, 130
journals,
literary 35–6, 143
'thick' 50–1
unofficial 74–5, 79

Kagarlitsky, Boris 78
Kalashnikov, Vladimir 171
Kalugin, Oleg, Major General 144
Kanatchikov, Semyon 26
Kapitsa, Academician 57
Kaputikyn, Sil'va 90
Kazakhstan 107, 109, 199–200, 202
Kennedy, Paul 2
KGB 47, 87, 139, 144, 164, 168, 178, 215
Khristoradnov, Yuri 127
Khruschev, Nikita 5, 6, 17, 42, 44, 56, 59, 120, 142, 216
and 'class struggle' 156
Kirghizia 107, 200, 202
Kirill, Archbishop of Smolensk 127
Klebanov, Vladimir 47–8
Klub 81 71
KOI (Circle for Social Initiative) 77
Kolbin, Gennadii 109
Komi people 208
Kommuna (anarchist group) 78
Komsomol (party youth organisation) 69–70, 77, 139, 165, 190
Korotich, Vitalii 112
Kostava, Merab 92
Kozhinov, Vadim 115
kruzhki (circles, coteries) 35, 43, 45, 123–4
Kunaev, Dinmukhamed 109
Kunyaev, Stanislav 176
Kurashvili, Boris 77, 172
Kuzbass Workers' Union 183

labour camps 9, 42, 51–2, 59, 119
labour movement, independent 184–5; see *also* trade unions
Lakshin, Vladimir 51
Landsbergis, Vitautas 167, 191
languages,
non-Russian 85–6, 87, 89, 97, 98, 99, 102–3, 105, 111
Russian 83, 106–7, 186
Latsis, Otto 148, 152
Latvia 95, 96–8, 99, 187–8, 189, 191, 197, 209
law,
rule of 43–5, 139, 141–2, 161–9
'telephone' 163
see *also* reform
leader, power of 8
legality, socialist 162
Legasov, Valeri 62–5
Lenin, *State and Revolution* 155–6
Lenin, V. I. 15, 28, 29, 37, 55, 155–6, 167, 174
criticism of 115, 143
and nationalism 83–5, 115

and totalitarianism 7
Ligachev, Egor 168
Lion Society, Lvov 104
literary journals 35–6
literature,
and glasnost 71
post-Stalin 43, 50–4
and revolution 36, 39
see *also* writer; 'village prose'
Literaturna Ukraina (newspaper) 103
Literaturnaya Gazeta 145
Lithuania 66, 95, 98–9, 106, 136, 153, 167, 188–91, 207, 209
Loshchenkov, F. 79
Lotman, Yurii 49
Luchinskii, Petru 199
Lutheranism 119
Lysenko, Vladimir 174

Makashov, General 177
Mao Zedong 16
market economy, move towards 116, 146–55, 179
Marx, Karl 36–7, 158
Marxism, and Gorbachev 158–9
media,
foreign 42
and glasnost 143–5
party influence in 8, 10
see *also* intelligentsia; journals; *samizdat*; writers
Medvedev, Roy 3, 167
Medvedev, Vadim 158
'Meeting-87' 79–80
Memorial group 73, 114, 172, 180
Men, Father Alexander 128, 131
mental hospitals, confinement in 47
Mill, John Stuart 158, 168
Minenergo (Energy Ministry) 65, 66, 67
miners' strikes (1989–90) 180–3, 184
Miners' Union 183–4
Minvodkhoz (Ministry of Water Resources and Melioration) 60–1, 168
Minzdrav (Ministry of Health) 65
mir (peasant community) 24–5, 26, 31–2
Mironenko, Victor 70
Moldavia (Moldova) 84, 189, 198–9
Mutalibov, Ayaz 193–4
mutual protection associations 31–2, 41

Nagornyi Karabakh 88–91, 106, 191, 192, 194, 195
Nakhichevan 192–3
narod (common people) 39
Nash sovremennik (journal) 113–14, 176
National Bolsheviks 114
National Democratic Party (Georgia) 93, 196–7
National Forum, Georgia 197
nationalism 82–3
in Baltic states 96–9
and environment 89–90, 104–5

Index

and 'Interfronts' 99, 111, 175, 187, 198, 204
liberation movements 186
role in revolution 84
Russian 110–16, 175–8, 179
Nazi-Soviet Pact (1939) 93, 97, 167, 187, 189, 198
'Nevada-Semipalatinsk' movement (Kazakhstan) 202–3
NKVD economic network 59
nomenklatura system 8, 10, 11, 15–18, 69, 81, 87, 107, 154–5, 165, 178
Nove, Alec 147
Novyi mir (New World) (journal) 50–2, 113
nuclear power programme 55, 103–4, 106
  see also Chernobyl explosion
nuclear weapons 202

Obolenskii, A. 166
Obshchina (Community) (religious journal) 124
Ogarkov, Marshal 190
Ogonyok (magazine) 106, 112, 130, 171
Ogorodnikov, Aleksandr 123–4, 128
Oktyabr (literary journal) 143
Orthodox Church *see* Russian Orthodox Church
Orwell, George 38, 45
Ossetian Popular Shrine Movement (Ademon Nykhas) 196

Pamyat (Memory) organisation 111–13, 116
Pan-Armenian National Movement 194–5
Panakhov, Nemet 192
'party clubs' 171–2
Party Conferences, *see* Communist Party
pass books 87, 162
Pasternak, Boris, *Essay in Autobiography* 9
Patiashvili, Dzhumber 94
patronage *see nomenklatura* system
Pavlychko, Dmytro 102–3, 104
Pazukhin, Evgenii 131
peace movement 67, 120, 202
peasants 3, 8, 28–30, 33–4, 142–3
  mir 24–5, 26, 31–2
  religion 122–3
People's Fronts *see* Popular Fronts
perestroika 7, 8, 18, 50, 72, 78, 95, 105, 111, 175, 216
  early version 139–41, 147–8
  evaluation of 155–8
  later development 141–8, 160–9
  opposition to 111–13, 141
Perestroika Club 73–4
Perestroika-88, 78
Peter the Great 22, 34
petitions 66, 68, 89, 95
Petrakov, Nikolai 153
Pimen, Patriarch 117, 125
Pinochet, General 8, 10
Pipes, Richard 7
pluralism 6, 14–15, 21, 49, 97, 150–1, 179
Podrabinek, Aleksandr 74–6
  Punitive Medicine 74

Poland 17, 84, 119, 153, 172, 191, 203
Politburo 178
political prisoners 157
politics, underground 5, 14, 43–7
pollution 89–90, 91, 93; *see also* Chernobyl explosion; environment
Polozkov, Ivan 177
Popov, Gavriil 168, 174
Popular Fronts 77–81, 172, 178, 179, 187
  Armenia 90
  Baltic states 97–9
  Belorussia 105–6
  Georgia 195, 197
  Moldavia 198
  Moscow 172
  Ukraine 104–5
population 3–4
Pravda 1, 149
Preobrazhenskii, E. 37
Presidency, increasing powers of 160, 175, 178, 188
press freedom *see* media
private enterprise 146–7, 172
privilege *see nomenklatura* system
public opinion,
  changes in 13, 19–20, 64–5
  influence of 61–2
Pugo, Boris 215–16

queueing 18

radicals 173–4, 175
Rashidov, Sharif 108, 109
Rasputin, Valentin 58, 61, 116
  Farewell to Matyora 122
rationing 18
Reagan, Ronald 68
reform,
  agricultural 138, 149–50
  economic 3, 18–19, 49–50, 115–16, 146–55, 181, 185
  electoral 3, 74, 76–7, 93, 159–62, 164–9, 174–5, 215–16
  legal 161–5
  necessity of 7, 213–16
  opposition to 1–2, 18
  political 3, 8, 155–9, 164–9, 170–85
refugees 192, 212
religion,
  and nationalism 90–1, 95
  persecution of 118–20
  post-Stalin 53–4
  and revolutionary movements 34–5
  and science 37
  and social solidarity 118–21, 127–8, 131–2
Repentance (film) 142
'revivalists' 114
revolution, Russian 27–9, 35–40, 84, 115, 143
  see also Bolsheviks; Lenin
river diversions 55, 59–60, 108, 142
Rodionov, General 168–9
Romania 186
RSFSR *see* Russians

Index

Rukh ('Popular Movement for the Support of Perestroika') 203–6
Russian Orthodox Church 35, 114, 118–31, 133, 136
Russians 143, 146–7, 171, 173, 175–8, 207–9
and nationalism 83–5, 106–7, 110–16, 179, 208
Rybakov, Anatolii, *Children of the Arbat* 115
Ryzhkov, Nikolai 148, 154, 182, 209

St Il'ya the Righteous, Society of 197
St Petersburg Soviet 28
Sajudis (the Movement) 66, 98, 106, 167, 188
Sakharov, Andrei 3, 48–9, 57, 65, 141, 165, 166, 168, 172, 173, 183
samizdat 5, 43–6, 71, 104
Schadov 182
Schumacher, Ernst 116
science,
and dissent 48–50
and nationalism 95
and revolution 36–7, 38–9
secession, right of 93, 97
security police *see* KGB
self-determination 84
see also nationalism; Popular Fronts
Selyunin, V. 148
Sergii, Metropolitan 118–19, 120
Shakhnazarov, Georgii 158
Shalamov, Varlam 9
Shanin, Theodor 212
Shatalin 154–5
Shcherbak, Yurii 103, 104
Shcherbitskii, V. 101–2, 203
Shchit (trade union for army) 190
Shevardnadze, Edvard 94
Shidlovskii Commission 27
Shmelyov, N. 116
Sholokhov, Mikhail 57
shortages 148, 151, 215–16
Sinyavskii, Andrei 44–5
skhod (communal assembly) 24–5, 28–9
Sobchak, Anatoli 174
sobornost (spirit of community) 22–40, 54, 118, 120–1, 123–4, 128
Social Democratic Association 172
Social Democratic Party (Azerbaijan) 193
socialism, under Gorbachev 76, 78, 141, 147–50, 153–9, 179, 214–16
'socialist legality' 162
'socialist realism' 39
society, created by party 9–11; *see also* civil society
Soloukhin, Vladimir 114–15
Solovyov, Yurii 80
Solzhenitsyn, Alexander 107, 143
A Day in the Life of Ivan Denisovich 51–2
The Gulag Archipelago 52, 143
Songaila, Ringaudas 98
Soviet Committee for the Protection of Peace 67
Soviet Sociological Association 72
Soviet of Workers' Deputies 27–8
soviets 3, 27–30, 182

Sovremennik (radical journal) 37
Soyuz faction 215
Stakhanov, Alexei 139
Stalin, Josef,
annexation of Baltic states 94, 96, 97
collectivization of agriculture 113, 114–15, 149
and intelligentsia 38–40, 41–2, 112
memorial to victims 96, 105
and nationalism 87–8
opposition to 1
and religion 119–20
and rule of law 161–2
system 5, 8–9, 15–17, 88, 141
terror 51, 105, 112–15, 142–3
Stankevich, Sergei 80, 160
Stepniak 25
strikes,
in Azerbaijan 192
by miners (1989–90) 180–3, 184
Stus, Vasyl' 104
Sufi brotherhoods 134–5
Suleimenov, Olzhas 202
Supreme Soviet 167–8, 178

Tadjikistan 107, 135, 200, 202
Tatar Popular Front 208
Tbilisi massacre (1989) 93–4, 168–9, 195, 196
technology 2–3
'telephone law' 163
Ter-Petrosian, Levon 195
Tolstoy, Leo 36
totalitarianism ix, 5–20, 29–34, 38–9, 57, 60–1, 79, 161–2, 211
crisis of 1–2, 15, 81
resistance to 106–7
trade unions,
for armed forces 48, 190
independent 47–8
official 182, 183, 184
Travkin, Nikolai 184
Trust Group 67–9
Tsipko, Alexander 173
Turchin, Valentin 3
Turkestan, proposed establishment of 202, 203
Turkmenia 107, 202
Tvardovskii, Alexander 50–2, 113–14
Tyumen oil workers 185

Ukraine 84, 86, 87, 97, 100–5, 106, 119–20, 144, 171, 176, 189, 203–6
Communist Party 100, 105
and nuclear power 64–5, 66
Ukrainian Autocephalous Orthodox Church 204
Ukrainian Catholic Church 129–31, 203, 204, 205
Ukrainian Culturological Club 104
Ukrainian Helsinki Group 104
Union of Evangelical Christians and Baptists 131–3
Union of Sovereign Soviet Republics,

proposed treaty 190–1, 197, 205–7, 209–10, 214
Union for Spiritual Rebirth of the Fatherland 176
Union of Writers *see* Writers' Unions
United Nations 97
United States,
  informal links with 67–9
  Strategic Defence Initiative 2
United Workers' Front 176, 185
'Unity' Association of Lovers of Russian Literature 176
unity movements *see* international fronts
urbanisation 3, 30–1, 53, 86–7, 150
Usmankhodzhaev, Inamzhon 109
Utilitarians 36
Uzbekistan 107–10, 199–200, 201–2

Vaino, Karl 96, 98
Vasilyan, Ramzik 195
Vazgen, Catholicos 90–1
Vendrov, Academician 59
Vezierov, Abdul-Rakhman 193
Vikulov, Sergei 113–14
'village prose' 52–3, 113–14
Vlasov, Yurii 168
Voinovich, Vladimir 13
Volodymyr, Metropolitan 129, 131
Vol'skii, Arkadi 192
Vokuta miners 183

women,
  in education 4
  revolutionary vision of 37
  rights of 46
workers 180–6
  rights 17, 26–8, 47, 76, 148
writers,
  and dissent 50–4, 61, 62
  and nationalism 89–90
  and religion 120, 123–4
  rural 52–3, 113–14
  status of 82–3
  see also intelligentsia
Writers' Union 12, 39, 61, 62, 69, 96, 145
  Belorussia 106
  Latvia 96–7
  Moldavia 198
  Russian 113–15, 155
  Ukraine 64–5, 102–5

Yakovlev, Aleksandr 112
Yakut people 208
Yaroshinskaya, Alla 81
young peope 68–73, 103, 105
  in Georgia 93
  and religion 122–5
Yugoslavia 147

Zalygin, Sergei 62, 113
Zaslavskaya, Tatyana 49, 72, 112, 116
Zel'dovich, Academician 57
Zinoviev, Aleksandr 11, 32–4